CHRISTIAN EGYPT

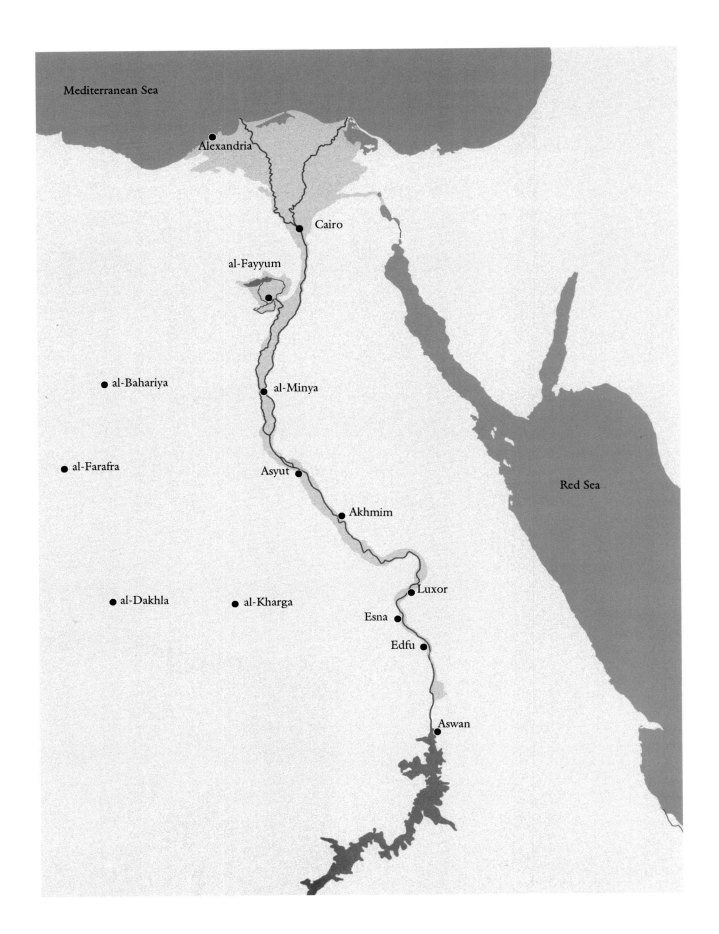

MASSIMO CAPUANI

CHRISTIAN EGYPT

Coptic Art and Monuments Through Two Millennia

With the contributions of

Otto F. A. Meinardus
and
Marie-Hélène Rutschowscaya

*Emendations and introduction to
the English-language edition by*

Gawdat Gabra

THE LITURGICAL PRESS
Collegeville, Minnesota

www.litpress.org

Library of Congress Cataloging-in-Publication Data

Capuani, Massimo.
    [Egitto copto. English]
    Christian Egypt : coptic art and monuments through two millennia / with the contributions of Otto F.A. Meinardus and Marie-Hélene Rutschowscaya ; emendations and introduction to the English-language edition by Gawdat Gabra.
       p. cm.
    Includes bibliographical references and index.
    ISBN 0-8146-2406-5 (alk. paper)
      1. Coptic church buildings—Egypt. 2. Coptic Church—History. I. Meinardus, Otto Friedrich August. II. Title.

NA4829.C64 C3713 2002
726.5'8172—dc21

                                                2002069482

CONTENTS

Introduction

Gawdat Gabra

The Copts, who number more than nine million according to unofficial estimates, represent the largest Christian community in the Middle East. They consider themselves the true descendants of the ancient Egyptians; Coptic texts called them "the people of Egypt." Christianity was introduced to Egypt as early as the first half of the first century. The Coptic Church, which is one of the oldest in the world, takes pride in the tradition recorded by the church historian Eusebius that St. Mark the Evangelist preached the gospel in Alexandria. The patriarchs of Alexandria played a crucial role in the theological controversies of the fourth and fifth centuries. The most important contribution of the Copts to world civilization is undoubtedly monasticism, which influenced the development of European monasticism. Coptic art and religious architecture represent significant aspects of the oriental Christian legacy in general and of the Coptic heritage in particular.

In the second half of the twentieth century, several factors provided an impetus for the rapid growth of Coptic studies and a quickening of interest among educated laypersons in Coptic Egypt. The general public began to be aware of Coptic civilization when the Brooklyn Museum mounted an exhibition of Coptic art in 1941. Another followed in 1944 at the Society of Coptic Archaeology in Cairo. That same year, the discovery of the Nag Hammadi gnostic library, with its manuscripts written in Coptic, encouraged many scholars to study the language in order to investigate gnosticism, a complex religious movement that, in its Christian form, spread in the second century. Under UNESCO auspices, scholars from different countries cooperated to publish these remarkable texts, which engendered a vast awareness of the Coptic heritage. The exhibition of Coptic art in 1963 at Villa Hügel, Essen, Germany, began a series of successful Coptic exhibitions in several great European cities such as Vienna, Munich, Zurich, and Geneva, with the latest at the Institut du Monde Arabe in Paris in 2000. To enhance the benefits of such cultural events, catalogs were provided that included accounts of Coptic history and culture, as well as wonderful color illustrations and bibliographical references. Since its foundation in 1976, the International Association for Coptic Studies has organized six international congresses that considerably furthered Coptic studies. The appearance of the eight-volume *Coptic Encyclopedia* in the United States in 1991 greatly advanced the knowledge of Coptic civilization and continues to facilitate research of both the scholar and general reader. It is noteworthy that visitors to Coptic monuments in Egypt include more than one million foreign tourists each year, in addition to the many Egyptians.

Although Coptic art and religious architecture never enjoyed the patronage of the court, and the Coptic Church suffered many waves of persecution throughout its long history, including the destruction of churches and the confiscation of property, the artistic heritage of the Copts is enormous and of special charm. Not surprisingly, the majority of Coptic buildings were made of mud brick, which was plastered, whitewashed, and decorated with paintings—inexpensive materials and techniques. The stone architectural sculpture of older Coptic monuments usually consisted of capitals for columns, friezes, and niches. While many Coptic art collections have been carefully published and their masterpieces introduced to the general public in elegant museum catalogs and volumes devoted to Coptic art, a considerable number of the ancient Coptic monasteries and churches are documented solely in very old publications, available only in academic libraries. In the last two decades, campaigns of excavation and conservation have led to the discovery of several Coptic buildings and wall paintings; the majority of these new discoveries have so far been published only in specialized periodicals.

Therefore, the need for an up-to-date, beautifully illustrated book on Egypt's Christian buildings has become imperative. The present volume is intended to provide just such a timely description of ancient and medieval Coptic constructions. The broad scope of Dr. Massimo Capuani's volume covers most of the Coptic sites throughout Egypt, including ruined monasteries like those of St. Jeremiah (Saqqara) and St. Apollo (Bawit). Famous architectural sculptures and wall paintings from these two monasteries are exhibited in the Coptic Museum, Cairo. No other book on Coptic architecture contains such a substantial amount of illustrative material; photographs of excellent quality contribute substantially to the understanding of the text. Many of the professionally photographed monuments do not appear elsewhere with such clarity and beauty, thanks to the author's dedication: his personal photographic record of architectural features and wall paintings greatly enhances the value of this volume. Dr. Capuani also supplies a chronology of Egypt from 332 B.C. to 1952 and an essay on the typology and architectural evolution of Egyptian churches to enable the reader to appreciate fully the abundant material. The volume is enriched by the contribution of Professor Otto Meinardus, who introduces readers to Christian Egypt with discussions of basic issues such as the patriarchs of Alexandria and the theology of the World Church during the fourth and fifth centuries, the history of the Coptic Church, monasticism, the attitude of Egypt's rulers toward the Copts, and the Coptic renaissance during the pontificates of the Patriarchs Cyril VI (1959–71) and Shenuda III (1971–). In a valuable, concise account, Dr. Marie-Hélène Rutschowscaya elucidates several aspects of Coptic art: wall paintings, icons, and illustrated manuscripts, as well as textiles, perhaps the most characteristic product of Coptic art. Thus the volume offers readers a comprehensive picture of the artistic achievements of the Copts. The work is furnished with a practical selected bibliography.

I believe that the richness of the Coptic civilization should be conveyed to a wider general public. I am convinced that the interested layperson, the student, and the scholar alike will all benefit from the text and illustrations of this book and that it will serve to promote knowledge about this important segment of the Christian Egyptian legacy.

Dr. Gawdat Gabra
St. Mark Foundation for Coptic History Studies,
Coptic Orthodox Patriarchate, Cairo

Coptic Christianity, Past and Present

Otto F. A. Meinardus

The first part of this essay surveys the history of the Coptic Church from the first century, at the time of the evangelist St. Mark, to the middle of the twentieth century. The second part describes a few specific aspects of the renewal of the church of Egypt that have occurred since the middle of the twentieth century. After a description of the return to the election of the patriarch by the biblical casting of lots, the biographies of the popes of the reform, Cyril VI and Shenuda III, are summarized. The characterization of the Sunday schools as the mainspring of this renewal must be interpreted in the light of what Christian education means within an Islamic society. The unprecedented resurgence of monastic communities is a help to understanding the new vitality of the whole Coptic community because it is from the monks' ranks that the leaders, the members of the episcopate, are chosen. Lastly, the passage concerning the spiritual support of the present renewal refers to certain recent discoveries and the translation of the relics of martyrs and confessors of the faith as well as to appearances of the Holy Virgin and the revitalization of Coptic pilgrimages.

Historical Developments of the Coptic Church

From the First to the Twentieth Century

The term "Copt" originally derived from the Arabic word *Qibt,* which in its turn is merely a shortened form of the Greek word *Aigyptios,* Egyptian, from which the initial diphthong "ai" and the adjectival suffix "ios" have fallen away, leaving the form *gypt* or *Qibt.* This means that the Coptic Church is the Egyptian Church, which can trace its origin to apostolic times. Following the flight of the Holy family from Bethlehem to Egypt (Matt 2:13-23), St. Luke informs us that Egyptians were also present on the first day of Pentecost when the Holy Spirit descended upon the faithful in Jerusalem (Acts 2:10). There is good reason to believe that some of these Egyptian Jews returned to their homes where they established Christian congregations. Jews had flourished in Alexandria and throughout the Nile valley from the early days of the Ptolemies, who ruled Egypt for about three centuries (323–30 B.C.E.). And early Egyptian Christians owed a great deal to the philosopher Philo, a contemporary of Jesus and the apostles, who during his lifetime was perhaps the most influential Jew in Alexandria. In fact, the works of Philo served as a model for the Christian theologians of Alexandria. He provided the young Christian community in Egypt with a way of reconciling their Christian message with the Egyptian cultural background.

The Christians of Egypt maintain that St. Mark the Evangelist visited Alexandria, where he preached the gospel and founded the apostolic see of Alexandria. In Acts, Mark is mentioned as a companion of Saul and Barnabas (12:25; 13:13); he is also portrayed as a co-worker of St. Peter, the Apostle to the Jews (12:12), and of St. Paul, the Apostle to the Gentiles (Col 4:10; 2 Tim 4:11). According to the historian Eusebius of Pamphylia (fourth century), Mark appointed his first convert in Alexandria, the cobbler Anianus, to serve as bishop of Alexandria in his place. Moreover, he ordained three priests, Milus, Cerdon, and Primus, all of whom became patriarchs of the see of Alexandria. The unbelievers of the city were greatly annoyed by the rapid spread of the gospel and planned to entrap the evangelist during the Easter celebrations of 68 C.E. In the course of the Divine Eucharist, the furious mob seized Mark, put a rope around his neck, and dragged him through the streets of Alexandria. The following day they once again dragged him by the rope until he died. Thus, just as Roman Catholics consider Peter the founder of their church, Egyptian Christians regard Mark as their divinely appointed patron.

The early history of the Coptic Church is both glorious and tragic. It is glorious because of the number of its illustrious children, such as the theologians Athanasius and Cyril the Great and the monastic fathers and mothers St. Anthony, St. Pachomius, and St. Syncletica. At the same time, the Christians of Egypt were exposed to the most severe persecutions. To this day, the Egyptian martyrs are commemorated in the Coptic calendar, which dates the years according to the "Era of the Martyrs" (A.M.), thus recalling the violent persecutions during the reign of the emperor Diocletian. The Era of the Martyrs began on August 29 (Julian calendar) or September 11 (Gregorian calendar), 284, the year in which Diocletian ascended the imperial throne. Following Diocletian's persecutions, which lasted in Egypt from 303 to 313, Christianity emerged victorious and dynamic, so much so that Alexandrian theology and christology were to leave a lasting impression upon the whole Church. These outstanding contributions of the Alexandrian theologians were produced in the famous Didascalia. In this celebrated catechetical school, Christians labored to demonstrate that reason and revelation, philosophy and theology were not merely compatible but essential for each other's comprehension. The major theologians of this school were Pantaenus, Clement of Alexandria, and Origen, who succeeded each other as heads of the institution. Very little is known about the theologians who followed Origen as heads, be it Heracles or Dionysius, later surnamed the Great. Eventually, both ascended the patriarchal throne of St. Mark. According to Coptic tradition, Heracles (d. 246) was the first prelate in Christendom to bear the title "pope." The reign of Dionysius the Great was severely troubled by Decius' and Valerian's persecutions in 251 and 257, which drove the patriarch into hiding. At a later date, St. Athanasius entrusted Didymus the Blind (315–398) with the headship of the catechetical school. He lived during the tempestuous age of the Arian heresy and the first ecumenical council of Nicaea in 325. Among his pupils were such outstanding theologians as St. Gregory of Nazianzus, St. Jerome, and the historian Rufinus.

The reign of Constantine the Great ushered in the triumph of the Christian Church over paganism and at the same time a reversal of the policy of persecution: Christians now began to harass those who still adhered to their pagan or non-Orthodox theological beliefs. The early patristic period was also marked by the appearance of numerous heresies. In upper and lower Egypt, several sectarian doctrines gained considerable ground. The various forms of gnosticism and Arianism disturbed the peace of the Church. For the Gnostics, "revealed knowledge of God" or "gnosis" was the central factor in the redemption of humanity. This revelation was attained only by the "illuminati" through metaphysical speculation and occult incantations. Gnosticism was ultimately superseded by a considerably more menacing heresy in which both emperors and patriarchs became involved. In the course of the Arian controversy, which began during the patriarchate of Achillas (d. 314), two Alexandrian theologians faced each other. Arius, presbyter of the historic and important church of St. Mark in Bucalis in Alexandria, maintained that Jesus Christ, although of divine origin, was only of "like" essence, therefore unequal to the Father. The patriarchs Alexander (d. 328) and later Athanasius (328–373) held that the Father and the Son were of one and the same essence. The christological impasse appeared insurmountable until the emperor Constantine yielded to the recommendations of the ecclesiastical hierarchs by summoning an ecumenical council to meet in Nicaea in Bithynia in the summer of 325. Three hundred and eighteen bishops, representing the whole of Christendom, convened to settle the major dogmatic differences. The Nicene deliberations provided the Church with a creed which has survived to this day. Arianism was condemned and Arius and four Arian bishops were deposed and banished. In Egypt, another controversy centered around Bishop Melitius of Lycopolis (Asyut) and Peter I about the return of those who had "lapsed" during the persecutions. The latter emerged from the dispute not merely as the twentieth pope and patriarch of Alexandria but also as the universally accepted and revered champion of orthodoxy and doctor of the whole Church.

The role of the Egyptian Church in the formation of the canon of holy Scripture was of utmost importance, owing to the advantages of its theological position and the biblical learning of the theologians from the catechetical school of Alexandria. The testimony of the Alexandrian church to the biblical canon provided uniformity. In addition to the universally acknowledged books, the Epistle to the Hebrews and the Apocalypse of St. John were also received as divine Scripture. In his *Thirty-ninth Festal (Paschal) Letter*, St. Athanasius provided a list of the canon of the Old and New Testament, which has retained its validity to this day. Furthermore, he noted the Old Testament Greek books—Wisdom of Solomon, Sirach, Esther, Judith, Tobit—as well as the

Teaching of the Apostles and the Pastor of Hermas as being useful for young converts, although they were not part of the canon.

Christian monasticism had its origin in the deserts of Egypt, from where the movement spread to other lands. According to the historian Sozomen (fifth century), the first anchorites fled to the desert for the sake of safety during the Decian persecutions in the middle of the third century. In some cases anchorites occupied tombs in upper Egypt, which often had habitable cells attached, used by priests in pagan times. The first anchorite who made his permanent abode in the desert is believed to have been St. Paul of Thebes, who fled at the age of sixteen to spend the rest of his life in the Eastern Desert and died in 340. By 270 however, there were many anchorites living near their own villages. Among them was St. Anthony, who is generally considered the true founder of Egyptian monasticism. He was the first anchorite to gather followers in order to establish a monastic community life, and he laid down formal rules for the spiritual guidance of his disciples. Gradually these anchoritic communities retreated into the inner desert to avoid the distractions of the "world." At the same time, monasteries also existed along the edges of the cultivated land near villages and towns. Throughout the Nile valley many monastic communities for men and women were established. In the diocese of Oxyrhynchus (al-Bahnasa) alone there were ten thousand monks and twelve thousand nuns. Monastic settlements existed on both banks of the Nile from Crocodilopolis (al-Fayyum) to Hieraconpolis (al-Minya) to Hermopolis Magna (al-Ashmunein). Monastics occupied the pharaonic tombs on the slopes of the mountains west of Lycopolis (Asyut) and east of Panopolis (Akhmim) as well as in and around the regions of Chenoboskion (Qasr al-Sayyad) and Dandara. On the west bank of the Nile a chain of monastic establishments extended from Naqada to Qamula and Thebes. Literally hundreds of monastics inhabited the monasteries and hermitages in and around Hermonthis (Armant), Latopolis (Esna), and as far south as Apollinopolis Magna (Edfu) and Syene (Aswan).

To some extent independent of this line of monastic evolution in the Nile valley and upper Egypt, which was originally inspired by St. Pachomius and later by St. Shenuda (Shenute in Coptic), monastic colonies emerged in the desert of Scetis (Wadi al-Natrun), the Eastern Desert between Cairo and Alexandria. Here, under the leadership of St. Macarius, St. John the Short (Colobus the Little), and St. Bishoi (Pshoi in Coptic), monastics settled as anchorites and in small and large communities. The fame of the desert fathers and mothers of Scetis spread to distant lands and attracted pilgrims from Syria and Palestine, Ethiopia and Mesopotamia, Asia Minor and even Ireland. Indeed, the desert of Scetis became the focus of the monastic movement which spread from Egypt to almost every part of early Christendom. During the latter part of the fourth century, Coptic monasticism showed its intercultural character. According to Coptic tradition, Maximus and Domitius, sons of Valentinian, emperor of the West (364–375), settled in the inner desert of Scetis, where they were instructed in the disciplines by St. Macarius the Great. After their death, their cell became known as that of "the Romans" or Paromais (al-Baramus). Palladius, bishop of Helenopolis in Bithynia (fourth century), mentions the Ethiopian robber Moses the Black, who joined St. Isidore at the cell of the Romans. Other visitors from overseas included the historian Rufinus, who travelled with the Roman lady Melania and spent eight years in Egypt. St. Jerome, a great admirer of monastic life, was in Jerusalem in 386 and went from there to Egypt to visit the monastics in Scetis. In 390, St. John Cassian went to Egypt with his friend Germanus; and around 420, he compiled two important works in Latin about his experiences in the East, which greatly influenced Western monasticism. In fact, the multicultural aspect of early monastic life in the Egyptian desert was considered more important than adherence to theological orthodoxy. In spite of the decisions of the third ecumenical council at Ephesus in 431, which had condemned Nestorius and his followers for their christological heresies, Nestorian monastics like Rabban Sari, Abraham of Kashkar (492–586), and Rabban bar Idta visited the Coptic monks to be instructed in ascetic discipline, and the monks of Scetis served as a model for many Nestorians like Rabban Hudhwi, Rabban Yunan of Anbar, and Mar Yuhannan of Qanqal.

The popularity of desert monasticism also inspired several notable women to follow the example of the male "athletes of God." Hilaria, the daughter of the emperor Zeno (474–491), clothed herself in the monastic habit and joined the monks of Scetis. The same is reported of Eugenia, the daughter of the Alexandrian prefect Philippus; Apollonia, the daughter of Anthemius, emperor of the West (467–472); and the distinguished women Theodora, Euphrosyne, and Anastasia. Having assumed male attire, these women lived in the caves and cells just as the monks did. Only after their death was the truth of their identity revealed. This practice was so widespread that one of the canons of the synod of Gangra in Paphlagonia (345) stated, "If a woman, under pretence of asceticism shall change her apparel, and instead of a woman's accustomed clothing, shall put on that of a man, then let her be anathema."

10

In the middle of the fifth century the Egyptian Church played a significant role in the christological controversies which sadly divided the whole Church. In the fifth-century dispute, the Alexandrian patriarchs and theologians Sts. Cyril the Great and Dioscorus were the two principal personalities representing the miaphysitic christology as opposed to the dyophysitic views of St. Leo, pope of Rome, and the hierarchs of Constantinople. St. Dioscorus (444–454) stood firm in the christological faith of his predecessor, St. Cyril the Great (412–444), who had stated, "One nature (physis or hypostasis) of the incarnate God-Logos," giving to the term *physis* its primary meaning of "nature." The definition of faith, as set forth by the theologians of the fourth council of Chalcedon (451), that "Our Lord is to be acknowledged in two natures, without confusion, unchangeably, indivisibly, and inseparably," was categorically rejected by the Egyptian theologians as a form of "splitting the very nature of Jesus Christ." Thereupon, the council fathers proceeded to condemn and depose St. Dioscorus, though, be it noted, not for heresy but because he "had disobeyed the canons of the holy fathers. . . ."

The post-Chalcedonian developments, the struggle for supremacy in Alexandria, the irenic attempt of the emperor Zeno (474–491) to heal the theological estrangement with the "Edict of Unification" by omitting the word "nature" from the document merely led to additional schisms. By the end of the fifth century, the Church was sadly divided into Miaphysites and Dyophysites, Arians and Nestorians.

The Arab conquest of Egypt under Omar's general Amr ibn al-As (639) introduced a radically new and altogether different situation for the Copts. In the beginning, the Arabs were welcomed by many Egyptian Christians as deliverers from the imperial Byzantine yoke and exploitation since the Arabs displayed an appreciable amount of political and religious tolerance. Coptic sources mention that several thousand monks from the desert of Scetis went from Terenuthis, a town in the delta, to salute the Muslim conqueror and to implore his protection for them and for their monasteries. Yet only a few years later, an increasing number of Christians had accepted the new religion of Islam. The Coptic patriarch Benjamin I (623–662) was the first hierarch to represent the Coptic community and church in an Islamic environment. During his administration, Islam penetrated into the Nile valley, and already by the beginning of the eighth century Arabic had become the official language. The first Arabic document in Egypt is dated 709.

Up to that period, Coptic and Greek had been spoken by the Egyptians in upper and lower Egypt. Coptic originally derived from later linguistic developments of hieratic and demotic Egyptian. The Coptic alphabet employs all the characters of the Greek alphabet and in addition seven letters, taken from the demotic, to express certain sounds that do not occur in Greek. There are four main dialects in the language, Saidic, Bohairic, Fayyumic, and Akhmimic; Saidic and Bohairic, however, are the most important. In the eleventh century, the Bohairic dialect was officially declared the liturgical language of the church. However, a century later many biblical and liturgical texts appeared in Coptic and Arabic, a practice that continued well into the seventeenth century. In some upper Egyptian villages, Coptic was still spoken in the seventeenth century. Today, Pope Shenuda III tries to revive the Coptic language by offering classes in the Coptic schools in Egypt and the diaspora.

One of the consequences of the Arab conquest was the increasing taxation of the Copts by their Muslim rulers. In the very beginning, although churches were occasionally destroyed, religious life seemed to have suffered relatively little. Still, Islamic pressure provoked resentment which expressed itself in at least six insurrections between 725 and 773. The political failure of these revolutions only increased the prestige of the conquerors so that from then on even more Copts accepted the faith of Islam. At any rate, by the ninth century Muslims were the majority in Egypt, and parallel to the decrease in the number of Christians was the decline in the number of dioceses.

The financial pressure exerted upon the Copts, the confiscation of ecclesiastical treasures, and the temporary imprisonments of members of the hierarchy were largely responsible for the introduction of the *cheirotonia*, or simony, the payment of sums of money for an ecclesiastical position.

During the reign of the Tulunids (868–905), the Ikhshidids (935–960), and the Fatimids (969–1171), the Copts experienced a general attitude of toleration, which, however, was unfortunately interrupted by the violent persecutions of the insane caliph al-Hakim. Thus, during the years 1012–1015, many churches and monasteries were destroyed, and Christians who were public servants were persecuted and expelled from government offices. But al-Zahir, al-Hakim's successor, permitted those who had been forced to embrace Islam to return to their original faith. The patriarchate of Christodulus (1047–1078) constituted one of the significant periods in the history of the Coptic Church. During this time, the patriarchate was moved from Alexandria to Cairo, a transfer which symbolized a certain accommodation to the Fatimid dynasty. The sympathetic attitude of the Fatimid rulers toward the Copts, which expressed itself in their participation in

Christian feasts and the unprejudiced employment of Christians in the government, was largely due to the Ismaelite nature of their faith, which the Egyptian Sunnis never accepted.

With the invasion of Egypt by the Turkoman general Shirkuh, an uncle of Salah al-Din, the Fatimid rule came to an end and the Ayyubid dynasty came to power (1171–1250). Although this period was not marked by major persecutions and outbreaks of violence, none of the Ayyubid rulers displayed any particular sympathy for the Copts. While the crusaders had challenged the supremacy of Islam, the Copts as well as the other Eastern Christians had accepted their minority position, and thus, they had little choice but to play the role of loyal Christian subjects.

During the thirteenth and fourteenth centuries, there was a brief Christian renaissance in the fields of theology, apologetics, ecclesiastical history, and canon law. In fact, the thirteenth century is generally considered the age of Coptic theology and dogmatics, and one of the great theologians of the Coptic Church in this period was al-Rashid Abu'l-Khair ibn al-Tayyib. Being both priest and physician, he served as secretary to the *wazir* (vizier) of Salah al-Din (Saladin, 1193–1198). The nucleus of thirteenth-century Coptic theology was composed of three brothers with the family name of Ibn al-Assal. Al-Safi Abu'l-Fada' il ibn al-Assal, the oldest of the three, was primarily engaged in polemics against Islam and the study of Coptic canon law. In his apologetic commentaries, he testified to the deity of Jesus Christ, based upon personal experience, the witness of the Gospels, the miraculous power of Christ, and the miracles which were wrought by the apostles in the name of Christ. Abu'l-Farag Hibatallah ibn al-Assal, a brother of al-Safi, wrote between 1231 and 1253. His literary efforts stand out because of his versatility. The younger step-brother of al-Safi and Abu'l-Farag was al-Mu'taman Abu Ishaq Ibrahim al-Assal, a student of philosophy, linguistics, homiletics, and liturgy. His major effort was his theological summa, the *Compendium of the Foundations of Religion,* in five parts and seventy chapters.

Shams al-Riasa Abu'l-Barakat ibn Kabar, commonly known as Abu'l-Barakat, was without doubt the most prominent and the last of the great Coptic-Arabic theologians of the Middle Ages. In his day, the great persecutions of 1321 occurred, which gave the final blow to the Copts. Abu'l-Barakat, who had served as secretary to Rukh al-Din Baybars al-Mansuri al-Khitayi, was seized by the Muslim authorities, but fortunately protected by the Mamluk prince whom he served. As a theologian and priest at the church of the Holy Virgin al-Muallaqa in Cairo, he wrote the *Lamp of Darkness,* a monumental encyclopedia of theology and ecclesiastical knowledge in twenty-four chapters.

Between 1279 and 1447, the Mamluks tried to expel all Coptic civil servants from government posts eight times. By the fourteenth century, the number of Copts in Egypt had significantly decreased. Moreover, Coptic history, that is, recorded history, comes to an end with the thirteenth and fourteenth centuries. This means that for the period between the fourteenth and nineteenth centuries we are largely dependent upon the occasional references by Muslim authors or the observations of Western pilgrims and travellers.

From the study of the history of the monasteries, which no doubt reflects in some measure the general conditions of the church, one gets the impression that during this period the Coptic Church declined sadly and had lost almost all of its former spiritual vitality. This spiritual impoverishment is also revealed by the almost complete absence of theological creativity from the fourteenth to the twentieth century. True, there were no longer any serious persecutions or destruction of Coptic property and the church as a whole was tolerated, yet the poll tax was collected from Copts until the middle of the nineteenth century. It is noteworthy that neither the French nor the British succeeded in winning the cooperation of the Copts as a group for their respective politics. Although individual Copts, just as some Muslims, aligned themselves with the interests of the European invaders, the church as such remained aloof and continued its conservative adherence to the traditions of a more glorious past. This aloofness, especially during the French expedition, may have been one reason for Muhammad Ali's ready acceptance of many Copts into the civil service.

If it was Muhammad Ali (1805–1848) who did the most to wrestle Egypt into the modern world, it was the patriarch Cyril IV, the Reformer (1854–1861), who tried to do the same for the Coptic Church. Thanks to his enlightened leadership, Christians gained a new sense of ecclesiastical prestige and position. Education was one of Cyril's primary interests, and he established schools at the patriarchate and at Harat al-Saqqayin with emphasis on language study. Schools for girls were also opened and the upper classes of Coptic society did not hesitate to send their children to these schools, which helped to prepare much of the lay leadership later in the century. As part of the educational efforts, the patriarch purchased a printing press from Austria and had it paraded through the streets of Cairo from the railway station to the patriarchate. Cyril was also concerned about the education of the clergy and introduced regular theological discussion classes and seminars;

from the priests he demanded church discipline. He also reorganized the management of church property and instituted strict bookkeeping.

The rule of the khedive Said (1854–1863) closely paralleled the patriarchate of Cyril IV, with whom he had a rather ambiguous relationship. He gave more equality to the Copts by ordering their young men to do military service along with all other Egyptians, while also canceling the traditional discriminatory poll tax on Christians and Jews. Unfortunately for the Copts, Said's measures towards equality backfired because conscription came to be used as a tool against the Christians; for example, every male in Asyut, a city with a large Christian community, was drafted. The patriarch was able to intervene and get the khedive to restore the Christians' exemption from military service.

The latter part of the nineteenth century as well as the first part of the twentieth were characterized by intense struggles between the various patriarchs and the *maglis al-milli,* the Community Council, centering mainly upon the issue of responsibility for the administration of the ecclesiastical endowments *(awqaf).* When the idea of a lay community council crystallized in 1874, Butrus Pasha Ghali asked the khedive for his permission, which he granted. The story of the Community Council reflects the power politics between the patriarchs, the clergy, and the laity. Immediately following his enthronement, Cyril V (1875–1927) even rejected the idea of having a Community Council. Throughout his administration, which lasted more than half a century, there was constant strife between the three parties. The situation did not improve under Cyril's successors, John XIX (1928–1942), Macarius III (1944–1945), and Yusab II (1946–1956). On the contrary, more than once, the government was forced to intervene to settle the disputes between the laity and the patriarchs, and compromises lasted for only brief periods. In June 1955, the Copts grew increasingly rebellious and demanded that Yusab II resign. Finally, under pressure from the Holy Synod and the Community Council, he was deposed and some of the responsibilities of the Council (like the personal status laws) were passed to the government. The story of the emergence of the lay movement in the Coptic Church is one of unfortunate disputes about the exercise of power, control, authority, and influence between the patriarchs, the clergy, and the laity.

THE COPTIC RENEWAL OF THE TWENTIETH CENTURY

The Revival of the Biblical Altar Lot

Throughout the centuries Egyptian Christians employed several methods for nominating and electing their successors to the apostolic throne of St. Mark. We can distinguish between the following five practices: 1. nomination and appointment of the candidate by his predecessor; 2. nomination by consultation and election by members of the clergy and the laity; 3. nomination by consultation of the clergy and the laity in conjunction with the government; 4. nomination and/or election by means of a dream or vision of a devout Christian; 5. nomination by consultation and election by casting the altar lot (see Acts 1:23-26).

During the first few centuries, it was customary for the patriarch to nominate and prepare his successor. Dionysius the Great had served Demetrius (d. 230) and received the nomination from him, which he solicited. The custom of serving a "spiritual apprenticeship" for the patriarchal office is attested in numerous instances. Athanasius the Great (328–373) served as a scribe for Alexander (311–328), and Theophilus (384–412) was the secretary of Athanasius. Theophilus, uncle of Cyril I (412–444), diligently prepared his nephew for the patriarchal office, and Dioscorus II (516–518) was the scribe of John II (505–511).

By far the majority of the patriarchs between the second and twelfth centuries, however, were nominated by consultation and elected by the Orthodox people gathered in Alexandria. After the Arab conquest, the Islamic government became increasingly involved in the administrative affairs of the church. By the middle of the twelfth century, its influence in the internal affairs of the church had increased so much that at the time of the election of John V (1147–1166), the episcopate, priests, and archons met in the government center in Alexandria. When a dispute concerning the candidate arose among the electors or the electors were divided into two or more interest groups, then a supernatural revelation in the form of a dream or vision experienced by a devout person determined the future patriarch. In some cases, the dream or revelation served as a divine confirmation of the electoral deliberations and consultations.

The first reference to the apostolic practice of casting lots in the election procedures for the Coptic patriarchate is mentioned in the vita of John IV (777–799). The bishops assembled in Alexandria and many names were mentioned. They wrote the names on small sheets which they placed in the sanctuary. Then they brought a young child, ignorant of sin, who drew out one of the sheets. They promoted the one whose name was drawn to the patriarchal dignity. This method was employed in only eleven out of the one hundred and seventeen elections. Both Cyril VI (1959–1971) and the present pope and patriarch Shenuda III ascended the throne through election by the biblical practice of the altar lot.

The Patriarchate of Cyril VI

On August 2, 1902, Azir Yusuf Ata, the second of three sons, was born in Tukh al-Nasara, governorate of al-Minufiyya in the delta. After his graduation from secondary school, he worked for a while in the firm of Thomas Cook and Sons. At twenty-five, he joined the monastery of al-Baramus in Wadi al-Natrun, where the monk Abuna Abd al-Masih al-Masudi became his spiritual father. In 1931, he was ordained priest and given the name Abuna Mina al-Muttawahad al-Baramusi. For several years he lived as an anchorite in a cave in the vicinity of the monastery, which had previously been occupied by Abuna Sarabamun, who was well known for his strict asceticism. Miles away from civilization, Abuna Mina met with the prophet of the desert, Abuna Abd al-Masih al-Habashi (the Ethiopian), who lived in a cave until 1970. This fellowship strongly influenced the asceticism of Abuna Mina al-Muttawahad. In 1936, Abuna Mina retreated to the slopes of the al-Fustat hills, outside Old Cairo, where he lived in one of the deserted Napoleonic windmills until 1942. It was during this time that he was appointed abbot of the monastery of St. Samuel at al-Qalamun, in the desert sixty kilometers south of al-Fayyum. With the donations and gifts he received he bought a piece of land where he built the small church of St. Menas along with a hostel for students.

On April 19, 1959, the altar lot was cast in favor of Abuna Mina as he celebrated the Divine Liturgy in his simple church of St. Menas in Old Cairo. Immediately after his enthronement, Cyril VI, his pontifical name, devoted his attention to the eighty-year-old thorny problems regarding the relation of the Copts to the Ethiopian Church. In the same year, on June 19, the two churches signed a joint declaration whereby the new patriarch-catholicos of the Ethiopian Church received the right to consecrate bishops for Ethiopia while still recognizing the supremacy of the pope of Alexandria. Then, on November 27, 1959, he laid the foundation stone of the ninth monastery of the Coptic Church, the monastery of St. Menas, built on a historic site in the desert of Maryut (Mareotis). During his patriarchate the church entered into ecumenical dialogues with Western and Eastern churches. Already in 1954, the Coptic Church was officially represented at the second general conference of the World Council of Churches, held in Evanston, Illinois. In 1962 the patriarch consecrated Abuna Makari al-Suriani as Bishop Samuel for Social and Ecumenical Affairs of the church, thereby initiating an active participation of the church in theological and organizational discussions with Eastern and Western churches. One of Cyril's major accomplishments lead to the translation of the relics of St. Mark from Venice to Cairo in June 1968.

The 1960s will be remembered for an active program for the construction of churches and monasteries, crowned by the building and inauguration of the new cathedral of St. Mark in Cairo, an occasion which brought together representatives from most of the Christian communities throughout the world. In terms of social and economic reconstruction, the endeavors of the rural and urban diakonia were milestones in the offering of relevant Christian services to the needy and alienated. Cyril's patriarchate left a lasting impression upon the life of the Egyptian Church. Throughout the critical time of the Six Days' War, in June 1967, the church identified itself with the national aspirations of the people, calling upon its sons and daughters to withstand the threat of the Israeli army. On March 19, 1971, Cyril VI, one of the truly great patriarchs of the apostolic see of Alexandria, died of a heart attack at the age of 69.

Following the death of Cyril, Archbishop Antonius of Sohag served as vicar until Sunday, October 31, 1971, when a new pope and patriarch of the see of Alexandria and all Africa, the 117th successor of St. Mark, was elected by altar lot. Six hundred twenty-two electors participated, and for the first time the church of Ethiopia was represented by forty electors. The three candidates who received the highest number of votes were Bishop Samuel (440), Bishop Shenuda (433), and Qummus Timotaus al-Maqari (306). Under the supervision of Dr. Kamal Ramzi Stino, the minister of tourism, and Mr. Ibrahim Nagib, president of the Coptic *awqaf* (religious foundations), the names of these three were placed in a silver case, which for the past three hundred years had been used to keep the holy chrism. On the appointed day of the drawing of the lot, many distinguished members of church and state attended the celebration of the Divine Liturgy. At the beginning of the service the names of the three candidates, which had been kept on the altar since the preceding Friday, were publicly announced. The deacons had assembled ten young boys. The smallest of them, Ayman Munir

Kamel, was chosen by Archbishop Antonius to select one of the three papers on the altar. Bishop Shenuda was proclaimed the 117th successor of St. Mark the Evangelist.

The Patriarchate of Shenuda III

Nazir Gayed Rufail was born on August 3, 1923, in the province of Asyut in upper Egypt. His schooling began at the Coptic school in Damanhur. Subsequently, he attended the American school in Banha and the Secondary Eman Coptic school in Shubra. At the age of seventeen he joined the Sunday school of the church of St. Anthony in Shubra. In 1943, Nazir matriculated at the University of Cairo and four years later received his B.A. in English and history. The following year he completed his compulsory military service. Being a reserve officer, he participated in the first Arab-Israeli war in 1948. Afterwards, he received his degree in theology from the theological college, which led to his appointment as lecturer at the theological school for monks at Helwan. Then, on June 18, 1954, he joined the monks of the monastery of the Syrians at Wadi al-Natrun, where he was placed in charge of the library. Under the religious name of Abuna Antonius al-Suriani he excelled in spirituality and asceticism. In 1959, Pope Cyril VI appointed him his personal secretary; however, Abuna Antonius returned to the monastery, preferring a life of solitude. He selected a cave some ten kilometers from the monastery at the edge of Wadi al-Faregh. On several occasions, Cyril had wanted to ordain him bishop. Finally, in September 1962, the pope summoned Abuna Antonius to the patriarchate in Cairo. As he bowed his head to receive the pope's blessing, His Holiness laid his hands on the anchorite and said, "I consecrate you Shenuda, bishop for the theological college and the Sunday schools. . . ."

Under his tenure as bishop and dean of the seminary, the number of full-time students increased from 100 to 207 and of part-time students from 30 to 300. Furthermore, women were admitted for the first time, some of them being appointed lecturers. In 1969, he was elected president of the Association of Middle East Theological Colleges. As bishop for education, Shenuda began his weekly spiritual meetings, which attracted thousands of people. An important feature of these meetings was the innovation of devoting the first part of each evening to replying to questions on theological and social issues. Deeply attached to the monastic life, Bishop Shenuda continued to spend half of the week in Cairo, lecturing and delivering sermons, the other half at the monastery in prayer and contemplation. He represented the Coptic Church at numerous ecumenical conferences. The last conference he attended as bishop for education and the Sunday schools was the *Pro Oriente* conference between the Eastern Orthodox Churches and the Roman Catholic Church, held in Vienna in September 1971, just one month prior to his election as pope and patriarch of Alexandria. At this conference, the participants agreed to the christological formula, once expressed by St. Cyril of Alexandria: "The one nature of the incarnate Word of God."

This christological formula was officially accepted when Pope Shenuda III visited with Pope Paul VI in Rome in May 1973. This was the first meeting between an Alexandrian and Roman pontiff since the great schism in 451. Both popes signed the common declaration, containing among other things, the confession of common faith in the mystery of the Word Incarnate.

Following the enthronement of Shenuda as the 117th successor of St. Mark, he continued his concern for the religious education of the Copts. Owing to his personal attention, the theological seminary expanded and enlarged. Six branches of the institution were established in Egypt: Alexandria, Tanta, Minufiya, Minya, Balyana, and the monastery of the Holy Virgin al-Muharraq. In the diaspora, three seminaries were opened, two in the United States and one in Australia. At the centenary celebrations of the theological seminary on November 29, 1993, the pope officially opened the Institute of Pastoral Affairs in order to develop the training of clergy and church workers.

Shenuda responded to the increasing problems with fundamentalist Muslims with his denunciations of fanaticism and sectarian strife. At the same time, President Anwar al-Sadat and members of the government made repeated allegations against the patriarch and Coptic community. Misunderstandings between the president and the patriarch culminated in the presidential decree of September 3, 1981, ordering the pope's exile to the monastery of St. Bishoi and the imprisonment of eight bishops, twenty-four priests, as well as a significant number of the leading laypersons. President Sadat set up a papal committee to discharge the duties of the patriarchate. However, the Holy Synod issued a decree confirming Pope Shenuda as the spiritual head of the church. For forty months, Shenuda was confined to the desert monastery. In the meantime, many loyal Copts played an important role in ensuring that he be released. Bishop Domadius of Giza paid weekly visits and served as principal mediator between the government and the exiled patriarch. On January 2, 1985, President Mubarak revoked President Sadat's decree. Accompanied by fourteen bishops, the patriarch departed from the monastery of St. Bishoi on Thursday, January 4, 1985. Over ten thousand people filled the cathedral to receive their pope, who after the prayer of thanksgiving, greeted his people by saying: "I have no residence except your hearts, which are full of love. I have never been away from your hearts, not even for the twinkle of an eye." Since his release, Coptic-Muslim relations have somewhat improved as a result of his efforts in promoting a spirit of love and unity.

Because of his deep commitment to the monastic movement, Pope Shenuda has been instrumental in renovating the established desert monasteries and in rebuilding the numerous deserted monasteries in upper Egypt. A papal residence was constructed at the rear of the monastery of St. Bishoi; it houses a chapel, large conference halls, an amphitheater for lectures, and guest houses. Here the pope has hosted many ecumenical conferences, including the Joint Commission of the Coptic and Roman Catholic Churches in February 1986, the Inter-Orthodox Joint Commission in June 1989, the Eastern Orthodox and Anglican Forum in March 1990, the World Federation of Orthodox Youth Seminar in May 1991, the *Pro Oriente* forums, and the conferences of the Association of Theological Institutes of the Middle East, etc.

Moreover, the patriarch has established several monasteries in the diaspora: St. Anthony in California, United States; St. Anthony in Kröffelbach and Sts. Mary and Mauritius in Höxter, Germany; St. Anthony in Melbourne and St. Shenuda in Sydney, Australia; St. Shenuda in Milan, Italy; St. Anthony in Nairobi, Kenya; and St. Anthony in Windhoek, Namibia. Because of the continued exodus of Copts from Egypt, large diaspora congregations have been established in the West: in the United States, about seventy; Canada, fifteen; Australia, twenty-seven; South and Central America, four; Great Britain, eight; and Central Europe, thirty. These overseas communities are guided by seventeen bishops.

To help the Holy Synod function more effectively, Pope Shenuda has divided its responsibilities into several subcommittees, for example, pastoral affairs, liturgy, ecumenical relations, monastic affairs, education, diocesan affairs. Also, the community council *(maglis al-milli),* chaired by the pope, is divided into subcommittees such as public relations, construction, legal affairs, financial affairs, rural development, education. Moreover, he has organized the clerical council, which now has two divisions, a disciplinary tribunal for priests and an ecclesiastical tribunal for divorces and annulments.

The Sunday School Movement,
Cradle of the Coptic Renewal

To understand the Coptic renewal towards the latter part of the twentieth century, it is imperative to recognize the dynamics of the so-called Takris Movement, in which the participants consecrated their lives, their time, their property to service for and in the Coptic Church. Although from the years 1948 to 1962 most of the members of the movement were laypersons, 1962 many of them had joined monastic communities, especially the monastery of the Syrians under Bishop Tawfilus (Theophilus), or had been ordained parish priests.

Four major Sunday schools left a lasting impression upon the theology and piety of its members, thereby determining the spiritual and educational climate of the church. The Sunday school center near the church of St. Anthony (established in 1934) was in the eastern part of Shubra, behind Kitchener Hospital. Spiritual growth through prayer and ascetic practices was a main concern of the founders of this institution. The examples of the saints, both martyrs and confessors, played an important educational role. The members of this school had to accept a strict and coherent spiritual life of prayer as well as ascetic discipline over a period as long as two years. In the 1950s and 1960s, several pioneers of this institution joined monasteries; the most important was Nazir Gayed, Pope Shenuda III, who had joined the school at age seventeen. Metropolitan Athanasius of Beni Suef and al-Bahnasa (d. 2000) was also an active member of this school, as was Bishop Gregorius (d. 2001), responsible for advanced theological studies.

The Sunday school center of Giza was located in the church of St. Mark. Among its pioneers were Saad Aziz (Bishop Samuel, assassinated October 6, 1981) and the renowned Abuna Bulus of Damanhur. Here, emphasis was placed on Bible study and social outreach and service. Service to the less fortunate in city and country led to the work of the urban and rural diakonia. The creation of good, solid relationships with the Muslim majority was an integral part of this movement.

The school center of Gezirat Badran was near that of St. Anthony in east Shubra. Its principal purpose was the total involvement of its members in the social and educational program of the church. Besides the traditional course of study, members participated in study trips to churches and monasteries. A new policy of the center was the religious and social education of young women.

Lastly, the center at the church of St. Michael in Tusun, Shubra, combined the various aspects of the other three. Almost all of the young men who had joined monasteries in Wadi al-Natrun, the monastery of St. Samuel at al-Qalamun, or the hermitages in Wadi al-Rayan (1960–1969) had attended one of the four schools, whose character had impressed itself so strongly upon their members that their future roles as church leaders were largely determined by the theology and piety of their Sunday school experiences.

The Resurgence of Coptic Monasticism

In January 1985, President Hosni Mubarak released Pope Shenuda III from forty months in exile at the monastery of St. Bishoi, and there was great rejoicing in the Coptic community. A few weeks later, I met with the pope. "To be sure," he commented, "the revival of Coptic monasticism and the spiritual reawakening of the church was not endangered by my absence. On the contrary, the experiences of our ancestors proved to be important. During my days at the monastery, I was able to ordain almost one hundred men as monks. Moreover, two new monasteries in upper Egypt were established at this time."

The spiritual revival of the Sons of the Pharaohs is one of the remarkable developments of Eastern Christianity at the present time. This renewal is visible in Coptic parishes throughout the country from Alexandria to Aswan; it is felt in the work of the Sunday schools, the social and educational institutions, and in the rural and urban diaconia. Every aspect of Christian life seems to be touched by it, including ecclesiastical art and architecture. The twentieth century reawakening, made possible through the reforms in the nineteenth century by Pope Cyril IV (1854–1861), can be dated to the period following the patriarchate of Yusab II. With the accession of Abuna Mina al-Muttawahad al-Baramusi as Pope Cyril VI in 1959, the original monastic ideals in their anchoritic and cenobitic forms regained their initial vitality, thus determining the spiritual life of the church in general and of the monasteries in particular. In the late 1950s, and especially throughout the 1960s and 1970s, many academically trained young people took monastic vows and repeopled the desert monasteries. This resulted in a steady change in the average age within the monasteries so that today, many of the monks are between twenty-five and fifty. At the same time, the difference in the level of education between the older and younger monks was obvious, a problem that could be solved only by patient, fraternal love. After all, many of the monks from the fourth to sixth centuries cherished their simplicity and biblically inspired anti-intellectualism. Indeed, the majority of them were peasants: St. Macarius the Great was a camel-driver; St. Macarius the Alexandrian had been a seller of sweetmeats; St. Apollo of Bawit had been a goatherd; Sts. Pambo and Paphnutius were illiterates like so many of the desert monastics who had memorized large portions of holy Scripture. Of course, there were exceptions to the rule: Sts. Evagrius, Albanius, Maximus, and Domitius were members of the intellectual or hereditary aristocracy. Today, the great majority of desert monks come from middle or even upper-middle class families. They join monasteries after having completed their military service and having spent some time in their respective professions as engineers, chemists, architects, pharmacists, surgeons, teachers. But this does not mean that there are no longer fellahin among Coptic monks.

It is difficult to measure the degree of spirituality, and yet there is no doubt that today the ascetic disciplines practiced in the officially recognized monasteries are considerably more severe than a generation or two ago. This is unquestionably due to the motivations which have led young people to enter the desert monasteries. Some of them join the desert monasteries because of a genuine religious experience, be it in the form of a vision, a dream, or an inspiration resulting from contemplation. A profound sense of guilt has led many to accept a life of asceticism in the hope that by self-denial they may atone for their sins. St. Anthony the Great was moved to his decision to forsake the world upon hearing the teaching of holy Scripture: "If you wish to be perfect, go, sell your possessions, and give the money to the poor" (Matt 19:21). Consequently, he retired to a cave in Wadi al-Araba near the Red Sea. For the majority of Copts, monastic life is still considered spiritually and morally superior to that lived in the world. Thus, the monks are often referred to as "angels of God." To follow their example is thought to be a surer way to eternal salvation than remaining in the world. Then, there are those monks, such as the late pope Cyril VI and now Shenuda III, who have radiated such a deep spirituality that they have attracted others by their personal example.

To join a monastery means the total identification of the person with the church. This is an important witness in a country or region where the church represents the faith and morality of a religious minority. Again, others embrace monastic life as a sign of protest against the laxity and worldliness of the church. Moreover, it should not be forgotten that the higher ranks of the Coptic clergy are nowadays selected exclusively from among monks. This means that there may be cases where a man may enter monastic life out of a desire for eventual leadership. These men would thus regard monastic profession as a means rather than an end.

In order to attain a spiritual monastic motivation, the novice acknowledges in the initiation pledge, "Monasticism is a complete death to the world and all that is in it in the way of wealth and possessions, in the way of relatives and friends, and in the way of appointments and occupations; and it is a life of worship and dedication to God, a life of penitence and deprivation and of perfect obedience and poverty." The novice promises to live in continence and separation from the world, following the true monastic life, obeying the canons and instructions of the true monks. The novice also promises that he will not solicit any appointment in the world or request to enter the priesthood.

From the seventh to the thirteenth centuries, most Coptic popes came from the monastery of St. Macarius, which served as the pontifical residence during the early Middle Ages. From the seventeenth to the nineteenth centuries, the Red Sea monastery of St. Anthony provided the ecclesiastical leaders for the church. During those years, the popes of Alexandria as well as the heads of the Ethiopian Church and the metropolitans of Jerusalem had been monks of the same monastery. In the middle of the twentieth century, largely due to the personal authority and pastoral qualities of Bishop Tawfilus, the monastery of the Syrians provided the leadership during the important years of the Coptic renewal. Since 1972, the monastery of St. Bishoi has supplied most of the bishops. This is understandable since Shenuda III selected this monastery as his desert residence.

Whereas the revival of Coptic monasticism in the four monasteries of Wadi al-Natrun (al-Baramus, St. Bishoi, the Syrians, and St. Macarius), the Red Sea monasteries of St. Anthony and St. Paul of Thebes, as well as the monasteries of St. Samuel at al-Qalamun, St. Menas at Maryut, and the Holy Virgin al-Muharraq at al-Qusiya has been sufficiently published, there exists virtually no literature about the recent reoccupation of some of the medieval monasteries south of Asyut in upper Egypt.

Only five of these monasteries have been officially recognized by the Holy Synod, namely, those of St. Shenuda at Sohag (the White Monastery), the Holy Virgin at al-Hawawish, St. Pachomius at Minshat al-Ammari, near Luxor, St. George at al-Riziqat, and St. Pachomius at Edfu. The other formerly abandoned monasteries, which are situated where the desert meets the cultivated land, are smaller places occupied by just one or two monks or a few women monastics. Nevertheless, this development is significant, for it demonstrates the dynamism of the current monastic movement among young Coptic men and women who identify themselves wholeheartedly with the church by accepting the ascetic life in pioneer situations.

The significance of monasticism in upper Egypt, until recently of interest only to historians and archaeologists, has been called to our attention because of the present monastic renewal and reoccupation of some of the abandoned monasteries. Relatively little is known of the history of these places. Most of them were devastated in the ninth century, during the patriarchate of Shenuda I (859–880). The Islamic historian al-Maqrizi (d. 1441) listed altogether fifty-nine upper Egyptian monasteries. Of these, only eleven were inhabited, five of them by only one or two monks; thirteen were still visited for the annual festivals in honor of their patrons; at least twelve were either deserted or completely destroyed. As for the rest, he simply mentions their names and locations.

Today, the following monasteries in upper Egypt are occupied by monks originally from St. Bishoi. The monastery of the Holy Virgin near Durunka is located about ten kilometers south of Asyut, on the slopes of Istabl Antar. Through the efforts of Metropolitan Michael of Asyut, the site as been rebuilt to accommodate large numbers of pilgrims from August 7 to 22, when the sojourn of the Holy Family at Asyut on their flight to Egypt is commemorated. The monastery of St. Shenuda is located about five kilometers west of Sohag, near the edge of the desert. The British architect Somers Clarke wrote in 1912 about this place, "This monastery is the noblest church of which we have any remains in Egypt, the chief monument of the Christians." It was founded by St. Bigol (Pjol), the maternal uncle of St. Shenuda, who became abbot in 385, and followed the rules laid down by St. Pachomius. In the eleventh and twelfth centuries, it served the Armenian community in Egypt; in the Middle Ages the relics of the apostles Sts. Bartholomew and Simon the Canaanite were kept there. The Mamluks destroyed it in the eighteenth century and only the church of St. Shenuda has survived. The monastery of St. Michael the Archangel is the northernmost on the mountain ridge east of the village of al-Hawawish, east of Akhmim. Special services are conducted on the feast of St. Michael as well as June 19 and November 21. The monastery of the Holy Virgin, the southernmost on the same ridge, is located within an extensive necropolis and has been rebuilt upon the foundations of a former church or monastery. The monastery of the Martyrs is situated between these monasteries. The monastery of St. George, on the edge of the desert near al-Riziqat and southwest of Armant, has served as a site of pilgrimage for many years. It is well known throughout upper Egypt because of the annual pilgrimage from November 10 to 16 commemorating the consecration of the church of St. George, and large numbers of Copts and Muslims gather for this feast. The monastery of St. Matthew the Potter, one of the oldest monasteries in the region, having been founded during the patriarchate of Pope Alexander II (704–729), is seven kilometers west of Asfun, two kilometers beyond Nag al-Zineiqa on the edge of the desert. Although destroyed by the Bedouins in the tenth century, it was rebuilt. The monastery of St. Pachomius at Edfu, five kilometers west of the celebrated temple of Horus, was reoccupied in 1975 and today has more than thirty monks living there.

In addition to these monasteries, there are three monasteries for women: the monastery of Sts. Theodore and Acladius at Madinat Habu on the west bank of the Nile opposite Luxor; the monastery of Sts. Pisentius and Abshai in the village of Tod on the east bank of the Nile south of Armant; and the monastery of St. Ammonius and the thirty-six hundred martyrs of Esna, about four kilometers southeast of Esna at the edge of the desert; its construction should be assigned to the second half of the eleventh century.

Spiritual Supports of the Coptic Renewal

A spiritual and organizational renewal of this magnitude, involving every aspect of Coptic church life, is accompanied by and embedded in a variety of religious events, some of which are typical of the Eastern Christian tradition. Also, the support of the early saints has been manifested by the discovery and translation of holy relics. Besides the relics of St. Mark, which were returned from Venice in June 1968 and repose in the crypt of the new cathedral of St. Mark in Abbasiya, Cairo, Pope Shenuda III received the relics of St. Athanasius of Alexandria from Pope Paul VI in May 1973 and also placed them in the cathedral. In Lent of 1976, the monks of the monastery of St. Macarius claimed to have discovered the relics of St. John the Baptist and the prophet Elisha in the ancient church of St. Macarius; they are now kept in the monastery. In October 1986, a group of Roman Catholic pilgrims from Zurzach, Switzerland, presented Shenuda III with a relic of the city's patron saint, Verena, who is said to have accompanied the Theban Legion from upper Egypt to Switzerland, where she suffered martyrdom during Diocletian's persecutions in the beginning of the fourth century. Two years later, relics of St. Maurice, the leader of the Theban Legion, were translated from the Benedictine abbey of St. Maurice in Tholey, Saar, Germany, to Cairo by two Roman Catholic priests, who presented these relics to the patriarch on April 14, 1989, at the monastery of St. Bishoi. In November 1991, it was my pleasure and honor to offer the patriarch the relics of the Theban martyrs Sts. Cassius and Florentius from the cathedral in Bonn, Germany. They, too, had suffered martyrdom under Diocletian.

In the monastery of St. Anthony on the Red Sea the incorruptible body of the great theologian Yusab al-Abahh, metropolitan of Girga and Akhmim (1735–1826) has recently been discovered and placed in a glass reliquary in the church of the Holy Apostles. The monks of the monastery of St. Samuel, in the desert of al-Qalamun, testify that in December 1976, the incorruptible body of St. Pisada, kept in the church of St. Misail, bled.

During the summer of 1990, the relics of twelve Coptic martyrs were unearthed near the monastery of St. Gabriel of Naqlun in the oasis of Fayyum. The bishop of the Fayyum distributed many of these relics to Coptic churches throughout Egypt and also in the United States, Australia, and Europe. In March 1990, large numbers of mummies were discovered near the monastery of the Martyrs, east of al-Hawawish. Many of these relics, believed to be those of Christian martyrs, were distributed to churches in Egypt and the diaspora. In the course of archeological work at Abu Fana, thirty kilometers south of Minya near Qasr Hor, workers discovered in 1992 the mummy of Apa Bane, a famous monk of the fourth century from upper Egypt, who is venerated by the faithful of the diocese of Mallawi. In August 1991, workers also found the remains of the tenth-century saint Simeon the Tanner in the church of the Holy Virgin of Babylon al-Darag (Old Cairo); the relics were divided between the churches of the Holy Virgin al-Muallaqa, Old Cairo; St. Simeon the Tanner, Muqattam, Cairo; and the Holy Virgin of Babylon al-Darag. At no other time in the recent history of the Coptic Church have so many relics been discovered as in the past fifteen years. One is reminded of the severe admonition of St. Shenuda, the fifth century abbot from upper Egypt, who strongly opposed the growth of this practice.

Moreover, appearances of the Holy Virgin and phenomena of light have provided celestial confirmation. There have been a number of appearances of the Holy Virgin: on the dome of the church of the Holy Virgin in Zeitun, a suburb of Cairo, in the spring of 1968; on the dome of the church of St. Damiana (Dimiana) in Shubra in the spring of 1986; in the church of the Holy Virgin in Edfu in upper Egypt in August 1981; in the church of the Holy Virgin in the delta village of Shetana al-Hagar in 1997 and 1998; and in the cathedral of St. Mark in Asyut in the fall of 2000. In all these instances, Christians of various denominations and Muslims have witnessed the manifestations, which are interpreted as signs of special grace in time of social and political adversity. For the biblically oriented Copts, an Arabic pulpit Bible provided the assurance of divine election when, on Sunday, June 13, 1976, this Protestant Bible, floating on the Nile, came to rest on the riverbank at the church of the Holy Virgin in Maadi, a suburb of Cairo. Bishop Gregorius of the theological seminary verified that it was open at Isaiah's prophecy, "Blessed be Egypt my people" (19:25).

The widespread veneration of the great wonderworker of the twentieth century, Pope Cyril VI, is significant. Even during his life he was the most beloved person because of his charismata. His cave, three kilometers from the monastery of al-Baramus in Wadi al-Natrun, and his tomb, in the crypt of the new basilica of St. Menas in the monastery in Maryut, have become popular shrines of pilgrimage for large numbers of Copts.

In conclusion, we should consider one new development. Because of the reclamation of desert land by both the government and the monasteries, one can now reach all desert monasteries by paved roads. For the first time in their sixteen-hundred-year history, these monasteries nowadays sit at the edge of the secular world, of consumer society; only a few gallons of gasoline separate them from golf-courses, beauty shops, fast-food restaurants, and the noise of village life. The silence surrounding them is broken. These venerable fortresses of spiritual austerity are being rapidly integrated into the life of the Coptic Church. Every weekend literally hundreds of pilgrims from cities and villages descend upon the monks. For the sake of the visitors they have installed souvenir kiosks selling pamphlets, medals, leather crosses, and textiles. The days of quiet, solitude, and isolation are gone forever, except for those few anchorites who have left their monasteries and fled from the world to live in the caves of the inner desert, miles away from the noise of our civilization: "Ama nesciri et pro nihilo reputari" (you should love to remain unknown and to be held for nothing).

The Arts Using Color

Marie-Hélène Rutschowscaya

Wall Paintings

The foundation of Alexandria in 332 B.C.E. irrevocably marks the Hellenization of Egypt and is at the root of a hybrid style in which the tradition of pharaonic Egypt is progressively overlaid with the forms and images spread abroad first by the Greeks and then by the Romans. In the absence of mosaics, probably because of their being costly and their taking a long time to execute, Coptic edifices were decorated with carvings often enhanced by colors and with paintings whose evolution can be traced without discontinuity from the Roman period to the Middle Ages.

The oldest Christian paintings in Egypt, no longer in existence, were in the catacombs of Karmuz in Alexandria (end of the third century). The semi-circular apse of the antechamber, probably serving as a chapel, was decorated with a frieze depicting those miracles of Christ which prefigure the Last Supper and the Eucharist. Christ was enthroned between Sts. Peter and Andrew, who were shown presenting the loaves and fishes to him. The baskets placed at their feet as well as the banquet scene to the right—where an inscription said that the people "ate the eulogies," that is, the bread Jesus blessed—pointed to the multiplication of the loaves and fishes. To the left, inscriptions identified Christ and the Holy Virgin among the guests who were witnesses to the changing of water into wine at the wedding in Cana. The scenes with wooded backgrounds, the supple and natural poses of the people (bodies seen from the back or in three-quarter, variety and liveliness of the gestures, fluid and floating clothing) link this work to Roman art, whether pagan or paleo-Christian, and in particular to the art of the catacombs both in Egypt (catacombs of Alexandria, temple dedicated to the worship of the emperor in Luxor) and in the rest of the Roman world (Rome, Libya, Bulgaria). In Bagawat, in the oasis of al-Kharga, the paintings of the funerary chapels exhibit a notable change in style and an enrichment of the iconographic repertory. The Chapel of the Exodus (fourth century) derives its name from the picturesque narration of the journey of the Hebrews toward the Promised Land under Moses' leadership. The center of the cupola is covered with a network of vine branches full of birds; this theme, which originated in the East, was most favored by the Roman world and was used again and again in the decoration of Christian monuments (mausoleum of St. Constantia in Rome, fourth century). The lower tier is occupied, without apparent order, by diminutive silhouettes rapidly sketched; other scenes from the Old Testament are added to that of the Exodus (sacrifice of Abraham, cycle of Jonah, Daniel in the lions' den, the three young men in the furnace, Noah's ark, and so on); there are also saints (St. Thecla and other holy women). In contrast, the Chapel of Peace (fifth century) presents large hieratic figures arranged in perfect order. Scenes from the Old Testament predominate: Adam and Eve after their sin, the sacrifice of Abraham, Daniel in the lions' den, Jacob, Noah's ark; the annunciation, placed after Noah's ark, symbolizes the new covenant between God and God's people while the following scene of St. Thecla conversing with St. Paul illustrates the theme of the teaching imparted to the faithful. These two styles appear also in the art of Roman catacombs as well as in the baptistery of Dura-Europos in Syria (beginning of the third century). In Antinoe, the lady Theodosia had herself represented in her funerary chapel as an orant, that is, with her arms outstretched in the attitude of prayer, between St. Colluthus and St. Mary, both natives of the region of Antinoe. Theodosia's high social status is shown in her sumptuous garments with woven decorations but also

1. Bagawat, Oasis of al-Kharga. Cupola of Chapel of the
Exodus, painting (4th century).
2. Monastery of Bawit, chapel 3. David and Saul, painting
(6th–8th centuries).
3. Monastery of Bawit, chapel 17. St. Phoibammon on
horseback, painting (6th–8th centuries).

4. Monastery of Bawit, chapel 28. The Holy Virgin and
Child in a medallion, painting (6th–7th centuries).
5. Monastery of the Martyrs, Esna. St. Claudius on
horseback, painting (11th–12th centuries).

by the painted decor of this monument where Christ between two angels was also represented. The animal and vegetal decor serving as background to the figures, the hieratic poses, the faces, and the folds of clothing treated in the antique manner, however with simplified forms, place the whole work in the Byzantine context of the fifth-sixth centuries, which is the time when the oldest icons and the mosaics of Ravenna (northern Italy) were created. In a house at Wadi Sarga, south of Asyut, a painting depicting the three young men in the furnace adopts a more lively style by means of the swaying of the bodies, the floating cloaks, and the varied attitudes of the men and the angel who, armed with a long staff, comes to save the martyrs surrounded by flames.

The oldest places of worship were established in the pharaonic temples, whose carved walls were covered over with paintings of which only scant vestiges remain (Philae, Abydos, Deir al-Bahari, Dandara, Luxor, Karnak, Madinat Habu, temples of Wadi al-Sebua and Abu Hoda in Nubia). For this reason the rock church of Deir Abu Hinnis near Antinoe, hewn within an ancient quarry, is home to one of the oldest examples of ecclesial painting (end of the sixth century). A long frieze at the base of the ceiling narrates the episodes of Christ's life, among which one can recognize the massacre of the innocents before Herod, the flight of Elizabeth and John, the dream of Joseph, and the flight into Egypt. The frieze, which continues uninterrupted between the scenes, is characterized by the variety of poses and the liveliness of the silhouettes. The sketches of the enthroned king, the sleeping person, the journey have their replicas in Mediterranean works of the same period (seat of Maximianus, ivory, Ravenna, sixth century). In the eighth century, in the same church, another cycle devoted to Zechariah's life was painted, with more rigid poses and stiff folds in the clothing. Two miracles of Christ, the wedding at Cana and the resurrection of Lazarus, were treated separately, a sign of things to come: compositions in panels. This method was adopted for a large part in the monastic complexes of Bawit and Saqqara, which flourished between the sixth and eighth centuries. In the oratories of the cells and in the churches, the walls may present up to three tiers of decoration: above the lowest tier, made of large panels with geometrical or floral motifs, the upper tiers show tall figures of standing monks and saints or scenes telling a story. Before that time (third century B.C.E.–second century C.E.), in the pagan necropolises of Tuna al-Gebel and Alexandria, the same devices were reminiscent of both the methods of pharaonic painting and those of Greek and Roman pictorial art. These paintings, discovered at the beginning of the twentieth century, show cycles that are unique because of their early date, the variety of the images, and the superb quality of their artisanship. The scenes from the Old and New Testaments (story of David, the three young men in the furnace, the cycle of the nativity and the annunciation, the baptism of Christ, and so on) are side by side with figures of equestrian saints, rows of saints and monks. Certain niches are occupied by the Holy Virgin seated on a throne holding the Child in front of her or nursing him; these representations are references to the divine motherhood of the Holy Virgin defined at the council of Ephesus in 431. The theme of nursing brings to mind the numerous representations of the goddess Isis nursing her son Horus. The most astonishing images depict the apocalyptic visions drawn from the biblical texts of Ezekiel, Isaiah, Daniel, and John: Christ, seated on a fiery chariot, is surrounded by the figures of the four living creatures flying on seraphim wings strewn with eyes; two angels bow as a sign of veneration; on the background of a starry sky, the sun and moon, personified by busts as was the convention in antiquity, symbolize the renewal of time, that is, eternity. On the lower tier, the Holy Virgin stands among the apostles in the traditional manner, as an orant, or is seated on a throne with the Child, whom she may nurse. This composition, which manifestly suggests the ascension, links the apocalyptic vision with the twofold event of the death and resurrection of Christ and then his second coming at the Last Judgment.

These great compositions and the narrative scenes are absent from Kellia (the Cells). A bust of Christ, warrior saints, a St. Menas between two camels appear as theophanic visions, like the portable icons. On the other hand, allegorical figures (unicorn, lambs, the Nile) and a multitude of animal pictures (lions, ducks, quails), plus lush vegetal compositions, have their roots in a daily life conditioned by the Nile and the desert, a life that was the anchorites'. As in other semi-anchoritic monasteries (Esna, Deir al-Dik), the cross is ubiquitous, whether bejewelled, enveloped by foliage, or weighed down by pomegranates, censers, or small bells. The theme of the crucifixion is not attested in Egypt before the twelfth century. The decorated cross evokes not Christ's torment but his triumph over death and his glory. One of these crosses has the particularity of showing in its center the bust of Christ giving a blessing (sixth–seventh centuries), which also appears in a Coptic manuscript dated from 906 (New York, Pierpont Morgan Library, M 600). However, it is an image which is also found in Ravenna, Italy (mosaic in St. Apollinaris in Classe, sixth century), on flasks from the Holy Land in Monza and Bobbio, Italy (sixth century), in Armenian manuscripts from the fifteenth–seventeenth centuries, and in the Nubian paintings of Faras and Abdallah Nirqi (ninth–eleventh centuries).

The Arab conquest did not stifle the artistic productivity of the Egyptian Christians. In fact, it was even a period when wall painting blossomed, creating great iconographic programs often covering over more ancient works. This was the case particularly in the monasteries of Wadi al-Natrun. In the church of the Holy Virgin, an annunciation was discovered in 1991; in about 1225 it had been overlaid with an ascension but could go back as far as a date before 710, when the Syrians bought the monastery. This magnificent work is remarkable because of its style and also because of the richness of its iconography: the Holy Virgin, seated on a throne, listens to the archangel's message; the group placed in the foreground of the town of Nazareth is surrounded by four prophets holding phylacteries (scrolls) with Coptic inscriptions. They are Moses, Isaiah, Ezekiel, and Daniel. This iconographic depiction, unique in Egypt, appears only in 1294 in the Peribleptos Church in Ochrid. A large part of the walls had been covered with up to three coats of paint. Thus two paintings of the Virgin and Child, dating from the second half of the seventh century, were discovered, as well as the group of Abraham, Isaac, and Jacob holding the souls of the blessed in Paradise. Later paintings are located in conchas: the ascension, annunciation, nativity, and dormition. There are Syriac inscriptions within the field of the compositions; the models are incontestably Byzantine, but the style is akin to the rock paintings of Cappadocia. The monasteries of al-Baramus and Anba Bishoi (Pshoi in Coptic) have also given us vestiges of paintings, among which is the encounter of Abraham with Melchizedek, showing a simplicity of drawing and colors characteristic of the oldest monastic paintings. In the monastery of St. Macarius, the sanctuary of Benjamin in the church of St. Macarius is remarkable for its use of wood panels as the base for paintings. For example, the twenty-four elders of the book of Revelation were seated on thrones embellished with precious stones and each held an ornate chalice, but each of their heads was painted on a wooden disk. At the base of the cupola, each triangular wooden panel had been painted with an immense figure of a winged seraph who seemed to unfold its wings to protect the sanctuary. The intrados of the entrance arch was covered with woodwork on which there were medallions showing the still recognizable scenes of the embalming and burial of Christ. On the west wall, Christ between two angels was side by side with equestrian and other saints. It is possible that these vestiges date from the restoration that took place under the patriarch Jacob (d. 830). In contrast, the decoration of the adjacent sanctuary of St. Mark could date from the years 1010–1050, when the evangelist's reliquary was brought to the monastery, a date which would tally well with the characteristics of the Fatimid style (pointed arches, decoration of the squinches). The iconographic program is much more complex and is divided into two tiers at the level of the pendentives and in their squinches at the base of the cupola. While the lower tier shows figures of angels, saints, a head of Christ, seraphim, and the scene of the three young men in the furnace, the upper tier illustrates scenes from the Old and New Testaments, the former prefiguring the latter. Moreover, the saints, monks, and martyrs of the lower tier appear as the witnesses of Christian faith and its intercessors, either by their ascetical life or their martyrdom.

In the desert in the vicinity of Esna, two monasteries, Deir al-Shuhada and Deir al-Fakhuri, preserve the vestiges of twelfth century paintings. Three times in Deir al-Shuhada, Christ is represented on his throne; two of these paintings show the apocalyptic vision so widespread in Egypt. On one of them, the busts of the Holy Virgin and St. John evoke the theme of the Deesis ("intercession" in Greek), which in the Byzantine world is linked with the Last Judgment; in the lower part, the Holy Virgin and Child, between the archangels Michael and Gabriel, is akin to the tradition of Bawit and Saqqara. On the other, Christ's feet rest on the sea of crystal mentioned in the book of Revelation (4:6) to symbolize the slaking of the saints' thirst and the separation of the heavenly world from the earthly.

In contrast, in the east apse of Deir al-Abiad (the White Monastery) in Sohag, Christ is enthroned among the four living creatures and the four evangelists at their writing, a unique example of this association; but similarly, the theme of the Deesis reappears in the south apse beneath an immense cross around whose arms a piece of cloth is wound (eleventh–twelfth century). In the nave of the church, now open to the sky, the walls show a variety of crosses, some of them identical with that of the south apse. Other crosses, arms covered with large intertwined designs, are identical to those decorating manuscripts of the twelfth–thirteenth centuries and to that in the apse of the church of Deir Abu Fana, also from the twelfth–thirteenth centuries.

Near the Red Sea, the church of St. Anthony in the monastery of the same name, has the particularity of not having had other phases of construction than the original one in the beginning of the thirteenth century. The decoration was immediately undertaken by Master Theodore about 1232–1233; before 1436, another painter worked there, called the painter of the paschal cycle (the holy women at the tomb, the appearance of Christ to the two Marys). Thus, the paintings follow an iconographic program established from the start, a fact which confers to the ensemble a cohesion rarely found elsewhere: at the entrance to the church, the faithful are welcomed by large equestrian saints and holy monks; as they advance toward the sanctuary, other saints and patriarchs meet them. As in Wadi al-Natrun, the sanctuary has several tiers leading the onlookers' gaze from Old Testament scenes to the twenty-four elders of the Apocalypse, then to the Holy Virgin and Child on the east wall, and to the enthroned Christ above. In the cupola there is a bust of Christ Pantocrator (ruler of the universe) surrounded by angels and seraphim. In addition, the theme of the apocalyptic vision of the enthroned Christ, between the Holy Virgin and St. John, appears once more in the adjacent chapel, called Chapel of the Four Living Creatures.

Paintings on Wood and Icons

One can consider that the large number of small painted wooden panels discovered on the site of the south church of the monastery of Bawit (middle Egypt) were either part of the screens separating the sanctuary

6. Monastery of Phoibammon, Deir al-Bahari(?). Bishop Abraham, painting (end of 6th century). Now in the Museum of Late Antique and Byzantine Art, Berlin.

7. Icon of St. Mark (6th century). Paris, National Library, Fr. 1129a.

8. Double icon representing the archangel Gabriel on one side and St. Theodore on the other (6th–7th centuries). Cairo, Coptic Museum, 9083.

9. Monastery of the Syrians, Wadi al-Natrun. The four sides of a chalice case with the representations of the Holy Virgin and Child, the Last Supper, Aaron, and Moses (18th century).

10. Cairo, church of St. Theodore the Easterner. Icon of St. Mercurius (18th century).

from the nave or part of the liturgical furniture (altar, chests, pulpit, and so on). Vestiges of carved woodwork, still in their places on the interior and exterior facades of the monument, attest that the painted panels could also have been part of the architectural decor. Thus, wooden panels representing narrative scenes, seraphim, and saints, dating from a later period, can still be seen in place in the monastery of St. Macarius at Wadi al-Natrun (ninth–twelfth centuries) and in Ethiopian churches (ninth–fifteenth centuries). Whether movable or fixed, these images must have been venerated as icons, with which, as texts assert, the Copts were familiar. The oldest go back to the fifth or sixth century. Seven among them come from a tomb in Antinoe (middle Egypt): an old man's bust, busts of saints, a veiled woman, an angel, all characterized by a style still very close to antiquity, and akin to the Roman-Egyptian portraits called Fayyumic, which disappear at the end of the fourth century when mummification was discontinued. Thus, the techniques of tempera painting and encaustic on wooden panels survived in the art of the icon, whether Coptic or Byzantine. In all probability, the Roman-Egyptian portraits were originally destined for domestic worship and were subsequently placed in graves; in the same way, the icons of Antinoe were reverently set down near the dead to obtain their intercession before God. Heirs to the Roman works, the paintings of Christ and Abbot Menas (Paris, Louvre Museum), Bishop Abraham (Berlin, Museum für spätantike und byzantinische Kunst), Saint Mark (Paris, Bibliothèque nationale, cabinet des médailles), Saint Theodore (Cairo, Coptic Museum) are characterized by a local, monastic style which differentiates them from the Byzantine works of the same period. The features of the faces are simplified and painted with flat colors; the folds in clothing are spare and either vertical or curved, drawn with one single brush stroke; the colors are muted.

Between the seventh and eighteenth centuries, icon-making seems to have been abandoned in Egypt since there is a total absence of production during this period. If this were not the case, one would have to explain the disappearance of these painted works—which reappear only in the first quarter of the eighteenth century—as the result of either iconoclastic violence or liturgical practice. From the eighteenth century on, icons are often signed and even dated. So we learn that many painters were foreigners, natives of Armenia, Greece, or Ethiopia. Nevertheless, the simplification of the forms, the use of flat colors and bold delineation seem to be genuinely Coptic characteristics, perhaps demanded by local customers attached to the tradition of monastic wall painting.

The Manuscripts

The oldest manuscripts in the Coptic language are the Gnostic codices written on papyrus discovered in Nag Hammadi (upper Egypt); they date from the fourth century. The calligraphy of individual letters, titles,

11. Annunciation, manuscript on parchment (913–914). New York, Pierpont Morgan Library, M 597, fol. 1v.

and beginnings of paragraphs in black, ocher, or yellow is the only decorative touch. We must wait until the fifth–sixth century (Codex Glazier, New York, Pierpont Morgan Library) to see a tau cross decorated with interlacing motifs and birds. The period called Coptic-Arab marks the beginning of a real miniature art characterized by a meticulous artisanship and an increased richness due to the use of gold applied either in sheets or with a brush. From the seventh century until about the year 1000, the manuscripts are decorated with monumental full-length figures deeply influenced by the wall painting in which frontality, the simplification of garments and shapes belong to the local tradition. The technique of linear drawing is also Egyptian; it is utilized much less often in Byzantium and the East.

From the twelfth century on, sumptuous Coptic manuscripts, adorned with gospel scenes characterized by a lively narrative style start to appear, imitating illustrated Byzantine and Eastern evangelaries (books of the Gospels). In general, the manuscripts begin with the portraits of the evangelists in the act of writing, a custom inherited from classical antiquity, which presented the portrait of the author at the beginning of the work. At the end of the twelfth century, Islamic influence becomes preponderant in the aniconic decorations, particularly the luxurious ornamentation of the headings of books and chapters. The artists follow the same artistic rules as the illustrators of the Koran: on a gold or silver background they deploy a complex network of geometrical figures which are inspired by Christianity (crosses) or are purely Islamic (arabesques). Moreover, the gospel characters move in an Islamized world which distances them from the Byzantine manuscripts. The two manuscripts, Coptic 13 at the Bibliothèque nationale in Paris (dated 1179–1180), and Coptic 1 at the Institut catholique in Paris (dated 1249–1250), form a unique iconographic ensemble in Coptic painting, which takes its place in the wider tradition, Armenian, Syriac, and Ethiopian; the figures wear caftans and turbans; the ornamentation of monuments and furniture is borrowed from Islamic decorative art (trilobed frames, furniture with inlaid work, brocade hangings, carpets); a rich polychromatic palette is used; scenes from contemporary daily life are represented.

The Fabrics

The fashion of wearing ornate garments appears as early as the New Empire (fabrics in the tomb of Thutmose IV [c. 1420–1411 B.C.E.], tunic of Tutankhamen [c. 1358 B.C.E.]) because of increased contacts with the Near East where material decorated with colorful ornamentation was a century-old tradition. This fashion reappears during the Roman period with the spread of the use of wool. Indeed, flax, exclusively used until the Greek period, was very difficult to dye, in contrast to wool which made it possible to obtain colors whose sumptuousness and freshness have persisted to our own time. Furthermore, we must add the shimmering silk materials adorning some pieces of clothing obviously of Eastern origin: caftans, leggings, tunics. This fashion seems again to have come from the East since it is in Syria—in Palmyra and Dura-Europos—that fragments of tunics dated from the second–third centuries and decorated with ornate braids and medallions made of flax and wool were discovered. The decorations in unbleached flax and purple wool reproduce geometrical and vegetal motifs identical with those of the sculptures and mosaics of the same period. In Egypt, the painted shrouds of the third–fourth centuries often represent the dead clad in garments ornamented in the same way. The custom spread throughout the whole Mediterranean basin, as one can easily see in mosaics (Piazza Armerina, Sicily) and paintings (Roman catacombs). However, it is only in Egypt, thanks to the dry climate and sandy subsoil, that fabrics have survived to our own time in an unrivalled state of preservation. Sites such as Antinoe and Akhmim have yielded tens of thousands of these textiles, especially in necropolises. Indeed, when mummification fell into disuse in the course of the fourth century, the dead were buried in their clothes, sometimes most sumptuous (tunics, cloaks, shirts of fine linen, shawls, headdresses with hair nets, shoes), and were surrounded with funerary furniture, sometimes a substantial amount. The large panels, with decorations identical to those of the clothing, may have been used originally as household furnishings (altar covers, blankets, curtains) and later on reused as shrouds. A particular series includes large printed linen panels—only fragments are extant—which, like the great "Antinoe veil" (fourth century, Paris, Louvre Museum), had several tiers of decoration. To obtain this effect, the material was immersed in a bath of dye, but certain parts of it were covered with a protective substance (clay, wax) to keep it undyed. In his *Natural History* (35.42), Pliny states that this technique was particularly utilized in Egypt. Printing on material is represented by fabrics of the fourth century at the earliest and continues until the Arab period.

The names of the great textile centers, like Alexandria, Panopolis, Oxyrhynchus, Tinnis, and Damietta, are known to us only through texts because any trace of a weaving shop in these locations has irremediably disappeared because of the fragility of wooden looms. It is only by studying the fabrics themselves that one can have any idea of their manufacture. The decorations in tapestry using the "Gobelins" stitch have backgrounds of cloth or tapestry; the decorations themselves and the background were rarely woven separately and later on sewn together. Most often, they were woven together on the loom; thus, tunics were made in a single piece or in three pieces and then assembled. The delicate dye work was done in specialized shops which used mostly vegetal dyes: madder and Mediterranean lichen for the reds; indigo and woad for the blues; reseda, pomegranate, saffron for the yellows. The animal dyes like the kermes of a Mediterranean red oak and the Armenian cochineal, which were very expensive, were rarely used in Egypt. Of the true purple, a color extracted from the shell of murex brandaris and highly prized in the Roman Empire, there is no trace in the Coptic fabrics.

Only two groups of fabrics have been dated with certainty. A pair of medallions and a band of flax and purple wool coming from a tomb in Hawara in al-Fayyum were found together with a coin dated 340 C.E.; their decoration is identical with that of painted Egyptian shrouds of the Roman period and fabrics discovered in Syria. In an Antinoe tomb, next to the body of Aurelius Colluthus, were sales contracts and his will, all written in Greek between 454 and 456 C.E. He was wrapped in a large tapestry whose upper tier shows

12. Band of fabric used for trimming, with network of grapevine leaves, flax and wool (4th–5th centuries). Paris, Louvre Museum, AF 5635.

13. Fabric with the representation of the birth of Aphrodite surrounded by a border of Nilotic decorations, flax and wool (6th century). Paris, Louvre Museum, AF 5470.

two busts under arcades supported by two large columns; a geometrical network with florets and leaves covers the space between the columns, a composition quite similar to the decorations in paintings and mosaics of the same period. It is essentially on the basis of iconographic, stylistic, and technical comparisons that one can attempt to establish a relative chronology. Among the oldest fabrics (second to fifth centuries), one must rank those which show naturalistic forms and those which, thanks to the gradation of colors, succeed in imitating the three-dimensional technique dear to Greek and Roman artists. In the course of the sixth and seventh centuries, the progressive disappearance of these effects entails an increasing use of flatly applied colors and an ever growing simplification of forms. During the Arab period, the dislocation of the elements, resulting in the loss of comprehension of the subject, leads to schematization and even to a purely ornamental abstraction. As in the pharaonic period, Egyptian fabrics kept their renown for a long time and in distant lands, to such an extent that in India they were called *kabati,* which comes from the plural form of the Arabic Qibt (Copt, Egyptian).

As happened to all regions which became part of the Roman Empire, Egypt was rapidly submerged by the artistic and iconographic formulas made fashionable by its new master, to the point of causing the nearly complete abandonment of pharaonic images despite their being several millennia old. One of the oldest is certainly that of the sign of life, the ankh, especially reproduced on Coptic objects because it was likened to the sign of the cross. Intended to breathe life into the gods and the dead, it was adopted by Christians because of its signifying resurrection and life and also because of its likeness to Constantine's cross, the labarum, made of a cross surmounted by a crown encircling the Chi-Rho (chrismon). The similarity between this sign and the Egyptian cross of life led many pagans to convert when, by order of the patriarch Theophilus, the Serapeum of Alexandria was destroyed in 391.

Nilotic subjects, which showed the fauna and flora of the Nile, became extraordinarily popular clichés throughout the Roman world: personification of the Nile, hunting and fishing activities, scenes of navigation on the river. However, if the flat application of colors can be reminiscent of a convention of pharaonic painting,

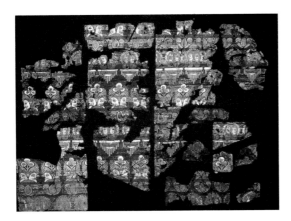

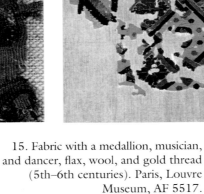

14. Fabric with griffins, trimming of a cloak from Antinoe (6th century). Paris, Louvre Museum, E 29212.

15. Fabric with a medallion, musician, and dancer, flax, wool, and gold thread (5th–6th centuries). Paris, Louvre Museum, AF 5517.

16. Fabric belonging to Aurelius Colluthus, flax and wool, Antinoe (middle of 5th century). Brussels, Royal Museums of Art and History, Tx 2470.

the treatment of human figures now follows Greek and Roman models. Thus Isis becomes the goddess Euthenia; Hapi, the personification of the Nile in pharaonic times, becomes a typically Roman river god sporting a thick head of hair and holding a cornucopia. The art of Coptic fabrics transforms in an original way the subjects drawn from the repertory of classic mythology. The god Dionysus, often accompanied by secondary divinities, was one of the favorites in the Roman period because he was likened to Osiris, the god of death and resurrection, called "master of the wine" in the texts of the pyramids. With the ascendancy of Christianity, the image of grape-harvesting cherubs and the vine became a frequent theme because of its funerary and symbolic meaning. The harvest of ripe fruit symbolized the gathering of completed human lives but also the idea of sacrifice followed by resurrection, essential to Christian faith: "I am the true vine, and my Father is the vinegrower" (John 15:1). Some of the impressive number of mythological scenes lent themselves to being Christianized in an effective way: Daphne is transformed into a laurel tree as the soul is transformed when it leaves the human body; the attribution of the purity of the pearl to Christ could be linked with the myth of Aphrodite's birth; Orpheus, holding the animals under his spell, was compared to Christ because the former had the revelation of "divine unity." Nevertheless, many of the scenes must be regarded as mere decorations empty of any meaning: Artemis the hunter, Bellerophon and the Chimaera, Jason and the Golden Fleece, scenes from Homer's poems and Euripides' tragedies, bucolic subjects, dancers, and so on.

Eastern motifs (double palms, floral backgrounds, winged animals, griffins, human heads arranged in staggered rows) which decorate wool tapestries may have been borrowed directly from silk materials found in Egypt in vast quantities and probably imported from the East, particularly from Sassanid Persia. Certain of these tapestries may have been made either in Egypt or in the East (leggings in the Louvre Museum and the Museum of Fabrics in Lyons, tapestry decorated with heads and palms in the Louvre Museum).

It is within this ambiance that the new religion, itself having originated in the East, was born and grew. If Christian themes appear to be less frequent than pagan ones, it remains that they constitute a most varied iconographic array which adorns without discrimination hangings, curtains, and items of clothing. Next to the representations of orants, holy persons, equestrian saints, and the motif of the cross, the Bible supplied the sources of inspiration for more elaborate projects. The scenes from the Old Testament which prefigure those of the New gave rise to astonishing works. The series of fabrics devoted to the story of the patriarch Joseph has the particularity of showing medallions and bands on garments depicting the episodes of his life as a continuous cycle: his father Jacob sends Joseph to his brothers; Joseph is plunged into the cistern and then removed from it; his tunic is dipped in a goat's blood; he is sold to the Ishmaelites; he travels to Egypt on the back of a camel; he is sold to Potiphar, the captain of the pharaoh's guard. Joseph's dream is often placed in the center of this narration because it foretold Joseph's destiny. The style of stocky bodies, with forms that are beginning to be dislocated and with square eyes, suggests the seventh or eighth century as a tentative date. According to their style, Jonah coming out of the mouth of the sea monster, the sacrifice of Isaac, and the ascension of Elijah belong to the same period. In contrast, the printed linen cloths, probably easier and quicker to execute, were often composed of several tiers and therefore represented several scenes: Jonah, Daniel in the lions' den, Moses receiving the tablets of the Law, the vision of the burning bush.

Gospel scenes appear on tapestries and printed fabrics as well as on silk embroideries. The printed fabrics are still strongly influenced by antique and paleo-Christian art. Embroideries belong to the Byzantine world; whether in wool, silk, or gold thread, embroidery work seems to have come from the East and had an unequalled importance in the Byzantine Empire. In Egypt, its use remained very restricted; workers were content with imitating tapestry decorations and copying Byzantine motifs. From the nativity to the miracles of Christ, the episodes which have been preserved attest to a custom anchored in a Mediterranean tradition of the use of ornamented textiles imitating paintings and mosaics. Certain printed fabrics were probably even created as icons kept in private dwellings or in churches, on a par with painted icons or those in mosaic, metal, or ivory. This is likely the case of the tapestry of the enthroned Holy Virgin (sixth century, Cleveland Museum). The composition seems to be a copy of a wall painting in a monastery church: the Holy Virgin is seated on a throne embellished with pearls and gems; she holds the Child on her knees and is flanked by the archangels Michael and Gabriel; above her, Christ on his throne is lifted up by two angels, an evocation of both the ascension and the apocalyptic vision of God. Twelve medallions containing the busts of the apostles are set off by a sumptuous vegetal border. The graphic style of the folds in the clothing and the schematic character of the faces, fashioned in a soft and nuanced way, situate this piece between the fifth and sixth centuries, the period of the oldest known painted icons.

Thus, the practice of wearing ornate garments, which began in the Roman period, naturally continued during the Christian period; it became customary to use not only secular subjects (see the Lady Theodosia,

Antinoe, a wall painting from the sixth century) but also often complex biblical narrative scenes like the cycle of Joseph. The most celebrated example in the Byzantine world is the renowned cortege of the empress Theodora, the emperor Justinian's wife, in St. Vitalis in Ravenna (sixth century): the court ladies are clad in luxurious garments covered with flowers, medallions, and squares with geometrical motifs. The empress wears an ample cloak whose lower part is adorned with the representation of the Magi bringing their offerings. As a consequence, the Fathers of the Church and members of the clergy rose up against these artifices and attempted to fight this "foolish industry. As soon as the art of weaving in imitation of painting was invented— an art both futile and useless—by combining the warp and the weft, which made possible the depiction of every kind of animal in fabrics, everybody hastened to purchase for themselves as well as for their wives and children garments covered with flowers and offering images of infinite variety. . . . When they show themselves in public in this sort of attire, they could be mistaken for painted walls. . . . One sees on these fabrics lions, panthers, bears, bulls, dogs, trees, rocks, hunters, in a word everything that the art of the painters who strive to imitate nature can imitate. . . . Those rich people who still have a veneer of piety take designs from the gospel stories and have their artisans execute them. They have them paint [weave or embroider] Jesus Christ in the midst of his disciples. . . . They believe they are doing something pleasing to the Lord when they wear these fabrics adorned with holy pictures; but if they want to follow my advice, let them sell such garments in order to honor the living images of God" (Asterius of Amasia, *Homily 1*, "On the Abuse of Riches").

Greek inscriptions on image: ΑΠΟC ΚΟΛΛΟΥΘΟC ΘΕΙCΙΑ ΟΓΙΑ ΜΑΡΙΑ

1. Theodosia between St. Colluthus and St. Mary, Antinoe. Reproduction in water color executed when the painting was discovered on the arcosolium of Theodosia (5th–6th centuries).

Following pages:

2, 3. St. Antony the Great and St. Paul of Thebes, paintings on wood (18th century). Cairo, Coptic Museum.

4. Christ and Abbot Menas, painting on wood, from the monastery of Bawit (6th–7th centuries). Paris, Louvre Museum.

5. The wedding feast at Cana, miniature on parchment (1179–1180). Paris, National Library, Coptic 13, gospel scenes.

6. Fabric with Jonah coming out of the mouth of the sea monster, flax and wool (6th century). Paris, Louvre Museum, E26820.

7. Fabric, called "Sabine's shawl," with mythological decorations (Artemis the hunter, Apollo and Daphne, Bellerophon and the Chimaera), wool, from Antinoe (6th century). Paris, Louvre Museum, E29302.

8. Fabric with fish, wool, from Antinoe (2nd–3rd centuries). Paris, Louvre Museum.

9. Tempera portrait from Antinoë
(4th century). Paris, Louvre
Museum, AF 6487.

Typology and Architectural Evolution of the Egyptian Churches

edited by Massimo Capuani

Beginning with the fourth century, during which Christianity triumphs over paganism, one sees in Egypt a sustained architectural activity whose primary aim is the building of churches. Except for the funerary monument, from now on the church is the only type of edifice to be considered in monumental terms; the other kinds of buildings (palaces, baths, stadiums, and gymnasiums) which characterized the Hellenistic-Roman period do not greatly interest the majority of people except under rather modest forms.

Among the churches of Coptic Egypt, one can distinguish urban churches and monastic churches. The typology of urban churches is further affected by the site on which a building is erected: large city or rural center. Indeed, the economic conditions enjoyed by large cities favor monumentality whereas the modest resources available to religious communities and farming villages limit their options to less prestigious edifices.

Another typological difference distinguishes the churches of the Mediterranean coast and the delta from those of the Nile valley. Whereas in the Nile valley one meets with characteristics proper to an indigenous cultural and artistic tradition, in the delta and along the Mediterranean coast, regions having a more direct contact with the Byzantine world and culture, one sees imperial architectural forms true to the traditional models of Constantinople's zone of influence.

With rare exceptions, monumentality is banished from monastic edifices. This is connected with the monastic ideal which by definition excludes the use of a rich and refined artistic technique. Monastics must not be led away from their ascetic ideal by the charms of a magnificent but ephemeral architecture. On the contrary, monastic architecture must suggest to them, through its unpolished and austere expression, an image of the spiritual world apt to foster contemplation and mysticism.

BASILICA WITH TRANSEPT

PERIOD

Fifth–sixth centuries

CHARACTERISTICS

The basilicas with transept are rare and found only in large urban buildings. The basilica has a nave separated from the side aisles by two ranks of columns which in general also encircle the transept. The north and south ends of the transept are either rectilinear or semi-circular. This type of church is found in the delta region and middle Egypt, to which it was "imported" from an architectural model of Constantinople and present throughout the Byzantine world.

EXAMPLES

1. Al-Hawariya (Marea), sixth century
2. Sanctuary of St. Menas, fifth–sixth centuries
3. Hermopolis (al-Ashmunein), fifth century

BASILICA WITH NAVE AND FOUR AISLES

PERIOD

Fourth–sixth centuries

CHARACTERISTICS

A few examples of churches with four side aisles—and even one with six—have been discovered; they are distinguished from equivalent imperial churches by a few particular traits. The central part, the nave and inner aisles, is encircled on its four sides by a relatively narrow ambulatory; the east part of the ambulatory gives access to the sanctuary. The nave is particularly narrow in relation to the inner aisles. From the middle of the fifth century this purely Egyptian type gradually disappears and is replaced by the traditional basilica with a nave and two aisles; it is found only in provincial areas.

EXAMPLES

1. Madinat Madi (Narmuthis), fifth–sixth centuries
2. Antinoopolis (Antinoe), fourth century
3. Pbow, fourth–fifth centuries
4. Armant (Hermonthis), sixth century

CHURCH WITH NAVE AND TWO AISLES

PERIOD

Fifth–seventh centuries

CHARACTERISTICS

The traditional basilica with a nave and two side aisles, the nave being wider and more impressive than the aisles, gains ground from the fifth century on. In the interior of Egypt, the architects usually retain the small western return aisle, which connects the side aisles and allows access to the two galleries on the upper story. In contrast, this architectural element is absent along the Mediterranean coast and probably in Alexandria, where churches are modeled on traditional imperial architecture. The sanctuary, either semi-circular or rectangular, is normally flanked by two adjacent rooms (*pastophoria*).

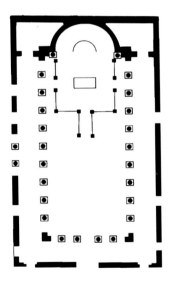

EXAMPLES

1. Sanctuary of St. Menas, sixth century
2. Kellia (the Cells), fifth–seventh centuries
3. Churches of Old Cairo, seventh century
4. Monastery of St. Jeremiah (Saqqara), seventh century
5. Umm al-Burigat, seventh century
6. Kom Namrud, sixth century
7. Monastery of Apa Bane, sixth century
8. Antinoopolis (Antinoe), fifth–sixth centuries
9. Monastery of al-Balayza, probably sixth century
10. Luxor, sixth century
11. Madinat Habu, seventh century

TRICONCH CHURCH

PERIOD

Fifth–seventh centuries

CHARACTERISTICS

The triconch church marks an evolution and the architectural enrichment of the presbytery of the basilican church with a nave and two side aisles. The sanctuary is characterized by three semi-circular apses on its north, east, and south sides arranged like a clover; the two rooms adjacent to the sanctuary are in the shape of a capital gamma. Present especially in middle Egypt, this type is found in both urban and monastic architecture. In the latter, the triconch sometimes takes on a particularly rich and monumental form.

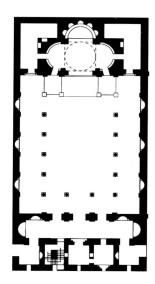

EXAMPLES

1. Monastery of Apa Bane, sixth century
2. White Monastery, fifth century
3. Red Monastery, fifth century
4. Monastery of St. Pachomius (Akhmim), sixth century

5. Dandara, middle of sixth century
6. Deir al-Matmar, sixth century
7. Deir Abu Matta, sixth century

CHURCH WITH A CENTRAL PLAN

PERIOD

Sixth century

CHARACTERISTICS

The edifices with a central plan are rather rare in Egypt and are found only in the delta region. These tetraconch structures have been used in both urban and monastic churches. In these examples, the tetraconch is formed by masonry walls delineating the perimeter of the edifice by means of four semi-circular apses, but it can also be outlined by four groups of columns arranged in semicircles within a rectangular space.

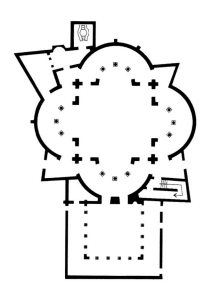

EXAMPLES

1. Sanctuary of St. Menas (east basilica), sixth century
2. Sanctuary of St. Menas *(martyrion)*, sixth century

CHURCH WITH A *KHURUS* (CHOIR)

PERIOD

Seventh–twelfth centuries

CHARACTERISTICS

The addition of the *khurus* (choir) around the middle
of the seventh century shows an evolution of the traditional basilican plan. The *khurus* is a complementary
space which lies crosswise between the nave and the
sanctuary, thus creating a clearer separation between
the area reserved for the laity and that reserved for
the clergy. This innovation was probably introduced
into monastic churches before being adopted by
urban architecture. Many existing edifices were modified by the addition of a *khurus*.

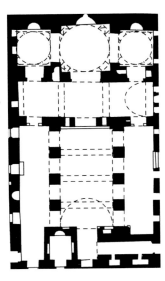

EXAMPLES

1. Monasteries of Sketis, seventh–ninth centuries
2. Churches of Old Cairo, seventh–ninth centuries
3. Monastery of the archangel Gabriel (Deir
   al-Naqlun), tenth–eleventh centuries
4. Monastery of St. Anthony, twelfth century
5. Antinoopolis (Antinoe), seventh century
6. Manqabad, seventh century
7. Al-Hayz, seventh or eighth century
8. Monastery of Ain Saaf, seventh century

CHURCH WITH NAVES ROOFED WITH CUPOLAS

PERIOD

Tenth–twelfth centuries

CHARACTERISTICS

The basilican edifice which was dominant up to the
tenth century undergoes a profound change when a
vaulted roof is adopted. In contrast to the wooden
roofs, this one is not threatened by either fire or insects
and bypasses the problems posed by the rarity of wood
suitable for construction. In lower Egypt, the barrel
vault is used to roof the central nave and *khurus;* but in
upper Egypt, architects have recourse to a church
structure comprising a nave roofed by two cupolas,
which around the twelfth century is transformed into
another structure comprising one cupola supported by
four massive pillars located in the center of the *naos*.

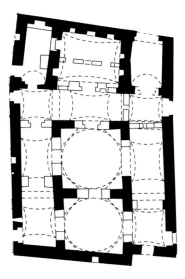

EXAMPLES

1. Monastery of St. Victor (Naqada), twelfth century
2. Monastery of the Potter, twelfth century
3. Monastery of the Martyrs, eleventh–twelfth
   centuries
4. Monastery of al-Kubbaniya, tenth–eleventh
   centuries
5. Monastery of St. Simeon, tenth–eleventh centuries

The Region of the Delta

For various historical and economic reasons which have contributed to the progressive disappearance of important artistic monuments, especially architectural ones, very few Coptic vestiges remain in the region of the delta. From the beginning of the nineteenth century, this region and its cities have shared the history of Alexandria: after centuries of decline and oblivion, this city has become again a cosmopolitan metropolis with a flourishing cultural and economic life. However, the development of urbanization has brought about the destruction of splendid religious and civil buildings whose memory is now found only in literary sources.

The region is rich in places of pilgrimage going back to antiquity, places of pilgrimage which Coptic families from all over Egypt are not willing to give up.

THE CHURCHES OF THE COASTAL CITIES

Alexandria

In our day there remain only scattered ruins of what was the splendor of ancient Alexandria, and practically nothing has come down to us from the monumental buildings going back to the time when the city was the glorious see of a patriarchate. Written documents describe the wealth of its palaces, its streets, its harbor, and in the Christian period, its churches. Indeed, it is obvious that from the fifth century on, triumphant Christianity had a marked influence on the aspect of the city, through the building of many new edifices, especially churches, and the adaptation of existing monuments to new uses. Where the Serapeum, an ancient temple dating from the time of the Ptolemies and dedicated to the god Serapis, had stood Justinian built a church in honor of St. John the Baptist and a monastery. The ancient Caesareum, the sanctuary established by Cleopatra and dedicated by Augustus to the worship of the divinized emperor, was transformed by Constantine into a church in honor of St. Michael; in the middle of the fourth century, this church became the see of the patriarchate of Alexandria. Among the most remarkable buildings of antiquity, we may also cite the church of St. Mark as well as those of the Holy Virgin, St. Theodore, Sts. Sergius and Bacchus, and St. Athanasius. Today, there remains no trace of all these churches, but one may hope that under the characteristic chaos of the modern city, some vestiges of its glorious past as the spiritual center of the Christian East may one day be discovered.

Alexandria honors the evangelist Mark with a vast cathedral erected in the center of the city, where the saint's head is preserved. That St. Mark evangelized Egypt is not only a venerated tradition of the Coptic Church but also the very foundation of the orthodoxy of the church of Alexandria, built on the uninterrupted succession of the Coptic patriarchs to the see of St. Mark. It is a fact that the Christian East used to connect the politically prestigious cities with one of the apostles in order to legitimate the apostolic character of the patriarchal see. In his *Ecclesiastical History* (2.16), Eusebius of Caesarea writes, "They say that this Mark, having set forth, was the first to preach in Egypt the gospel which he had also composed and was the first to establish churches in Alexandria itself" (Eusebius, 110). No one knows what the source of Eusebius' information is, but it is thought that this tradition originated in Rome about 200 and that Eusebius found it mentioned in the writings of Sextus Julius Africanus. The fact that Eusebius reports it very briefly and introduces it by the word *phasin* (they say) leaves its authenticity open to doubt—as though Eusebius were unwilling to insist on this argument because either he is not entirely convinced of its truth or he does not want to give too much "apostolic" importance to the patriarchal see of Alexandria. Indeed, in Eusebius' time this see was already beginning to openly oppose the other patriarchates of the Christian Church. Nonetheless, this tradition was fully accepted, and consequently, the patriarchal see of Alexandria was recognized as the third in rank after those of Rome and Antioch.

Mark, the disciple and companion of Peter, went to Rome with him, and Peter's recollections inspired him to write down his Gospel. Mark might have arrived in Egypt in the fifth decade of the first century (in 40, 43, or 49, depending on the sources). After having evangelized the region of the Nile delta, the Thebaid, Libya, and the Pentapolis and having established Christian communities in Alexandria, Mark would have died a martyr in 62 or 68. His martyrdom has been recorded by writings which tell how he was captured on Easter Day by a group of pagans who were celebrating the festival of the god Serapis, dragged through the streets of the city to a place outside the walls, on the seashore, and killed—unless he died from his wounds. He was buried in the place of his martyrdom, named Bucalis, a venerated goal of pilgrimage for the whole Christian world. In the wake of the doctrinal controversies and the break between the Coptic Church and the Melchite Church, the former appropriated the saint's head for itself while the rest of the body went to the latter. In 828, some Venetian merchants stole the body and carried it to Venice where it was placed in the basilica of St. Mark. In 1968, Pope Paul VI restored part of the relics to the patriarch Cyril VI, and they were transported to the new cathedral of Cairo (Anba Ruwais).

The Basilica of al-Hawariya (Marea)
In the harbor district of ancient Marea, now al-Hawariya, some twenty kilometers south of Alexandria, the remains of an imposing basilica have recently been excavated; it goes back to the sixth century and has a nave, two side aisles, and a transept. Its dimensions are very impressive: the church is forty-nine meters long and thirty-seven meters wide and its transept measures forty-five meters. The nave is separated from the two side aisles by two ranks of columns which do not end with the aisle but continue along the arms of the triconch

17. Large capital from the 6th century, reused as a baptismal font, from Alexandria and now in the Coptic Museum of Cairo.

transept. Up to the discovery of this basilica, that of Hermopolis was believed to be the only one in Egypt to have a transept with semi-circular extremities. But in contrast with that of Hermopolis, the basilica of Marea had neither small rooms on both sides of the apse nor an ambulatory on the west joining the north and south aisles.

Christian Buildings in Amriya

To the south of Amriya, a few kilometers from al-Hawariya, in Kom Abu Draa, the vestiges of a church with a nave, two side aisles, a narthex, and a baptistery have been discovered and are believed to go back to either the sixth or seventh century. Kom Abu Draa also has the ruins of a Christian complex including a church with a nave and two side aisles built over an ancient underground tomb.

North of Amriya, in al-Deir, are the ruins of a monastery which can be identified with the one early Christian sources call Oktokaidekaton.

The Churches in Abusir (Taposiris Magna)

Little is left of the ancient harbor of Taposiris Magna, called Abusir today, in the locality of the Mareotis. The name of the city is certainly derived from the temple of Osiris dating from the Ptolemaic period, whose vestiges have been recovered and which was transformed into a military fortress in the first half of the fourth century. In the east part of the court near the pylons of the temple, the ruins of a small church with a nave, which served the military garrison, are still visible.

In the western section of the city, the remains of a large church complex have been excavated: a basilica with a nave, two side aisles, and a chapel attached to the north wall. Two large courts flank the basilica to the north.

Near the village of Burg al-Arab, a few kilometers south of the ancient Taposiris Magna, stand the ruins of a basilica with two apses, both of which have a synthronon, a nave, and two side aisles; on the west side there is a crypt connected to the side aisles by two flights of stairs. Adjacent to the east apse is a building with an apse on the east side. In the south courtyard of the basilica one can see the remains of a baptismal font.

The Churches of Ain Makhura

On the seashore about fifteen kilometers west of Abukir stand the ruins of a site, dating from late Roman antiquity, whose origins and name are uncertain. The vestiges of two churches have been identified. One, the older of the two, probably goes back to the sixth century; built according to a basilican plan with a short nave and two aisles on either side, it has on the north, east, and south numerous rooms adjacent to the sanctuary, two of which were used as baptisteries. Some of these rooms are more recent than the original building. To the west of this first church, there is another one built with more care and materials of better quality: it is

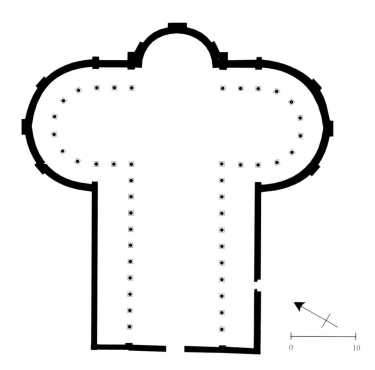

18. Al-Hawariya (Marea).
Plan of the basilica (6th century).

47

a basilica with a nave, two side aisles, an atrium, and a narthex. Its east side contains five rooms, the northern and southern ones protruding from the rectangular plan of the edifice.

The Basilica of Marina al-Alamein (Leucapsis or Antipharae?)

Some forty kilometers from the sanctuary of St. Menas, the seaside health resort of Marina preserves the vestiges of a small basilica from the fourth century. The church is characterized by a narthex on the west and a transverse space between the narthex and the nave; this space is divided into three bays, the middle one giving access to the aisle.

The Church of Tell al-Farama (Pelusium)

West of the ancient city of Pelusium, today Tell al-Farama, recent excavations have revealed a late Roman fortress, which dates from the second half or even end of the sixth century. At Tell al-Makhzan, in the eastern part of Pelusium, are the vestiges of a church. It is a huge basilica with a nave, two side aisles, a narthex, and an inner synthronon. The last features five steps within the apse. The baptistery is at the northwestern corner of the church. To the south of the apse there is a vaulted underground crypt with a bench for the clerics and an altar-block. The basilica dates from the fifth or sixth century.

THE SANCTUARY OF ST. MENAS
(DEIR ABU MINA)

The vestiges of the ancient sanctuary of St. Menas are located about seventy kilometers to the southwest of Alexandria, in the Mareotis (Maryut) district. About two kilometers separate the archaeological area from the monumental monastery of St. Menas, founded in 1959 by the patriarch Cyril VI; a few relics of the saint are kept there.

The Martyrdom of St. Menas

The history of the sanctuary of St. Menas is closely related to the life and martyrdom of this saint, one of the most revered in the Coptic Church. Menas' family belonged to the nobility and was from Nicopolis, an Egyptian city in the delta. According to ancient manuscripts, Menas was born about 275 in Phrygia, where his father, Eudoxios, was prefect. However, it is more probable that he was born in Libya because the Coptic language often confuses Phrygia (Taphrige) with Africa, understood as Libya (Taphryge), geographically and culturally close to Egypt. His parents, Eudoxios and Euphemia, gave Menas a Christian upbringing. At

19. Ampulla of St. Menas representing the saint at prayer between two kneeling camels.

48

their death Menas, still only an adolescent, inherited considerable riches and estates; however, he was intent before all else upon prayer and the reading of Scripture.

At the age of fifteen, Menas was constrained to enlist, but when an edict of the emperors Diocletian and Maximian imposed the pagan cult, Menas donated his wealth to the poor and withdrew to the desert. After a few years of solitude, Menas heard a celestial voice predicting his martyrdom, and he decided to present himself to the prefect in order to confess his Christian faith. The event took place on the occasion of the yearly celebrations in honor of the emperors and consequently in the presence of a great crowd. The prefect was obliged to inflict the worst tortures in an effort to make him abjure his Christian faith and sacrifice to the gods. But although he had been hung from the *hermetarium* and flogged, pulled by the feet, then burned with red-hot irons, Menas remained unshakable and serene in the face of martyrdom. Powerless against his persistent tenacity, the prefect had him beheaded and thrown into the pyre.

The martyrdom took place in 296. A tribune named Athanasius, a pious man, decided to collect Menas' remains and take them along to Egypt in order to protect himself and his retinue. After an eventful journey, during which sea monsters tried to steal the precious cargo, Athanasius and his companions reached Alexandria; they placed Menas' remains on a camel and crossed the Mareotis swamps, but when they reached the desert, the camel stopped short. Since the animal refused to budge, they transferred the load to another camel, stronger and fresher, but this one just as obstinately refused to move. The same thing happened with other camels. Athanasius then understood that he was dealing with a divine sign and the relics of the saint were to remain in this place. He made a wooden case, placed the relics in it, and buried them, but not without building a small temple on the spot.

Pilgrimages to the Sanctuary
Because signal miracles were worked at the saint's grave, the place quickly became the destination of pilgrimage. People sick with every kind of illness came there and the saint healed them all. During Constantine's reign (306–337), an oratory was built which subsequently was enlarged and transformed into a church by the patriarch Athanasius (328–373). All the while, the renown of the holy miracle worker was spreading throughout Eastern Christian communities.

Very soon the church Athanasius had built proved too small for welcoming the thousands of pilgrims coming from the whole ancient world. With the support of the emperors Arcadius and Theodosius II, the patriarch Theophilus began the construction of a vast basilica. This was completed only under the emperor Zeno (474–491), who created a whole city (inns, taverns, baths, markets) to serve the needs of the pilgrims during their stay at the sacred place. The city was named Martyropolis, and the emperor furnished it with a garrison of twelve hundred men capable of defending it against the incursions of desert pillagers.

A lamp burned day and night on the saint's tomb and, according to tradition, the oil was miraculous. Thus it came about that pilgrims collected a small quantity of this oil in a flask and took it along to their homelands as a protection against diseases. The earthen flasks were produced on the spot; they had two handles and were adorned with the image of St. Menas at prayer between two kneeling camels. These flasks were also used to collect the water from the spring near the saint's tomb; this water also was believed to have miraculous powers. Archaeological research has demonstrated, among other things, that near the basilica there stood two bathing stations where pilgrims came to plunge themselves into the miraculous waters.

The sanctuary of St. Menas was never attacked by the Bedouins, who in the course of the fifth and sixth centuries devastated the monasteries of the desert of Scetis, and it was also spared the raids of the Sassanid Persians, who conquered Egypt in the beginning of the seventh century. During the seventh and eighth centuries, the jurisdiction of the sanctuary was the object of intense conflict between the Melchite and Coptic patriarchs. Up to the end of the eighth century, it was in the hands of the Melchites; but about 750, the Ummayad governor Abd al-Malik, to whom the two parties had appealed to resolve the question, opted for the Copts, who thus regained jurisdiction of the sanctuary.

In 836, the caliph al-Mu'tasim decided to have the Gawsaq al-Haqani, his private residence, built in Samarra, in present-day Iraq, and he wanted it to be embellished with marbles and precious furnishings. To achieve this, he ordered that the marble ornaments and columns of the most beautiful churches in Egypt be used. It was thus that the sanctuary of St. Menas was shamefully despoiled of the splendid slabs of multicolored marbles that decorated its floor and walls. The limited restorations initiated by the patriarch Anba Yusab were of little help because the sanctuary was vandalized and partially destroyed a few years later. The saint's relics remained there until the end of the fourteenth century, at which time the progressive depopulation of the Mareotis region, the weakness of the patriarchate, and the unceasing raids of desert marauders did not allow the preservation of the sanctuary's integrity. The venerated relics were then transported to the church of St. Menas in Cairo, in the district of Fumm al-Khalig, where they remained until 1962. At that time, part of the relics were brought back to the Mareotis region and placed in the large monastery which Patriarch Cyril VI built between 1959 and 1961, not far from the ruins of the ancient sanctuary.

The Archaeological Area

Archaeological excavations were begun in 1905 at Deir Abu Mina by a German team headed by C. M. Kaufmann. At the time, the Bedouins living in the region called the locality Karm Abun, which means St. Menas' vineyard. At different times, German archaeologists have conducted excavations to unearth the vestiges of the ancient buildings. The sanctuary-town occupies a large area and contains the remains of numerous sacred edifices.

At the center of the sanctuary-town there is a cultic complex composed of three parts: the Great Basilica, the *martyrion* (martyry, "martyr-church"), and the baptistery. North of this, a vast rectangular plaza, where the pilgrims used to gather, is surrounded on all sides by a portico and has a fountain for ablutions at its center. The pilgrims' lodgings *(xenodochia)* stand north of this vast place. The tetraconch situated to the east, the north basilica, and the basilica of the baths are also particularly interesting.

The Great Basilica

The easternmost building of this three-part complex is called the Great Basilica because it was then the largest church in Egypt. Designed on an impressive scale and built with precious materials, it was used to receive the multitudes of pilgrims who flocked to the saint's tomb. It goes back to the end of the fifth century, more precisely, to the time of the emperor Zeno and was modified and enlarged at the beginning of the sixth century; an earlier, smaller building, probably erected during the first half of the fifth century, had not been completed.

The plan is that of a basilica and consists of a nave, two side aisles, and a large transept, whose columns form a continuation of the side aisles. At the intersection of the nave and transept was the presbytery, where

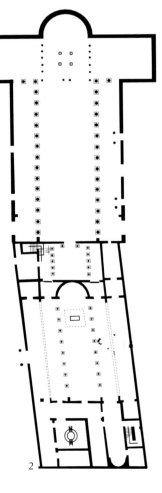

20. Sanctuary of St. Menas. Plan of the large cultic complex (Great Basilica, *martyrion*, baptistery) in the phases of its development.
Phase 1: 4th century
Phase 2: 5th century
Phase 3: 6th century
Phase 4: 8th century
In black: buildings still in use.
In grey: buildings in ruins.

50

the bases of the four columns which held the ciborium above the altar and the vestiges of the synthronon are still visible. The church was closed to the east by a semi-circular apse. The dimensions of the church are extraordinary: seventy-five meters in length (including the narthex); twenty-seven meters in width for the nave and side aisles and fifty-one meters with the transept. The main entrance of the church was on the north side, near the northwest corner, and opened onto the vast plaza where pilgrims gathered. A narthex with columns—those of the north and the south placed in a semi-circle—was attached to the great west entrance which led to the nave; it served as an intermediary space between the Great Basilica and the *martyrion*. Originally flanked by two columns, this entrance is today obstructed by the apse of the church built about the middle of the eighth century by the patriarch Michael I (744–768).

In the body of the church itself, one can still see many of the marble pedestals of the two ranks of columns which separated the nave from the side aisles, which were surmounted by galleries. When the church was first erected, it had only a nave; but it was enlarged, and the two aisles were added in the first half of the sixth century. At that time, the apse was shifted about five meters toward the east and the foundations of the external walls of the original transept were used as stylobates for the new transept.

The structure of the basilica of St. Menas is derived from that of the Constantinian basilica of the Holy Apostles in Constantinople (no longer extant), which is the source of all cruciform martyries and, indirectly, of all the basilicas which have a transept forming the arms of a cross. Like the basilica-martyries of the same period, this building must have been designed and built by the imperial architects of Constantinople. The character of its plan and the richness of the materials used indicate that the basilica was erected at the emperor's command. Multicolored marbles covered the limestone masonry; capitals with two tiers of acanthus crowned the shafts of the columns; and splendid mosaics very probably adorned the concha of the apse.

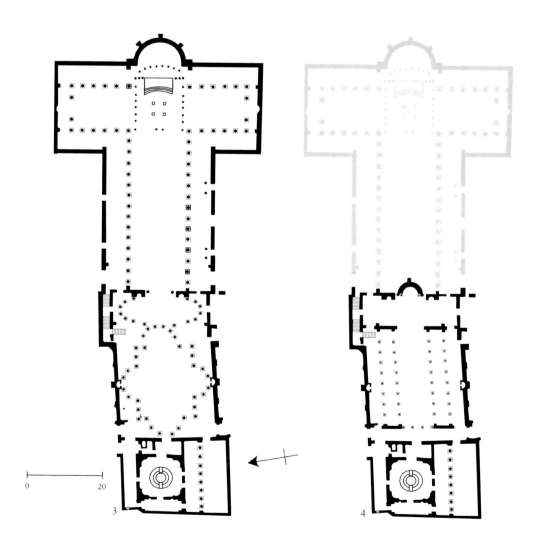

The Martyrion

The *martyrion* of St. Menas is placed at the center of the three-part sacred ensemble, west of the Great Basilica. It is above the crypt where the saint's body was kept; its structure underwent several extensive transformations which progressively altered its plan and size.

There are few traces of the first *martyrion,* dating back to the fourth century, because the original building was almost entirely demolished in the course of the successive phases of construction. Nevertheless, these vestiges allow us to conclude that the original building was almost square and made of unbaked bricks. It had been built around the cenotaph so that the latter was on its west side.

The next construction is from the fifth century and its nucleus is a small church with a nave, two aisles, and a tripartite sanctuary; the archaeologists call it the Little Basilica. Because it very rapidly proved too small, it was enlarged on all four sides: first, on the east, the "east annex," also with a nave and two aisles, gave access to the crypt; afterwards, perhaps two small aisles were added making the building a church with a nave and two aisles on either side. The baptistery goes back to the same period.

The phase of construction which has left the most important remains dates from the sixth century, probably from the reign of Justinian (527–565). The plan of the structure, which has four semi-circular apses, can be drawn within a rectangle. Delimited by columns whose pedestals are still visible, the east-west axis of the tetraconch is longer than its north-south axis. In front of the east semi-circle, one can see the traces of the square presbytery and the place of the altar. During the seventh century, all the buildings were damaged by a terrible fire and were restored only about the middle of the eighth century under the patriarch Michael I when the sanctuary came under the jurisdiction of the Coptic Church. The basilica with the nave and two aisles on either side was restored: today the main apse is still intact and occupies the west opening of the Great Basilica, which was no longer used in the eighth century.

The Saint's Tomb

The tomb of St. Menas is under the *martyrion*. The monument went through three successive phases of construction. Going back to a time difficult to determine, probably pre-Christian, the original structure was a hypogeum, an underground burial chamber, comprising three small rooms *(cubicula),* one of which was demolished to make room for the martyr's funerary chamber. The other two small rooms contain mortuary recesses in a starlike arrangement, each of which could accommodate two or three corpses.

The second phase dates from the fifth century and coincides with the erection of the Little Basilica. At that time, the funerary chamber was transformed to suit the demands of worship, and a staircase replaced the original vertical well which made access to the tomb difficult. The final funerary structure goes back to the middle of the sixth century and is probably contemporaneous with the construction under Justinian of the tetraconch edifice that surmounts it. What is most noticeable from this period is the addition of a second staircase, an incontrovertible proof of the enormous increase in the number of pilgrims wanting access to St. Menas' tomb. This new staircase was to serve only as the entrance into the chamber and the old one only as the exit to insure order in the flow of devotees. The room situated east of the funerary chamber corresponded to the west one, which was demolished when the martyr's tomb was installed. It might have been used as a chapel for commemorative celebrations and as a restful place for those pilgrims who desired to linger near the saint's tomb.

The Baptistery

The baptistery is located in the west part of this large tripartite complex. The steps of its construction correspond to those of the *martyrion*. The building, whose vestiges are impressive, goes back to the sixth century, to the time when the *martyrion* was transformed into a tetraconch. The plan shows that there was a narthex connecting it with the *martyrion,* two main chambers provided with semi-circular niches, and some rooms in which catechumens preparing themselves for baptism gathered and waited; on the south side were a portico and courtyard.

The two main chambers were reserved for the rites of baptism. The larger one, whose plan can be drawn within a square, is an octagon; it has exedras on the diagonal axes and a cupola surmounts it. In the center, the baptismal basin with its steps is still visible. The rectangular room located at the west end also had a baptismal basin; this duplication was perhaps due to the separation of the two sexes.

The Basilica of the Baths

Northwest of the tripartite Great Basilica were baths where pilgrims went to immerse themselves in the miraculous water and fill small ceramic double-handled flasks on which St. Menas was represented praying between two kneeling camels. There, one can see an edifice—probably not religious—going back to the sixth century; it is about sixty meters long and built on a basilican plan with a nave and two side aisles. The nave is especially interesting because it ends with an apse on both the east and west. Two series of six columns, whose bases are still extant, separated the nave from the aisles.

The North Basilica

In the north section of the sanctuary-town, near the cemetery, there are the vestiges of a church built on the basilican plan with a nave and two aisles; it can be dated from the second quarter of the sixth century. The nave ends on the east in a large apse to which are attached the two characteristic rooms where the services were prepared; these rooms gave onto the aisles. At the west end, these aisles are connected, thus forming a sort of ambulatory.

To the north, a small room with four columns; to the south, a chamber destined for baptisms; and to the west, a big atrium with columns are three more interesting elements.

The East Basilica

About one and a half kilometers east of the sanctuary-town, one can see the remains of a church whose plan is especially interesting. The building dates from Justinian's time, that is, the middle of the sixth century. It is a tetraconch, and each apse is semi-circular, accented by three columns on the inside and curvilinear masonry on the outside. The central room, intended to support the weight of the roof, probably a cupola, has four massive pillars. On its west side, the church is flanked by an atrium with porticoes on the north, west, and south sides. A room with a baptismal font occupies the northeast angle. The edifice was probably a monastic church. This hypothesis is plausible in view of its location outside the sacred complex and of the large number of monastic cells (about one hundred) discovered in its surroundings.

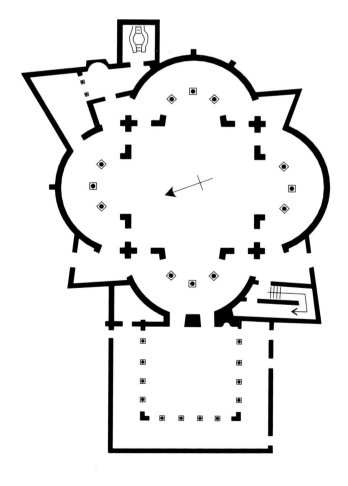

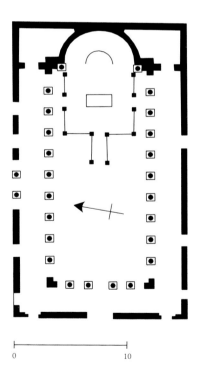

21. Sanctuary of St. Menas.

Left: plan of the east basilica (6th century).

Right: plan of the north basilica (6th century).

The region of the Nile delta is the site of many places of pilgrimage for the Coptic Church. Thousands of people come from all over Egypt in order to pay homage to the saints and martyrs whose relics are kept there and who are venerated there. The most important locations are the monastery of St. Dimiana near Bilqas, that of St. George in Mit Damsis, and the church of St. Rebekah in Sunbat.

The monastery of St. Dimiana (Sitt Dimiana) is in Zafaran, some ten kilometers north of the city of Bilqas. Having refused to marry in order to preserve her virginity and consecrate her life to God, Dimiana, the daughter of a Christian governor of Egypt in the third century, received from her father the gift of a monastery in which she retired with forty other religious women. During Diocletian's persecution, about 304, Dimiana and her sisters underwent martyrdom. The legend reports that Helena, Constantine's mother, came to the place of the martyrdom and had a *martyrion* built there in which the relics of Dimiana and her sisters were preserved; this church was subsequently destroyed. Today, it is the most important monastery for women in Egypt and a place of pilgrimage, especially during the month of May, on the occasion of the saint's feast day.

The monastery dedicated to St. George (Mari Girgis) is situated on the east bank of the Damietta branch of the Nile, east of the town of Tanta, near the village of Mit Damsis. Pilgrims come there in the month of August. Legend has it that this spot was occupied by a monastery dedicated to the Holy Virgin and that one day a boat filled with pilgrims from Jerusalem was sailing on these waters and suddenly stopped near the monastery walls; its crew and passengers were unable to move it. The pilgrims asked the monastery for hospitality, and during the night St. George—a relic of whom was on board—appeared to the abbot: he requested that the relic remain in this place and that a church be built where it would be preserved with due honor. Today this relic is kept in a modern church of the monastery.

Not far from Mit Damsis, near the west bank of the Damietta branch, pilgrims venerate the relics of St. Rebekah (Sitt Rifqa) and her five sons, martyrs under Diocletian, as well as those of two other martyrs, Sts. Piroou and Athom, natives of the place.

Nitria and Kellia

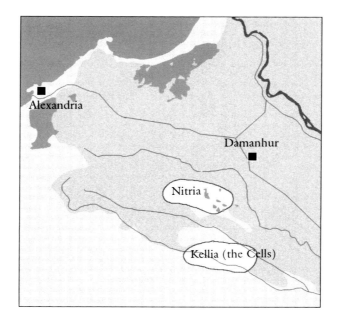

The prestigious monastic complexes of Nitria and Kellia, as well as that of Scetis, about which the following chapter will speak, were situated in the delta region, on the edge of the Western Desert, south of Alexandria. The result of an intense program of reclamation of the arid lands lying on the edge of the fertile zone, implemented in the twentieth century, was that the progressive advance of cultivated fields destroyed the remains of renowned monastic complexes, like that of Nitria, which were located in a desert area. The monasteries of Kellia were luckier: because they were deeper into the desert than Nitria, the irrigation and reclamation programs spared them until the 1960s. In the course of those years, the University of Geneva and the French Institute of Cairo undertook a systematic archaeological campaign which made it possible to study, photograph, and interpret during some thirty years the vestiges of Kellia, doomed to a rapid and practically unavoidable destruction.

NITRIA

Almost nothing remains from the celebrated monastic settlements of Nitria; they very probably were located near the present village of al-Barnudj, some sixty kilometers south of Alexandria. Greek documents call this locality the mountain of Nitria *(to oros tēs Nitrias)*, and the Egyptian documents, the mountain of Pernoudj (in Arabic, Gebel al-Barnudj). The Greek name Nitria indicates that the region is rich in natron (sodium carbonate), still extracted today and used to bleach flax and produce glass, and in antiquity also used to embalm corpses.

The word "mountain," found in Egyptian monastic literature, and its Arabic translation *gebel* must not mislead us. These words do not have their usual meaning of "mountain" in the strict sense but designate an "abandoned and desertic place" on the edge of a fertile area; in the Nile valley, this site is in general quite steep. In monastic literature, the word designates the desertic part on top of the bluff and at its foot, next to the cultivated fields. Therefore the "mountain of Nitria" is the desertic area in the vicinity of the village of Nitria, today al-Barnudj.

According to our sources, monastic life appeared in the first decades of the fourth century (about 320). The founder of anchoritic life, or at least one of the first people to embrace it, was Amun; he was a native of a small town in the delta where he was born about 280 into a rich family. Orphaned at a rather young age, he was raised by his uncle, who forced him to marry against his will when he was twenty-two years old. Because he had decided to consecrate his life to God, Amun succeeded in convincing his bride to live with him in the ascesis of chastity. Their house soon grew into a true monastery since the couple had also won over their slaves to the practice of continence. After some eighteen years of this kind of conjugal life, Amun was urged by his spouse to embrace a full and unmitigated anchoritic way of life, and he withdrew to Nitria, where a colony of anchorites attracted by his holiness quickly gathered around him because of his charismatic personality.

Having visited the region toward the end of the fourth century, the anonymous author (Flavius Rufinus?) of the *History of the Egyptian Monks (Historia Monachorum in Aegypto)* and Palladius in his *Lausiac History (Historia Lausiaca)* speak at length about Nitria and its anchorites. The *History of the Egyptian Monks* (20.5), describes Nitria in the following terms: "Then we came to Nitria, the best-known of all monasteries of Egypt, about forty miles from Alexandria; it takes its name from a nearby town where nitre is collected. . . . In this place there are about fifty dwellings, or not many less, set near together and under one father. In some of them, there are many living together, in others a few and in some there are brothers who live alone. Though they are divided by their dwellings they remain bound together and inseparable in faith and love" (*Lives*, 148).

And Palladius writes in his *Lausiac History* (7.1-5): "I . . . crossed over to Mount Nitria. Between this mountain and Alexandria there lies a lake called Marea seventy miles long. I was a day and a half crossing this to the mountain on its southern shore. Beyond the mountain, stretches the great desert reaching as far as Ethiopia, Mazicae, and Mauritania. On the mountain live close to five thousand men following different ways of life, each as he can or will. Thus some live alone, others in pairs, and some in groups. There are seven bakeries on this mountain serving these men as well as the anchorites of the Great Desert, six hundred in all. . . . On this mountain of Nitria there is a great church. . . . The guesthouse is close to the church. Here the arriving guest is received until such time as he leaves voluntarily. He stays here all the time, even for a period of two or three years. They allow a guest to remain at leisure for one week; from then on he must help in the garden, bakery, or kitchen. Should he be a noteworthy person, they give him a book, not allowing him to converse with anyone before the sixth hour. On this mountain there are doctors living, and also pastry cooks. They use wine, too, and wine is sold. All these work with their hands at making linen, so that none of them is in want. And indeed, along about the ninth hour one can stand and hear the divine psalmody issuing forth from each cell and imagine one is high above in paradise. They occupy the church on Saturdays and Sundays only. Eight priests have charge of the church; while the senior priest lives, none of the others celebrates or gives the sermon, but they simply sit quietly by him" (Palladius, 40–41).

According to the sources, the monasticism of Nitria was anchoritic in essence and its organization reflected this ideal by adopting a model based on the principle of cooperation. The monastic community was centered around the church, in which the monks gathered for the communal liturgy, celebrated only on Saturday and Sunday. Assisted by a council of seven other priests, the principal priest enjoyed a certain authority not only on the spiritual but also on the administrative level. The great number of anchorites (the figure five

22. The village of el-Barnudj, where the monastic foundations of Nitria were established.

10. Sanctuary of St. Menas. Ruins of the
Great Basilica (end of 5th century) and,
in the background, the large modern
monastery dedicated to the saint.

11. Kellia. Aerial view of the hermitages
at Qusur al-Izayla.

12. Kellia. Detail of a hermitage at Qusur
al-Rubaiyat.

13. Kellia. Detail of a hermitage at Qusur al-Rubaiyat.

14, 15, 16, 17. Kellia. Some examples of the representation of the cross in the hermitages.

Preceding pages:
18, 19, 20. Wadi al-Natrun, monastery of
St. Macarius. Remains of painted decorations
in the sanctuary of the main church (12th
century) with scenes from the nativity (the
adoration of the Magi, an angel announcing
the good news to a shepherd) and the bust
of St. John the Baptist.

21. Wadi al-Natrun. View of the
monastery of St. Pshoi.

22. Monastery of St. Pshoi, church of
St. Pshoi.

23. Wadi al-Natrun, view of the monastery of the Syrians.

24. Monastery of the Syrians, church of the
Holy Virgin. Wall painting representing the
annunciation (10th–11th centuries): the
traditional iconography of the Holy Virgin
with the archangel Gabriel is enriched by
the presence of Moses, Isaiah, Ezekiel, and
Daniel, all prophets of the annunciation.

Following pages:
25, 26, 27. Monastery of the Syrians,
church of the Holy Virgin. Wall paintings in
the choir (about 1225) with representations
of the nativity, the dormition of the Holy
Virgin, and the annunciation.

28. Wadi al-Natrun. The walls of the
monastery of al-Baramus.

29. Monastery of al-Baramus, church of the
Holy Virgin. Wall painting of
Abraham receiving communion from
Melchizedek (13th century).

Following page:
30, 31. Monastery of al-Baramus, church of
the Holy Virgin. Wall paintings of
Christ enthroned and the archangel Michael
(13th–14th centuries).

thousand given by Palladius is certainly questionable, but it nevertheless indicates that they were numerous) posed material problems with regard to the acquisition of food supplies, the care of the old and sick, and the hospitality extended to guests. The colony of Nitria therefore included gardens, bakeries, kitchens, storerooms, guest houses, and in all likelihood infirmaries—even though the sources do not confirm this. From the spiritual viewpoint, the organization of the monks of Nitria enabled them to freely live in their solitude while being supported by the presence and example of their confreres and able to have access to the help and spiritual advice of the elders.

The decline, and the subsequent abandonment of Nitria, probably took place in the first half of the seventh century—perhaps because of the devastation and ravages wrought by Persian invaders. When the patriarch Benjamin I passed through the area on his way to Scetis, Nitria was completely deserted. The sand and wind of the desert and, more recently, the reclamation and irrigation projects have apparently erased the remnants of its monastic settlements. However, it is possible that a campaign of diligent and systematic excavations may unearth a few traces of so extraordinary an anchoritic complex.

KELLIA
(THE CELLS)

The archaeological remains of the large monastic center of Kellia ("cells" in English) are in a desert area at the edge of cultivated fields, near the road from Alexandria to Cairo, half-way between the highway and the "desert road." The location is in the middle of a straight line connecting Damanhur to Sadat City. The ruins of the famed monastic center were identified in 1964. Unfortunately, the extraordinary remains of Kellia had been almost completely destroyed by the irrigation projects and land reclamation, a recently constructed railroad line, and the elements—particularly the rains, which irremediably wash away the paintings and wall inscriptions discovered by archaeologists. In an area of approximately one hundred square kilometers, some sixteen hundred monastic settlements have been identified. Archaeologists are in the process of tabulating and studying the monuments that had survived before the area became the object of an overall plan to transform the desert.

The Koms ("hillocks" in Arabic and used to designate Kellia), which comprised many hermitages, are in localities which today are called Qusur al-Rubaiyat, Qusur al-Izayla, Qusur Isa, Qusur al-Higayla, Qusur al-Arayma, and Qasr Waheida. To reach these places, one must leave the town of Dilingat, travel west, and go beyond the bridge over the Nubariya Canal; just before the railroad tracks, an unpaved, mostly sandy road on the right leads to the area of the hermitages, a few kilometers away.

23. Kellia.
Room of a hermitage at Qusur al-Rubaiyat.

The First Monastic Foundations

People leading a solitary life came to the region of Kellia about the middle of the fourth century, that is, a few years after the first monastic settlements in Nitria. The founder of Kellia was again Amun, who had established anchoritic life in Nitria. The monastic colony there had grown to such a point that it had become impossible for so many monks to find the solitude they needed. So Amun decided to establish a new monastic foundation farther south in a completely desertic area especially suitable to ascetical practice. This probably occurred in 338 on the occasion of St. Anthony's visit to Nitria. Indeed, that year Anthony left his hermitage close to the Red Sea in order to go to Alexandria and help the patriarch Athanasius (who was to become his biographer) in his fierce struggle against the Arian doctrine. Nitria was on his way, and it seems that he stopped there, if one believes what is related in *The Sayings of the Fathers (Apophtegmata Patrum) (Desert Christian,* Anthony, 34): "Abba Anthony once went to visit Abba Amun in Mount Nitria and when they met, Abba Amun said, 'By your prayers, the number of the brethren increases, and some of them want to build more cells where they may live in peace. How far away from here do you think we should build the cells?' Abba Anthony said, 'Let us eat at the ninth hour and then let us go out for a walk in the desert and explore the country.' So they went out into the desert and they walked until sunset and then Abba Anthony said, 'Let us pray and plant the cross here, so that those who wish to do so may build here. Then when those who remain there want to visit those who have come here, they can take a little food at the ninth hour and then come. If they do this, they will be able to keep in touch with each other without distraction of mind.' The distance is twelve miles."

Anchoritic Life in Kellia

Whether it is a legend or a historical fact, the tradition recorded in the *Sayings of the Fathers* concerning the foundation of Kellia confirms the relationship between Amun and Anthony and the influence of the latter on the beginnings of anchoritic life in Nitria, Kellia, and Scetis. In Kellia, as well as in Nitria and Scetis, the life was patterned on the spirit of Anthony's monasticism, which was fundamentally anchoritic and consequently different from the monasticism of St. Pachomius in upper Egypt, which was rigorously cenobitic.

The *History of the Egyptian Monks* (20.8) records that "beyond this there is another place, the inner desert, about ten miles away. This is called Cellia because of the number of cells there, scattered about the desert. Those who have already begun their training there (that is, in Nitria) and want to live a more remote life, stripped of external things, withdraw there. For this is the utter desert and the cells are divided from one another by so great a distance that no one can see his neighbour nor can any voice be heard. They live alone in their cells and there is a huge silence and a great quiet there. Only on Saturday and Sunday do they meet in church" (*Desert Fathers,* 148–49).

More exactly, the way of life in Kellia, Nitria, and Scetis was semi-anchoritic, which represents a balance between anchoritic and communal life; these monastic settlements can be seen as "cooperative communities" of anchorites in which the mutual obligations were very restricted whereas individual freedom was practically unlimited. The monks spent the week in their own cells and gathered on Saturday and Sunday in their churches for the synaxis (assembly). This was the only communal time in the anchorites' life at Kellia; it was punctuated by three important moments: Vespers, the eucharistic liturgy, and the agape. Vespers was celebrated

24. Kellia.
Niches in a hermitage at
Qusur al-Rubaiyat.

74

in the church on Saturday evening and consisted of a dozen psalms. After the anchorites had a few hours of rest, the great liturgy began during the night of Saturday to Sunday; it lasted several hours and comprised the recitation of psalms and the celebration of the Eucharist, in the course of which the monks received communion under both species, bread and wine. Once the liturgy was completed, the anchorites broke their fast by sharing a common meal called the agape.

The agape (the Greek *agapē* means "love," "charity") manifested the bond of charity uniting the monks to one another. All texts agree in stating that this meal was taken in the church where the Eucharist had been celebrated. In fact, as archaeological discoveries have confirmed, this meal was served in a large room adjacent to the church and set apart for this purpose. It is indeed likely that by the term "church" (*ekklesia* in Greek) the ancient writers meant not only the church proper, where the Eucharist was celebrated, but also the whole communal structure which besides the church contained the refectory *(agapeion)*, the food stores, and the kitchens. During the meal, it was permissible to converse; the fare consisted of a few dishes of vegetables, sometimes cooked; and contrary to the practice on weekdays, one could drink wine, but in limited quantity.

The eucharistic celebration entailed the presence of a priest among the monks. The best known of the anchorite priests at Kellia was Macarius—called "of Alexandria" to distinguish him from Macarius the Great, also called "the Egyptian," the founder of the anchoritic monasteries in Scetis. The priests exercised a certain authority over the other monks by presiding at the council of the elders, which periodically met to discuss communal affairs and mete out punishments to the monks who had committed a serious sin. But the priests' authority was chiefly spiritual in character because there were no written rules or vows to which the monks were bound. Besides priests, there were certainly other clerics to assist them during the liturgical functions and stewards to manage the common possessions. The monks handed over to the stewards the product of their weekly work in exchange for food and supplies for the next week. The assembly of the monks ended on Sunday morning and everyone went back to his own hermitage, often five or six kilometers away.

The hermitages (*kellion* in Greek, *kellia* in the plural) were normally occupied by one monk. But often the elderly anchorites welcomed into their cell one or two younger brothers, who were both their disciples and their servants. Inside the hermitage everyone enjoyed the freedom of organizing his life as he wished; but rather rapidly, a tradition was established which contributed to standardize the anchorites' life. Along with work, prayer was the most important occupation of the day. Monks got up in the middle of the night for the prayer called the "little synaxis," to distinguish it from the office recited in common during the night of Saturday to Sunday. To offer this prayer, the monk remained standing, with arms raised, and turned toward the east. This is why the space destined for prayer had a niche in the east wall in which a cross was represented. At the first light of dawn, the monk began his manual work, which in general consisted of weaving reeds and palms into baskets, ropes, mats. When completed, these artifacts were given to the stewards who were in charge of selling them in the neighboring villages and buying what the anchorites needed, especially wheat. The making of baskets and mats was widespread among the anchorites because this sort of work could be done in solitude inside the individual hermitages and because, far from hindering prayer, it fostered recollection. The prayer compatible with work was called *meletē* (meditation); this term did not mean mental activity but the repetitious recitation in a low voice of biblical invocations such as "Be pleased, O LORD, to deliver me; / O LORD, make haste to help me" (Ps 40:13).

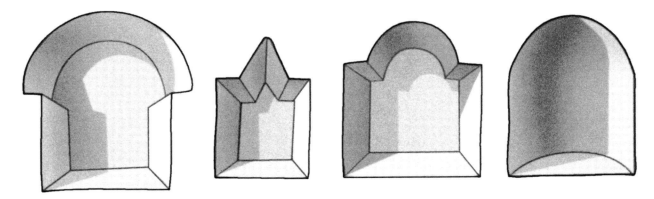

25. Kellia. Types of niches in the hermitages.

Some monks were scribes and copied sacred texts; these copies were either for sale, for the community church, or for the brothers. The most illustrious among them was Evagrius Ponticus, a native of Cappadocia, who had been the disciple of Sts. Basil and Gregory Nazianzus. As Palladius reports in the *Lausiac History* (38.10), Evagrius had retired to Kellia after spending two years in Nitria: "He lived there for two years, and in the third year he went off to the desert. Then he lived there fourteen years in the so-called Cellia, eating but a pound of bread [a day], and a pint of oil in the space of three months, and he was a man who had been delicately raised in a refined and fastidious manner of life. He composed one hundred prayers, and he wrote during the year only the price of as much as he ate. . . . Then he drew up three holy books for monks— Controversies they are called—on the arts to be used against demons" (Palladius, 113).

Work was interrupted about noon (the sixth hour) at the hottest time of the day for a period of rest which in general lasted until three in the afternoon, the ninth hour was traditionally devoted to the meal. The anchorite's food was limited to a daily ration of about one pound (three hundred grams) of dry bread, softened in water and seasoned with a little salt and, at times, with a drop of oil. The sick and old were entitled to bread and raw or cooked vegetables. The only beverage allowed was water. After this frugal meal, the anchorites returned to their work or went to visit a confrere either in order to bring succor to the elderly and sick or to receive spiritual advice. Charity obliged the monks to respect the rites of hospitality: one had to be totally available to welcome visitors; one washed their feet and offered them food specially kept for such occasions, lentils or other boiled vegetables. In this case, the visitor and host ate together, whatever the hour, because the love of neighbor had priority over fasting.

As evening drew on, the monk recited the last office, Vespers, sometimes alone, sometimes together with neighboring confreres. Finally, everyone went back to his own cell where he lay down on a mat placed on the floor or on a bed of palms.

The Architecture of the Hermitages

The site of Kellia comprised about sixteen hundred hermitages (*koms* in Arabic, "hillock") built in a little less than three centuries, between the middle of the fourth and the beginning of the seventh, and arranged in five groups, today called *qusur* in Arabic: Qusur al-Rubaiyat to the west, Qusur Isa and al-Izayla in the middle, and Qusur al-Higayla and al-Arayma to the east. The study of those structures which have been excavated allows us to observe the simplicity of the early constructions during the fourth and fifth centuries in contrast to the refinement characterizing those of the sixth and seventh centuries, built before the place was definitively abandoned in the course of the eighth century.

The few vestiges of the oldest hermitages that have survived to this day go back to the second half of the fourth century and the fifth century; their architectural elements are poor, made of tiny rooms, partially hollowed in the earth and covered by a vault, forming spare lodgings surrounded by a wall. About the end of

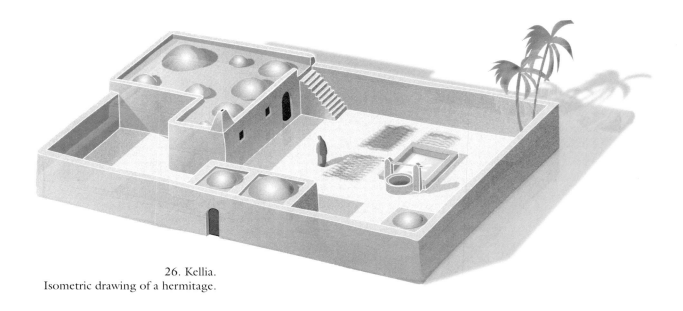

26. Kellia.
Isometric drawing of a hermitage.

the fifth century, there appears a more developed architecture characterizing the hermitages of Kellia for about two centuries until their abandonment. Thus, in a little over one century, its founders' conception of anchoritic life was undeniably transformed. This transformation is manifested by the increased facilities to receive others in the hermitage (originally destined to isolated anchorites, it progressively shelters several monks); it is also revealed in the decoration (simple and poor in the beginning, it grows richer and more complex) and finally, around the end of the seventh century, by large rooms which indicate that the hermitage has acquired a more important role in the life of the anchoritic colony.

The evolution of the hermitage reflects that of anchoritism itself: solitude becomes more and more relative and depends more on individual discipline than on the rigor imposed by this sort of habitat. The typical hermitage is a rectangular enclosure whose high walls measure thirty and twenty-five meters. The whole is oriented so as to present one of the longer walls to the most violent winds coming from the north and northwest. The living quarters are to the northwest and a large courtyard to the southeast. The entrance is in the middle of the south side through a portal protected by a vestibule inside the wall. The spacious garden-courtyard usually had a well and a latrine near the southeast corner.

The systematic study of the anchorites' lodgings clearly demonstrates the successive phases of the construction of the hermitage. Whereas the original building contained only the rooms necessary for the elder and his disciple, in the course of the seventh century the overpopulation of Kellia and the new conception of anchoritic life made it necessary to build cells for the newcomers.

The living quarters were made up of a "communal" section and a "private" one. The common part comprised an anteroom, a vestibule where manual work was done and visitors were received, a pantry, and a kitchen. The private zone included the elder's apartment and the disciple's cell. The elder's apartment had a large room for prayer (its walls had niches elegantly decorated, especially on the east wall), another room, smaller and less decorated, where the anchorite slept, and a third, which probably served as an addition to the prayer room. The disciple's cell was much simpler and had only one room where he both slept and prayed; the east wall had a niche adorned with the traditional painted cross. Both the elder's apartment and the disciple's cell had a recess, probably used for storage.

These rooms were vaulted; small windows placed high brought in a little light and fresh air. Niches were hollowed out in the thick walls; they were used for objects such as lamps, books, tools for work. Scarce in Egypt, wood was non-existent in the desert; as a consequence, it was rarely used and in general reserved to make doors.

Earth was the material almost exclusively used for the hermitages at Kellia and unbaked brick was the essential component of construction. The excellent quality of the bricks used at Kellia is due to two local characteristics: the presence of water some meters under the desert and of a rocky material called *gebal* in Arabic, which is composed of extremely fine particles and more granular components bonded by mineral salts, the whole thing being an ideal stabilizer in a dry climate. Water was added to this rocky material to form a mixture from which bricks were fashioned; regulations regarding their dimensions were particularly strict and always observed (20 x 40 x 7 and 40 x 40 x 7 centimeters).

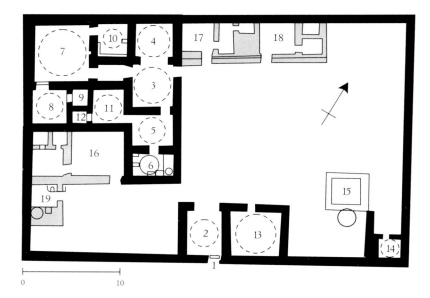

27. Kellia.
Plan of hermitage Qusur el-Izayla 48.
In black: first phase (6th century).
In grey: second phase (7th century).
1. Entrance
2. Vestibule
3, 4. Rooms for receiving visitors
5. Additional room
6. Kitchen
7. Elder's oratory
8. Elder's bedroom
9. Closet
10. Elder's workroom
11. Disciple's room
12. Closet
13. Storeroom
14. Latrine
15. Well
16, 17, 18. Apartments for anchorites
19. Kitchen

The clay brick was the only local product but it was not the only material used to construct the hermitages. Others were imported, such as lime, stone, and ceramic. The last was used not only for containers for water or food but also for water pipes, ornaments applied to vaults and arches, and the cylindrical openings, shaped like the neck of an amphora, whose purpose was ventilation and communication between rooms.

The Pictorial Decoration of the Hermitages

The hermitages of Kellia furnish an extraordinarily rich documentation on Coptic painting from the fifth to the seventh centuries. Here, painting is an integral part of architecture; the sophisticated use of color suggests fluted columns and pilasters, composite capitals, apses in the shape of shells, marble and alabaster plaques. The colors were applied over a very thin egg-based coating which had been carefully smoothed out and left to dry. Unfortunately, this base is so thin that, once brought to light by archaeologists, the paintings tend to disintegrate at an astonishing rate. Mineral pigments were used; mixed with lime or fixed with a binder such as casein, they produced various colors: ocher, green, black, white, and more rarely, blue. By mixing the primary colors or by painting them on top of one another, painters obtained chromatic variations: red, rose, purple, yellow, brown, and grey. The masterly use of white and black gave luminosity and transparency to figures.

The decorations offer an extremely varied iconography running the gamut from the suggestion or accentuation of architectural components to the representation of biblical scenes, figures of saints and monks, Christ in majesty, and innumerable types of crosses—cross as the tree of life, cross represented as a gold candlestick or adorned with precious stones or wreathed with leaves and flowers or ornamented with lamps and censers. The openings, doors, and windows are outlined by friezes with geometrical or floral motifs and are frequently decorated with the leaves of palm trees, tamarinds, or vine branches which grow from luxurious canthari (drinking vessels) and bear luxuriant clusters of grapes. There are also representations of animals: gazelles, camels, sheep, hares, snakes, crocodiles, hippopotamuses, doves, peacocks, roosters, fish, horses, donkeys, and lions. Besides real fauna, there are also fantastic and fabulous animals, such as unicorns and chimeras created by the imagination of the monks who painted them. Every animal has a particular symbolic signification: the peacock, whose flesh is regarded as incorruptible and whose plumage is renewed every year, is the symbol of resurrection; the dove, a messenger of peace, represents the Holy Spirit; the gazelles and deer, the catechumens; the sheep, the apostles Peter and Paul. The animals associated with evil, like the lion, the crocodile, and the hippopotamus, are inherited from ancient Egypt: they were objects of worship under the pharaohs, but they became objects of a sacred fear in the Coptic world.

All these decorations show a great many boats, always treated in red and black. In the Christian world, the boat is a symbol of the faith and of the church, but perhaps one should not overlook its ancient meaning of spiritual vehicle for the passage into the afterlife.

28. Kellia.
Fragment of an inscription in a hermitage at Qusur al-Rubaiyat alluding to a *presbyteros*, an elder or a priest, called George and ending with *amen*.

The Wall Inscriptions

The epigraphical witnesses in the hermitages at Kellia have an incalculable value because they are both abundant and enable us to study monastic epigraphy in its architectural context and are the oldest texts in Bohairic, the Coptic dialect of the delta region, that have come down to us. Owing to the humid climate of the area, the ancient manuscripts did not survive.

Most of the inscriptions at Kellia are from the seventh century and beginning of the eighth, a period in which monasticism saw its greatest expansion in the region. These inscriptions in Bohairic or Greek can be found in various rooms, but normally they are in the vestibule, the room where the visitors and pilgrims entered and sojourned. In general, the inscriptions are painted in reddish ocher, sometimes in black. The style of the handwriting is very diverse: in certain cases, the uncial, written with extreme care and typical of the manuscripts of the time, is the work of scribes or copyists; in others, the wavering and awkward writing is probably the work of monks.

Progress in interpreting the texts has made it possible for us to learn more about the way of life and especially the funerary rites of the monks residing in Kellia. The greatest number of inscriptions recall the memory of deceased monks according to stereotyped formulas such as "Our blessed brother (. . .) son of (. . .) native of (. . .) fell asleep on (. . .) day of the month of (. . .) at (. . .) hour. Remember him and may the Lord Jesus Christ grant rest to his soul at the same time as to the saints and all those who belong to him. Amen." Sometimes, though rarely, besides the day, month, and hour of death, the year is indicated according to the era of the martyrs, a dating system which appears in 284 C.E., the year Diocletian, the last great persecutor of Christians, acceded to the throne. In other cases, the inscriptions can be dated because they mention patriarchs of Alexandria—Theodosius (535–566), Agatho (655–681), John III (681–689), and Simon (692–700)—or Byzantine emperors like Justinian (527–565), Mauritius (582–602), Phocas (602–610), Constans II (641–668), and Justinian II (685–695, 705–711). In some cases, the chronological reference is given by the name of the nation governing Egypt; this is how the occupation by Arabs, called the Lami, is mentioned for the first time. As a rule, the commemorative inscriptions were read aloud, in accordance with the Egyptian tradition which held that in this way one was assured that the blessings wished for in the written formula would be realized.

Other inscriptions are legends accompanying the paintings of saints and animals. Those which accompany the decor, the cross in particular, are generally in Greek: the most frequent invocation is the Byzantine formula *IC XC NI KA* (*Jesus Christos Nika*, that is, "Jesus Christ, be victorious").

Churches and Refectories

The numerous churches which archaeologists have excavated at Kellia enable us to observe the evolution of the basic concept underlying the anchorites' life. Whereas isolation and solitude were favored at the beginning, one sees that with the passage of time, the very simple cooperative spirit of the early period yields to a

29. Kellia. Funerary inscription in Coptic in a hermitage at Qusur al-Rubaiyat, written by a monk named Elijah who speaks of a dead confrere named Menas, called *makarios* (blessed) because he has entered eternal life.

communitarian spirit; this cannot be identified with the cenobitism of St. Pachomius, but without any doubt, it can be interpreted as halfway between the anchoritic concept and the cenobitic one.

Archaeological discoveries at Kellia have confirmed the existence of architectural ensembles which can be called *ekklesia* and were essentially constituted by the buildings devoted to religious rites, church and refectory, where the anchorites came together from Saturday evening until Sunday for the synaxis, which began with Vespers, culminated with the eucharistic celebration, and ended with the common meal, the agape. Two such complexes of particular interest have been identified at Qusur Isa and Qasr al-Waheida. At Qusur Isa 1, three churches have been found. The first one (beginning of the fifth century) has a transverse nave and a sanctuary with two adjacent rooms to the north and south. Both the second church of Qusur Isa 1 (end of the fifth century) and the third (beginning of the seventh century) have a basilican plan with a nave, two side aisles, a sanctuary, and two adjacent rooms. The two churches of Qasr al-Waheida (fifth century) are in every respect identical to the two preceding churches: in the smaller one, the side aisles are separated from the middle one by two series of three columns, while in the larger one the central nave is surrounded on three sides by an ambulatory delineated by sixteen columns.

The two complexes of Qusur Isa and Qasr al-Waheida underwent a rapid decline from the middle of the seventh century on. At that time, the traditional church buildings—where the monks settled in the surrounding area gathered for the synaxis—were abandoned in favor of places of worship attached to the hermitages themselves which thus became true monasteries. Consequently, within the hermitages appear large halls with two bays, to the east of which is a sanctuary. At Qusur al-Izayla, the buildings of hermitages 16 and 45 are typical examples of monastic churches. These have undergone frequent transformations and have necessarily required the enlargement of the perimeter of the hermitage as well as substantial modifications in the living quarters. Originally conceived as a place conducive to asceticism where the anchorite sought by all means to separate himself from the exterior world, the hermitage at Kellia was transformed into a place where not only monks but guests and pilgrims lived in close contact. Near the church, extra rooms were added, such as refectory, kitchens, dormitories, latrines. At Qusur al-Rubaiyat and Qusur al-Izayla, very interesting examples of refectories from the second half of the seventh century have been discovered. They have the same architectural structure as the monastic churches: two or three bays, each one roofed with a cupola made of bricks.

The churches can be distinguished from the refectories by their orientation and the presence of the base of the altar to the east, while in the refectories one can see the bases of the tables used at meals, one to each bay.

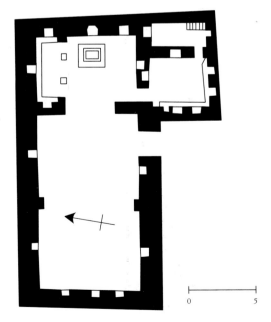

30. Kellia.
Plan of the church of the hermitage Qusur al-Izayla 16 (second half of 7th century).

0   5

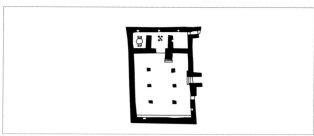

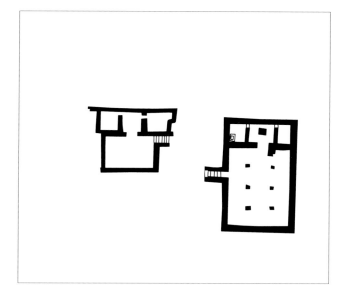

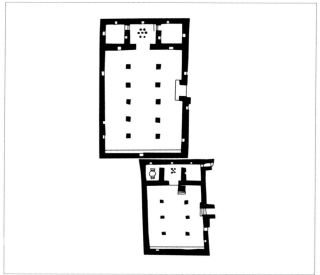

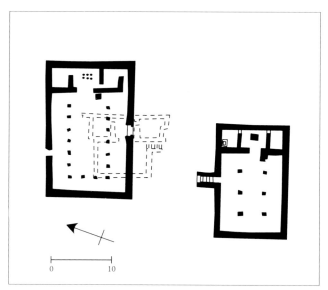

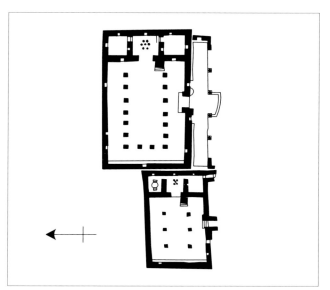

31. Kellia.
Left: evolution of the ecclesial center of Qusur Isa 1.
Right: evolution of the ecclesial center of Qasr al-Waheida.
Phase 1: beginning of the 5th century
Phase 2: end of the 5th century
Phase 3: beginning of the 7th century

The Abandonment of Kellia

When the severe harassment caused by the fiscal policy of the Arabs, the new lords of Egypt, resulted in the abandonment of Kellia in the beginning of the eighth century, only a few hermitages continued to be inhabited by the last monks, who gave hospitality to traveling pilgrims. But soon they also left the place and the hermitages were used as shelters by the nomadic people of the desert during their seasonal travels. In the course of the centuries, wind filled the anchorites' lodgings with sand, which protected the paintings and inscriptions from the elements. The landscape was so thoroughly remodeled that it was only in the beginning of the 1960s that a Franco-Swiss archaeological mission identified the place and resurrected it after centuries of oblivion.

Scetis (Wadi al-Natrun)

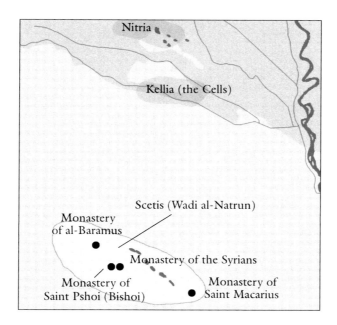

Wadi al-Natrun, which is the present name of the region of Scetis, is halfway between Cairo and Alexandria and west of the "desert road." This hilly area has its principal axis extending from the northwest to the southeast and is about thirty kilometers long and never wider than eight kilometers; its lowest reaches are twenty-five meters below sea level. The aspect of this region is desolate because of its desertic character and whitish color. This latter is due to the abundance of mineral salts, in particular common salt (sodium chloride) and natron (sodium carbonate) from which comes the present Arabic name Wadi al-Natrun (valley of natron). The latter is the incrustation formed by the seasonal drying up of the many ponds lying in the low places: the water level rises from December to March and then slowly falls in the following months, causing the complete desiccation of the ponds or their transformation into ill-smelling swamps infested with flies and mosquitoes. The only uses of natron in our day are in the bleaching of flax and the fabrication of glass.

From the fourth century on, this inhospitable region became one of the most important anchoritic centers, along with Nitria and Kellia (the Cells), not only for Coptic Egypt but for the whole of Christendom. Its ancient name of Scetis (Scetis in Latin, Sketis in Greek) is the hellenized form of the Coptic name Shiet which would mean, according to the monks' interpretation, "measure of the heart"—but the real etymology remains unknown. It is not impossible that the Greek term itself was coined to associate the name of the locality with the practice of ascesis (*askesis* in Greek; the place of *askesis* is *asketirion*). Before receiving its present name, Wadi al-Natrun, the place was also called Wadi Habib, after the Arab warlord who stopped there in the second half of the seventh century.

The birth of anchoritic life in Scetis is connected with the figure of St. Macarius the Egyptian, also called the Great, who withdrew there about 330 in order to live in solitude and asceticism. His virtuous life and his wisdom quickly attracted many followers who thus became the first monastic group in Scetis. The most illustrious among them are the charismatic figures Macarius of Alexandria, John the Little, Pshoi (Bishoi in Arabic), John Kama, and Moses the Black. The anonymous author of the *History of Egyptian Monks* describes the desert of Scetis in these terms: "This place is a waste land lying at a distance of a day's and a night's journey from Nitria through the desert. It is a very perilous journey for travellers. For if one makes even a small error, one can get lost in the desert and find one's life in danger. All the monks there have attained perfection. Indeed, no one beset with imperfections could stay in that place, since it is rugged and inhospitable, lacking all the necessities of life" (*Desert Fathers*, 113). The harshness of the life at Scetis was at the limit of human capacity. Palladius reports (*Lausiac History*, 18.4) that Macarius of Alexandria "condemned himself to sit naked in the marsh of Scete out in the great desert for a period of six months. Here the mosquitoes lacerate even the hides of the wild swine just as wasps do. Soon he was bitten all over his body, and he became so swollen that some thought he had elephantiasis. When he returned to his cell after six months he was recognized as Macarius only by his voice" (Palladius, 59).

THE MONASTERY OF ST. MACARIUS
(*DEIR ABU MAQQAR*)

Historical Information

St. Macarius the Great

The foundation of the monastery of St. Macarius is closely linked with the life of this holy ascetic who is one of the most prestigious figures in the Coptic Church and even in all the Christian churches. He is called Macarius the Egyptian or the Great to distinguish him from Macarius of Alexandria. His life is known to us thanks to the *Life of Macarius (Vita Macarii)*, falsely attributed to Serapion, bishop of Thmuis, a disciple of Anthony and a friend of Macarius.

Born about 300 in a village of the delta, where his father was a priest, Macarius became in his youth a camel driver and, in this capacity, often went with his caravans into the desertic area of Scetis, today Wadi al-Natrun, to harvest salt and natron. Extremely pious and attracted by ascetic life, Macarius decided at the age of thirty to withdraw to this solitude; some ten years later, he was ordained a priest. His first dwelling was a cavity in the rocks of the desert and this soon became a place which pilgrims, attracted by the reputation for austerity and holiness that Macarius had acquired, were eager to visit. Some of these pilgrims became his disciples and a monastic community arose. The location of this first settlement corresponds to that of today's monastery of al-Baramus. During this period of 343 to 352, Macarius visited Anthony the Great in his hermitage near the Red Sea.

About 360, Macarius left the community to retire once more into solitude, more to the south, in a cave where he would be able to devote himself to the more rigorous ascetic practice for which he yearned and which had been impossible because of the crowd of disciples gathered around his holy person. But in this new place too, where the monastery of St. Macarius stands today, many disciples followed him to profit by his example and his teaching. In 374, the emperor Valens, who had become an Arian, took strong repressive measures against the Orthodox, often condemning them to exile. This is why Macarius was forced to leave

Scetis, to which he returned a few years later and where he died in 390. Apparently, his disciple Paphnutius succeeded him in his function of superior of Scetis. It was from this time on that the hegumens of St. Macarius received the dignity of superiors of the monastic community of Scetis.

Development and Prestige of the Monastery

From the fifth century on, the monastery of St. Macarius suffered repeated attacks by desert pillagers. In the course of the third and bloody plundering in 444, forty-nine monks died, having refused to take refuge in the tower and preferring to accept martyrdom by following the example of their hegumen, Anba Yuannis (John). During the second half of the fifth century, the monastery enjoyed the beneficence of the emperor Zeno, who showered it with gifts and sent his own architects to see to the construction of adequate buildings. There were good grounds for Zeno's benevolence because the emperor's own daughter, Hilaria, had joined the monastery by disguising herself as a man. Despite this disguise, her femininity, even though hidden, caused her to be called Hilary the Eunuch.

The monastery of St. Macarius gained a special prestige about the middle of the sixth century when it became the official residence of the Coptic patriarch of Alexandria. The emperor Justinian had begun to inflict severe penalties on the Egyptians who had remained faithful to the Monophysite doctrine of Eutyches, condemned by the Council of Chalcedon in 451. The persecution reached its peak in 551 when the emperor sent Melchite troops under the command of Apollinarius to Alexandria in order to reestablish by force the orthodox doctrine defined at Chalcedon. All that the Coptic patriarch Timotheus II could do was abandon his see in Alexandria and retire with his retinue to the monastery of St. Macarius, making this the temporary residence of the patriarch. It is not known exactly how long the patriarch's see remained in the monastery, but it certainly had been transferred back to Alexandria by the beginning of the seventh century.

In 641, the Arabs conquered Egypt and, in the beginning of their occupation, adopted a politics of tolerance with regard to the Christian population and monastic communities. It was during this period that Anba Yuannis, the hegumen of St. Macarius, undertook to remodel the monastic complex and fostered the formation of small, less important religious centers, called *manshopis,* where the monks could live alone or in small communities, all the while continuing to depend on the principal monastery. But the Arab politics toward the Christian population changed about the middle of the eighth century, a time when the last Ummayad caliph, Marwan II, dealt with the monks with singular harshness.

In 817, Berber marauders launched a violent attack, sacking and burning the monasteries of Scetis, including St. Macarius. This event led the monks to erect a high wall and fortifications which would allow them to protect themselves and their churches against assaults. Among other things, the monks built emergency cells attached to the inner walls of the monastery to serve, in case of danger, as lodgings for the monks of the numerous *manshopis* which had proliferated in the immediate surroundings. Thus was born the prototype of the

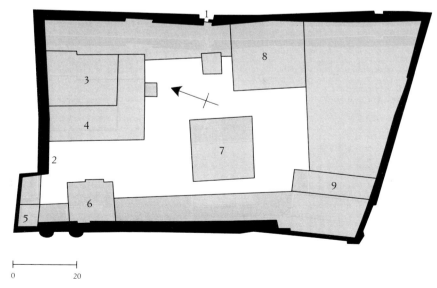

0   20

85

monasteries in Scetis where the buildings devoted to religious rites were concentrated and defended by massive fortifications while the monastic cells were scattered in the vicinity outside the enclosure. Only the priests and the monks in charge of the liturgical celebrations lived inside the fortifications. The rule was semi-anchoritic: every person lived his individual life, with the exception of Sunday when all the monks gathered to celebrate the Eucharist and agape.

During the period of persecutions directed against the Copts by the caliph Abu Ali al-Mansur al-Hakim bi-Amr Allah (al-Hakim, 996–1021), the patriarch Zacharias found refuge in the monastery of St. Macarius. It was also in this period that a certain Buqaira al-Rashidi gave the monastery the head of St. Mark, which had been sold to him by a Turk aristocrat for the sum of three hundred dinars.

The Dark Centuries and the Renaissance
The fourteenth century was the hardest and the most painful in the whole history of Scetis. A period of impoverishment and decline of monasticism began and was to last for over five hundred years until the renewal which began some thirty years ago. About the middle of the fourteenth century, the oppressive measures taken by the Mamluk sultan al-Salih ibn Qalawun against the Copts became extreme: churches and monasteries were destroyed, lands were expropriated, taxes were doubled, and any resisters were executed. The plague called the Black Death raged during the same years and, according to chronicles, caused the death of fifteen thousand people in one single day in Cairo alone. Monasteries were equally decimated: one hundred monks perished, and hunger and destitution forced the survivors to emigrate elsewhere.

During the following centuries, the monastery of St. Macarius, like all others in Wadi al-Natrun, had to contend with poverty, ignorance, the lack of religious vocations, and the ravages caused by the Bedouins. Between 1700 and 1969, the number of monks oscillated between a minimum of three or four individuals and a maximum of twenty-five. The renewal dawned in 1969 with the arrival of a dozen new monks who, coming from the desert located south of al-Fayyum, entirely renovated the monastery both from the spiritual standpoint, as well as from the material standpoint by restoring the ruinous buildings. In that year, there remained only six elderly monks; today there are one hundred. Having pursued various professions before devoting themselves to monastic life, some have university degrees; agronomists, physicians, veterinarians, pharmacists, engineers, and specialists in the humanities live in spiritual union according to the gospel ideal, each one bringing his precious contribution to the community.

The Monastic Buildings

The Portal
When one comes down the big staircase which leads to the courtyard onto which the monastery buildings open, one arrives at a large arch made of red brick. It probably goes back to the middle of the seventh century

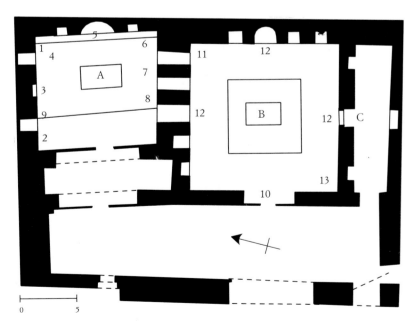

34. Monastery of St. Macarius. Plan of the church of St. Macarius (7th century).
A. Sanctuary of St. John the Baptist
B. Sanctuary of Benjamin
C. Little sanctuary
1. Nativity (concha)
2. Unidentified scene (concha)
3. The sacrifice of Abraham
4. Annunciation
5. Moses and Aaron
6. The announcement to Zechariah
7. Isaiah and the seraph
8. Abraham and Melchizedek
9. The dream of Jacob
10. Painting relating to the rite of the *myron*
11. Seraph
12. The twenty-four elders of the book of Revelation
13. St. John the Baptist

and was the north portal of the church rebuilt by the patriarch Benjamin I. As the dimensions of the church were reduced by the destruction caused by the Berbers, the arch ended by being incorporated into the defensive walls.

The Church of St. Macarius

What is left of the ancient church of St. Macarius is only a part of the majestic edifice of former times because the west part of the building was destroyed and today is occupied by the courtyard onto which the church of the Forty-Nine Martyrs opens. The very first church was erected in 360, but the oldest structures still visible today date from the reconstruction undertaken by the patriarch Benjamin I in 655. The edifice from the seventh century was especially impressive with its nave and side aisles separated by marble columns and its abundant decorative paintings. At the beginning, the church of the Forty-Nine Martyrs was very probably attached to the church of St. Macarius.

From the building of the seventh century, there remain only the walls of the middle sanctuary, dedicated to the patriarch Benjamin, the walls of the north sanctuary, dedicated to St. John the Baptist, and the walls of the south sanctuary. Benjamin's sanctuary is roofed with a large cupola eight meters in diameter, supported by an octagonal drum from the Fatimid period (eleventh–twelfth centuries), and decorated with wall paintings in poor condition, representing the twenty-four elders of the book of Revelation, John the Baptist, and the two equestrian saints Claudius and Menas. The representation of the tetramorph (from the Greek meaning "four forms") on the northeast pendentive of the octagon is particularly interesting. Painted on a wooden panel and going back to the twelfth century, it represents the symbols of the evangelists: on the left Mark's lion, on the right Luke's ox, on top John's eagle, and in the center a human figure, Matthew's symbol. Deriving from the visions of Ezekiel, the visions of Isaiah, and the book of Revelation, the tetramorph is a symbol of Christ: human in his birth, ox in his sacrificial death, lion in his resurrection, eagle in his ascension into heaven. The four figures also represent what is noblest, strongest, wisest, and cleverest in creation. The many eyes painted on the wings of the tetramorph symbolize universal knowledge and divine providence.

The sanctuary of John the Baptist, also dedicated to St. Mark, is on the north side of the middle sanctuary; its architecture goes back to the seventh century except for the drum supporting the cupola, which dates from the Fatimid period, and for the cupola itself, which collapsed in 1909 and was rebuilt in 1976. During the period of restoration and reconstruction conducted in the same year, bones were discovered on that spot; they could be those of the two great precursors of Christian monasticism, John the Baptist and Elisha. Tradition confirmed the presence of these two precious relics in the monastery of St. Macarius since the beginning of the tenth century when for unknown reasons they were carried there from Alexandria. Originally brought from Palestine around 360 and received by the patriarch Athanasius, they were kept in Alexandria in the church of St. John the Baptist, also called the Anghelion. It is probably not by chance that from the

35. Church of St. Macarius. Painting of the tetramorph (12th century).

beginning of the tenth century, the consecration of the Coptic patriarchs of Alexandria took place precisely in the monastery of St. Macarius. Up to that time, the investiture ceremony had been in the cathedral of the Anghelion, where the relics of both prophets were kept. The consecration of the new patriarchs in the presence of the relics of Elisha and St. John the Baptist had probably become a solid tradition. The sanctuary is also dedicated to St. Mark because his head had been kept there for almost five hundred years, from the eleventh to the sixteenth century, when it was brought back to Alexandria to the church where it is venerated to this day. Dating from the Fatimid period but partially obliterated, wall paintings executed with refinement decorate the sanctuary; the themes are taken from the Old and New Testaments (Moses and Aaron, Isaiah and the seraph, Abraham and Melchizedek, Jacob's Ladder, the sacrifice of Abraham, the announcement to Zechariah, the annunciation to Mary, and the nativity).

The south sanctuary, called the little sanctuary, probably dates from the seventh century and served for the preparation of the Eucharist. Medieval documents mention it also under the name of council cell because the bishops and priests went there to consume the eucharistic bread remaining after communion.

Ten patriarchs, St. John the Little and the three Sts. Macarius (Macarius the Great, also called the Egyptian, the founder of the monastery; Macarius of Alexandria; and Macarius the Martyr, the bishop of Tkow in middle Egypt) are buried in the church of St. Macarius. In Coptic iconography, the three saints are shown with different symbols: Macarius the Great holds a stick, the symbol of struggle and sacrifice; Macarius of Alexandria holds a ladder, the symbol of his progressive pursuit of virtue; Macarius the Martyr is clad in a white tunic and is accompanied by a lamb, the symbols of his function as shepherd and of his martyrdom.

The Church of the Forty-Nine Martyrs

This church is dedicated to the forty-nine martyrs of the monastery of St. Macarius, killed in 444 by desert marauders at the time of the third attack against Scetis. Originally, the church abutted the west side of the church of St. Macarius, of which it was probably a part. It has a vestibule, a *naos* (a single nave), a *khurus* (choir), and one sanctuary. The nave, at right angles to the main axis, is roofed with a barrel vault; four uneven arcades supported by three marble columns separate the nave from the choir, which is also roofed with a barrel vault interrupted in its middle by a low cupola. On the north side of the choir there is an urn in which the relics of the three Sts. Macarius and St. John the Little are placed during the penitential period preceding Christmas and on the saints' feast days; otherwise, they are kept in the church of St. Macarius.

The Chapel of the Myron

The square building called the Chapel of the Myron was formerly part of the large church of St. Macarius. Located in the northwest corner of the building, this room was used for nine centuries to prepare the holy oil *(myron)* for the whole of Coptic Egypt. The holy oil was prepared here for the first time in the years following the council of Chalcedon and for the last time in 1330. The rite of the preparation of the *myron* is not performed every year but only when the depletion of the reserve requires it. The patriarch himself conducts this particularly long and complex rite during Holy Week in the presence of his bishops.

The Church of St. Iskhirun

The church dedicated to the renowned Egyptian martyr St. Iskhirun, killed during Diocletian's persecutions, is situated south of that of St. Macarius, of which it was perhaps originally a part. It has a *naos* (a transverse nave), a *khurus,* and three sanctuaries. The nave is separated from the choir by a wall in which are three doors; in the south section, the nave and the choir are roofed with a barrel vault, while the north section is roofed with a splendid cupola in four parts. In all likelihood, this cupola was constructed in the thirteenth century after the collapse of the north part of the building. The middle sanctuary is roofed with a cupola in all respects identical, though smaller, with that of the sanctuary of St. Benjamin in the church of St. Macarius; it is therefore likely that this building was erected in the seventh century. On the north side of the choir, one can see the large portal, with its decoration in red bricks, which originally gave access to the church of St. Macarius.

The Tower

The tower, dating from the thirteenth century, is one of the most important monuments of the monastery, and its impressive mass dominates all the other buildings. Its square base measures twenty-one meters and fifty centimeters on each side and is sixteen meters high.

The building was the ultimate defensive bastion against the attacks of desert raiders. It has three stories. A drawbridge on the second floor is the sole entrance to the tower. On the first floor are vaulted rooms where food reserves were stored; at its north end is a well insuring the water supply during periods of siege. The second floor is divided into two parts separated by a corridor along the north-south axis. On the east side is a chapel dedicated to the Holy Virgin (al-Adra) comprising a transverse nave and three sanctuaries. The iconostasis probably dates from the thirteenth century. The west part of the second floor contains three rooms used in the past to press grapes and olives.

Likewise, on the third floor a north-south corridor separates the east and west sides. The three west rooms do not present any special interest while the east rooms are used as chapels, dedicated respectively, from

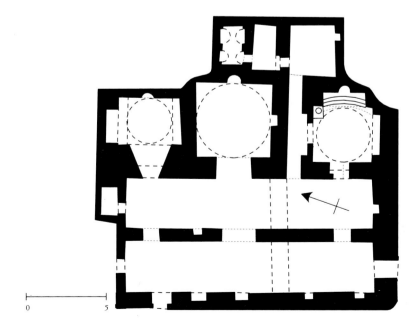

Facing page:
36. Church of St. Macarius. Painted decorations in the south sanctuary.

37. Monastery of St. Macarius. Plan of the church of St. Iskhirun.

north to south, to the archangel Michael; Sts. Anthony, Paul, and Pachomius; and the anchorites. The chapel of the archangel Michael, the traditional protector of Coptic monasteries, has the rank of patriarchal church. There are a nave and two side aisles separated by small and slender marble columns and only one sanctuary. A precious wooden iconostasis separates the sanctuary from the nave and aisles; furthermore, the latter are partitioned by a wooden screen which delimits the space reserved for the choir on the east side. The south wall is decorated with wall paintings representing a series of warrior saints: from left to right, Victor; Eusebius; Basilidas, Eusebius' father; Justus, son of the emperor Numerianus and nephew of Basilidas; Apali, son of Justus; and Thecla, wife of Justus and mother of Apali. The north wall shows a painting of St. Michael, and farther to the right, a female figure probably portraying St. Hilaria, daughter of the emperor Zeno.

South of the chapel of the archangel Michael is the chapel dedicated to Sts. Anthony, Paul, and Pachomius, the founders of Christian monasticism in Egypt; a wall painting on the north wall represents these three saints. The south chapel is dedicated to anchorites (al-Suwah) and decorated with paintings of the following anchorites: Anba Samwil (Samuel), hegumen of the monastery of Qalamun; Anba Yuannis, hegumen of the monastery of St. Macarius; Anba Nofer (Onophrius), an anchorite shown naked and covered only by his long beard; Anba Abraham, a disciple of Anba Yuannis; Anba Girgis (George); Anba Abullu (Apollo); Anba Abib, the companion of Anba Abullu; Anba Misail; and Anba Bigimi. These wall paintings, dating from the sixteenth century, are the work of an Abyssinian monk.

A staircase leads to the third floor of the tower, from which one has an unobstructed view of the surrounding desert and the impressive works of irrigation and agriculture accomplished by the monks during the last decades. In the past, the top floor of the tower served as a post of observation to watch for approaching raiders. A large wooden panel, rhythmically struck with a sledgehammer, announced the danger to all those outside the walls. The same instrument was used for calling the monks to the liturgical celebrations.

The Refectory

The old refectory is in the south wing of the monastery and probably dates from the eleventh and twelfth centuries. Rectangular in plan, it has five bays; the three southern ones are roofed with cupolas of brick while the other two are roofed with a barrel vault. One long masonry table runs the whole length of the room on the west side.

38. Monastery of St. Macarius. Wall paintings of Sts. Onophrius and George in the chapel of the anchorites in the monastery tower.

Historical Information

The Holy Monk Pshoi

The origin of this monastery is closely linked with the life of the holy monk Pshoi, its founder and patron saint. The name Pshoi means high, supreme. Born in the delta region, he was part of a large family that the mother had to raise by herself after her husband's death, which happened when her seven children were still very young. According to legend, an angel appeared to Pshoi and urged him to withdraw into the desert to devote his life to God; without hesitation, the youth, not yet twenty years old, went to the desert of Scetis, where he became the disciple of St. Pambo (also called Pemoa or Bamua), who had been the disciple of Macarius the Great. In Scetis, Pshoi met John the Little, whose very close friend he became and who was particularly known for his rigorous obedience to his superiors—which is confirmed by the legend recounting that Pambo ordered John to plant a stick in the desert and that John did not hesitate to obey and plant the stick which grew into a vigorous fruit tree.

When Pambo died, an angel appeared to Pshoi and commanded him to leave the monastic community and his friend John in order to live in ascetical solitude. Pshoi consented and withdrew to a cell on the site which is now occupied by the monastery of the Syrians and the monastery which bears his name. His piety was such that, to prolong his prayers as long as possible, he used to attach his hair to a rope hanging from the ceiling to keep from falling asleep. His devotion to Christ and his humility gave rise to numerous legends. One of them reports that one day, Jesus came to his cell under the guise of a pilgrim. As was his custom with the visitors who came now and then, Pshoi began to wash the pilgrim's feet in humble sign of hospitality, not recognizing his guest until the latter revealed himself by showing him the marks of the crucifixion.

Pshoi's reputation attracted many disciples who in time formed an important community of anchorites. But in 407, when the Bedouins made their first attack against the monasteries of Scetis, Pshoi was obliged to flee. He retired to the vicinity of Antinoe (today Ansina) in middle Egypt, where he met Paul of Tamwa, founded a monastic community, and died in the first decade of the fifth century. His body was transported to Antinoe, where it remained until it was transferred with that of his friend Paul of Tamwa to the monastery founded by the saint in Wadi al-Natrun.

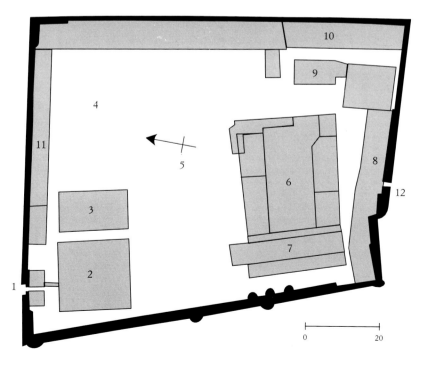

39. Plan of the monastery of St. Pshoi.
1. Main entrance
2. Tower
3. Guesthouse
4. Gardens
5. Well of the Martyrs
6. Church of St. Pshoi
7. Ancient refectory
8. Cells
9. Ancient mill
10. Library
11. Infirmary
12. Secondary entrance

Sackings and Devastation

In the course of the centuries, the monastery had the same fate as the others in the desert of Scetis and endured the raids and assaults of the Bedouins. It is here, according to legend, that the bandits stopped to wash their bloody swords after murdering the forty-nine martyrs of the monastery of St. Macarius. The patriarch Benjamin I (623–662) promoted vast works of remodeling and reconstruction, but in 817, the fifth attack on Scetis brought new massacres and extensive damage which compelled the monks to abandon their home.

However, the anchorites' tenacity brought them back to the monasteries of Scetis a few years later, under the patriarchates of Jacob (819–830) and Joseph I (830–849). A new raid damaged the monastery in 1096, but carpenter ants and other insects did still worse and little by little damaged the wooden structures beyond repair, thus accelerating the dilapidation and decay of the place. It was thanks to the patriarch Benjamin II (1327–1339) that the buildings were renovated so that once more the monastery recovered from its forsaken state. In order to honor the memory of Benjamin II and thank him, the monks of the monastery of St. Pshoi preserve the body of the patriarch, their benefactor, in their main church.

Pilgrims and Visitors

In the course of the following centuries, the monastery was visited by travelers from different nations; Arabs, French, English, and Germans describe it in their travel journals and indicate the number of monks living there: twenty in 1638, four in 1712, twelve in 1799, four in 1837, seven in 1875, fourteen in 1896, twenty-three in 1923. During the last thirty years or so, the number of monks has gone from a score to about one hundred and fifty today; many serve Egyptian churches and parishes while still belonging to the monastery. From September 1981 to January 1985, the patriarch Shenuda III spent a period of forced exile at the monastery of St. Pshoi at the end of which he was allowed to return to his patriarchal see in Cairo.

The Monastic Buildings

The Walls

An impressive enclosure built in the ninth century surrounds the monastery. The walls are about ten meters high and two meters wide and measure one hundred sixty-six meters on the east and west and ninety-five meters on the north and south. The plan of the monastery is rectangular. Originally, there were four entrances, one to each side. Today, only two remain, on the north and south, the others having been blocked up. The main entrance is on the north side and is in keeping with the traditional defensive scheme: a corridor roofed with a barrel vault, with portals at both ends, one opening to the outside, the other to the inside.

The Tower

The fortresslike tower is situated at the northwest corner of the monastery, and goes back to the late thirteenth century. As usual, one enters the tower on the second floor by a wooden drawbridge which was lifted when, in times of danger, the monks took refuge in the tower against the attacks of assailants. Only two of the three original stories have survived. On the first floor are rooms where food was stored and prepared; one can discern the traces of an oven, a mill for grains, a press for grapes, and an olive press; there is also a well some thirty meters deep. The second floor comprised the living quarters of the monks during the periods of siege. Recently, the rooms east of the corridor, which have cupolas supported by brick arches, have been transformed into a church, and so today the place is a church dedicated to the Holy Virgin; it has a transverse nave and triple sanctuary. But no tradition, whether oral or written, indicates that these spaces were used for worship at any previous time.

A staircase leads to the roof of the tower where the chapel dedicated to the archangel Michael is situated on the north side. It is likely that originally the chapel was not isolated but integrated into the architectural structure of the third floor which was destroyed at an unknown time.

The Church of St. Pshoi

The main church is dedicated to St. Pshoi, the founder of the monastery. Nothing remains from the first church, probably destroyed by the Berbers in 817. The principal structures of the building we see today probably date from the middle of the ninth century. However, many structural elements are part of the restoration and remodeling conducted about 1330 by the patriarch Benjamin II.

The plan of the church comprises a *naos,* which has a nave, two side aisles, and a western return aisle, a broad *khurus,* and a triple sanctuary. The tomb of the patriarch Benjamin II, the benefactor of the monastery, is located in the southwest corner of the south aisle. The nave has a precious wooden pulpit, while the wooden door separating the two bays of the nave has decorative hexagonal panels with arabesques and ivory inlays and probably dates from the fourteenth century. The choir is rectangular in plan and placed transversely in relation to the nave. The tomb of the founder, St. Pshoi, and St. Paul of Tamwa, his friend who was like a brother to him, is placed near the north wall.

The north sanctuary is dedicated to the Holy Virgin; it is separated from the choir by an arched portal. It is a particularly long and narrow room whose structure probably dates from the ninth century. The middle sanctuary, dedicated to St. Pshoi, communicates with the choir through a high portal with ornate wooden panels dating from the Fatimid period. Its square plan probably goes back to the ninth century and its cupola to the fourteenth. The south sanctuary, dedicated to John the Baptist, also dates from the time of the renovation of the buildings in the fourteenth century.

The Chapel of St. Iskhirun

The entrance to the chapel of St. Iskhirun (Abu Iskhirun) is located on the south side of the choir of the main church. Its construction dates from the eleventh century; only its cupola is part of the renovation accomplished by the patriarch Benjamin II about the middle of the fourteenth century. The plan is almost square and on the east opens onto a semi-circular apse which serves as a sanctuary; the relics of the holy martyr St. Iskhirun are kept under the altar. An icon from the seventeenth century placed on the iconostasis separating the choir from the sanctuary represents the saint on horseback. As is customary, a wooden partition separates the nave from the choir.

North of the sanctuary, a narrow passage leads to a small room used as a baptistery. The diameter of the stone baptismal font is ninety-five centimeters. The monasteries of St. Pshoi and al-Baramus are the only ones possessing a baptistery. That there is a baptistery is due to the fact that many Coptic families either visiting the monastery on their way to or coming from the surrounding towns and villages wished their children to be baptized in holy and particularly venerated places.

The Chapel of the Holy Virgin

Dedicated to the patriarch Benjamin I, the chapel of the Holy Virgin (al-Adra) is on the northeast side of the main church and is entered from the *khurus* through a door set to the left of the tomb of St. Pshoi. The

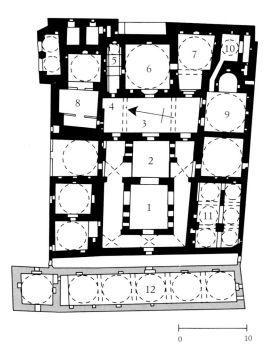

40. Church of the monastery of St. Pshoi.
Above: illustration from *Description de l'Égypte* (1809).
Left: plan. 1. Nave: west bay, 2. Nave: east bay, 3. Choir, 4. Tomb of St. Pshoi, 5. Sanctuary of the Holy Virgin, 6. Sanctuary of St. Pshoi, 7. Sanctuary of St. John the Baptist, 8. Chapel of the Holy Virgin, 9. Chapel of St. Iskhirun, 10. Baptistery, 11. Chapel of St. George, 12. Ancient refectory.

room features a nave roofed with a barrel vault. The sanctuary, almost square in plan, is separated from the nave by a finely worked wooden iconostasis and surmounted by a cupola.

The Chapel of St. George
The entrance to the chapel of St. George (Mari Girgis) is near the southeast corner of the main church. Built in the eleventh or the twelfth century, it has two sanctuaries and is roofed with six low cupolas.

The Refectory
The ancient refectory is located west of the church of St. Pshoi and connected to it by a long, narrow corridor. Its entrance is in the middle of the corridor, opposite the west entrance of the church. After the Sunday liturgy, the monks used to go directly from the church to the refectory to celebrate the agape. The hall measures twenty-seven meters in length and four and a half meters in width. Four arches at right angles to the main axis delimit five distinct spaces. The central space is roofed with a beautiful quadripartite vault while the other four have cupolas in which some openings admit light. A long stone table fills the room from north to south; it is strangely low, being only thirty-six centimeters high. It is evident that the monks sat cross-legged on the floor. Today, the refectory is a museum exhibiting ancient objects, sacred and secular.

The Well of the Martyrs
Opposite the north entrance to the church of St. Pshoi, one can still see the well where the Berbers are supposed to have washed their bloodied swords after the massacre of the forty-nine monks of the monastery. The well is twelve meters deep and its water, which is limpid and fresh, is regarded as miraculous.

THE MONASTERY OF THE SYRIANS
(DEIR AL-SURIAN)

Historical Information

The Julianist Heresy
The monastery of the Syrians was founded in the sixth century. Its beginning is closely connected with Julian's heretical doctrine which spread throughout Egypt under the patriarchate of Timothy III (517–535). The Julianist heresy, also called Aphtartodocetism, owes its name to its principal exponent Julian, a theologian and bishop of Halicarnassus in Ionia, from which he was exiled to Egypt for having defined the doctrine of the incorruptibility of Jesus' body. The Aphtartodocetae denied that human beings were corruptible by nature and held that this corruptibility was a consequence of original sin. Christ was considered the new Adam in his "natural" humanity, which was anterior to sin and therefore incorruptible. The Orthodox Church rejected Julianism: in its eyes, the Logos had taken the form of a humanity that was not ideal and abstract but fallen after sin and therefore corruptible. Thus, the Orthodox Church reaffirmed and clarified the notion of the complete and real human nature of Christ.

However, Julian's doctrine was so successful in the desert of Scetis that the majority of the monks embraced it. Those who refused to do so obtained from the governor Aristomachus permission to erect new churches and new monasteries in which they could settle apart from the Julianists. Consequently, new monasteries appeared beside the old ones; they kept the same name but added to it the title Theotokos (Mother of God), exalting in this way the significance of the incarnation—which Julian's doctrine tended to minimize—and reaffirming the charismatic dignity of the Holy Virgin.

The monastery of the Syrians was one of these. Founded by the Orthodox monks of the neighboring monastery of St. Pshoi, it took the same name but associated it with the Theotokos. In the beginning of the eighth century, the controversies between Orthodox and Julianists died out and it was no longer necessary to occupy two distinct monasteries. So the monastery of the Holy Virgin Theotokos was ceded to a group of rich Syrian merchants from Tekrit in Mesopotamia who had settled in al-Fustat in Old Cairo. As a consequence, the monastery became the home of Syrian monks and took the name of Monastery of the Holy Virgin of the Syrians.

A Center of Syrian Culture

That there were monks from Syria in the desert of Scetis is attested as early as the end of the fourth century. And the fact that the monastery was acquired by Syrians perhaps reflected the wish to constitute a monastic community which would be ethnically and culturally homogeneous.

In 817, the fifth raid of the Berbers caused disastrous damage to the monastery, which however was rebuilt and reequipped thanks to the persistent labors of two monks, Matthew and Abraham. It rapidly became an important and prosperous institution, possessing a library rich in Syrian texts and artistic treasures. The hegumen, Moses of Nisibis, a learned and cultured man, played the leading role in the formation of this collection; in 927, he traveled to Baghdad to ask the caliph al-Muqtadir bi'llah to grant fiscal exemption to monasteries. After the caliph had acceded to his request, Moses took the opportunity to travel to Syria and Mesopotamia in search of manuscripts. After three years of fruitful investigations, he returned to Egypt with 250 Syrian manuscripts which enriched the monastery library and made it a fundamental source for the history and culture of Syria.

At the end of the eleventh century, the monastery was home to some sixty monks according to the census conducted by Mawhub ibn Mansur, the coauthor of the *History of the Patriarchs of the Coptic Church*. It was then the third monastery after those of St. Macarius and St. John the Little. But in the course of the fourteenth century, the monastery was decimated by the scourge of the plague which left it in a lamentable state; in 1413, a visitor by the name of Moses, a monk from the monastery of Mar Gabriel in Tur Abdin, found just one monk. Thanks to the help of the patriarch of Antioch, Ignatius XI, who visited the monastery at the end of the fifteenth century and granted privileges and donations to it, the community of the Syrians recovered its former splendor. However, Egyptians were beginning to enter it, and in 1516, out of forty-three monks, twenty-five were Egyptians and only eighteen were Syrians.

Little by little, Egyptians replaced Syrians, all the while contributing to the prosperity of the monastery. Under the patriarchate of Gabriel VII (1526–1569), who had been a monk there, the monastery became so powerful that it was able to send to the communities of St. Anthony and St. Paul twenty and ten monks respectively in order to restore the monasteries damaged by Bedouin raids. Travelers from the West (French, German, and English) who visited the monastery in the seventeenth century report that there were two churches, one for the Syrians, the other for the Copts; they also mention a miraculous tree called "St. Ephrem's tree." Indeed, according to tradition, Ephrem, a fourth century Syrian theologian and ascetic from Nisibis, in his desire to meet the holy monk Pshoi, came to the monastic centers of Scetis and went to Pshoi's hermitage at the place where the future monastery of the Syrians would stand. The two men met but were unable to converse since Ephrem spoke only Syrian. Miraculously, Pshoi suddenly began to express himself in that language, enabling

41. The monasteries of St. Pshoi and the Syrians.
Illustration from *Description de l'Égypte* (1809).

95

his visitor to understand him. Moreover, the staff which Ephrem had leaned against the door of the hermitage all at once rooted and began to sprout. To this day, one can see near the church of the Holy Virgin this tamarind, miraculously born from Ephrem's staff.

The presence of Syrian monks is attested only to the end of the seventeenth century. In 1715 and 1735, when the Lebanese Joseph Simeonis (Yusuf Sim'an) Assemani was sent to Egypt by Pope Clement XI to seek ancient texts preserved in monasteries, he went to that of the Syrians but did not find anyone from Syria. Nevertheless, he was able to visit the very rich monastery library and succeeded in acquiring forty precious manuscripts which today are kept in the Vatican Library.

Between 1839 and 1851, the British Museum in London was able to procure about five hundred Syrian manuscripts from the library; they are not only religious texts but are concerned also with philosophy and literature. The dispersion in the West of the manuscripts from the library of the monastery of the Syrians triggered an absorbing research on the Syriac language and culture. Up until the time these manuscripts became available to Western scholars, many classical texts from Aristotle, Euclid, Archimedes, Hippocrates, and Galen were known only in their thirteenth century Latin translations, which themselves were often derived from earlier Arabic translations. Even though many among them have reached us only in a fragmented state, the documents from the monastery of the Syrians are the oldest copies of important Greek classical texts, some of them going back to the fifth century.

The Monastic Buildings

The Walls
The plan of the monastery of the Syrians is somewhat unusual among the other monasteries of Wadi al-Natrun. It has the shape of an almost rectangular quadrilateral whose width (the shortest sides measure 36 and 54 meters) is much smaller than the length (160 meters). The monks explain this anomaly in an intriguing but unlikely way: according to them, the monastery was built on the model of Noah's ark. The walls probably date from the end of the ninth century and their height varies between nine and a half and eleven and a half meters.

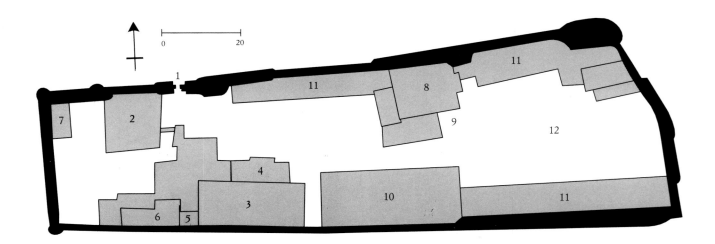

42. Plan of the monastery of the Syrians.
1. Entrance, 2. Tower, 3. Church of the Holy Virgin, 4. Church of the Forty-Nine Martyrs, 5. Cell of St. Pshoi, 6. Ancient refectory, 7. Cemetery, 8. Church of St. Mary, 9. Tree of St. Ephrem, 10. Library and cells, 11. Cells, 12. Garden.

The Tower

The majestic tower *(qasr)* rises west of the north entrance to the monastery. It was built in the middle of the ninth century and in any case antedates the walls. It comprises a ground floor and three stories above it. As usual, one gains access to it on the second floor through a wooden drawbridge, which insured the inviolability of the edifice against pillagers' raids. The first floor contains the rooms employed in the past for the storage of food supplies and the production of flour, oil, and wine. Also, a well insured complete autonomy for a long time. The second floor was for centuries the location of the library until the precious manuscripts were gradually surrendered to visitors and experts from the West who were seeking them to enrich the collections of the Vatican Library and British Museum. Some of the niches in the walls are still visible.

The third story of the tower is divided by a corridor onto which open four vaulted rooms on one side and two on the other. These rooms were probably cells used by the monks in periods of danger. In accordance with Egyptian monastic tradition, the top story (here the fourth) shelters a chapel dedicated to the archangel Michael. It comprises a nave and a choir separated by the traditional wooden screen and roofed with a barrel vault. The sanctuary is surmounted by a brick cupola resting on four pendentives decorated with stalactite motifs which could date back to the fifteenth century.

The Church of the Holy Virgin (el-Adra)

The church of the Holy Virgin goes back to approximately 645. If one leaves aside the court and a side chapel dedicated to the forty-nine martyrs of Sebaste, its plan is perfectly rectangular and measures twenty-eight meters in length and twelve meters in width.

The entrance to the church is on its north side through a square court which is surmounted by a cupola and opens onto the monastery courtyard. The main building can be divided into three sections: the *naos,* the *khurus,* and a triple sanctuary. The full length of the nave is roofed with a barrel vault and flanked by two small side aisles, which are joined on the west according to a typically Egyptian usage. A masonry balustrade one meter and twenty-five centimeters in height divides the nave into two sections. In the floor at its west end there is a *laqqan,* the marble basin which was used for the washing of the feet on Holy Thursday. The half-cupola above the west door of the nave is decorated with a very beautiful wall painting going back to the time of the church's construction or a period immediately following. It represents the annunciation in the traditional way with the Holy Virgin and the archangel Gabriel, but it is enhanced by the presence of four prophets (Moses and Isaiah on the left, Ezekiel and Daniel on the right) who foretold the incarnation. By juxtaposing the ancient expectations and their realization, the artist expresses the fulfillment of the divine plan through the intimate union of the Old and New Testaments.

Also on the west, at the end of the south aisle, a door opens onto a narrow corridor leading to the cell where, according to tradition, St. Pshoi lived. A hook is screwed into the ceiling of the small room; the saint used to attach his hair to it to avoid falling asleep during his hours of prayer.

43. Monastery of the Syrians. The defensive tower from the 9th century.

A magnificent wooden portal separates the center nave from the choir. A Syrian inscription bears the date 926. The ebony panels are richly inlaid with ivory. The figures of St. Peter, the Holy Virgin, Christ, and St. Mark are carved on its upper part. The architectural structure of the choir, transverse in relation to the nave, is typically Syrian and is akin to that of the church of the Holy Virgin of Hah in Tur Abdin. The middle part is surmounted by a cupola twelve meters high, flanked on the north and south by two half-cupolas embellished with fine wall paintings, whose date can be placed in the thirteenth century (c. 1225). The style is linear and incisive, the colors are pure and warm, and the inscriptions are in both Syrian and Greek characters.

The south half-cupola shows the annunciation on the left and the nativity on the right. The iconography is Byzantine. In the annunciation, Mary is seated and her attitude expresses surprise at Gabriel's announcement. In the nativity, the figure of Mary, lying by the manger in which the infant Jesus is resting, dominates the scene; above, angels proclaim the good news; to the left of the Holy Virgin, the shepherds are represented, and below her, St. Joseph. To the far right, the Magi approach the cave bringing their gifts; according to a very ancient convention of Christian iconography, they represent the three ages of life, old age, maturity, and youth.

The north half-cupola shows the dormition of the Holy Virgin, also in the Byzantine manner: Mary is lying on the bed of her *transitus* in the presence of the weeping apostles (John at her feet, Peter at her head). Behind the bed, Christ stands holding in his arms the Holy Virgin's soul in the form of a baby in swaddling clothes, a symbol of her birth to new life. On the west wall of the choir, one can see a Coptic inscription engraved in the stone: this is the epigraph of the tomb of St. John Kama, whose body was probably transferred to the monastery of the Syrians when the one dedicated to him fell into ruins.

Two large steps lead to the main sanctuary *(haykal,* from the Hebrew *hekal).* The door between the choir and the sanctuary is an extraordinary work of inlay from the beginning of the tenth century. This date is attested by a Syrian inscription written on the door itself and indicating that it was made under the patriarchates of Anba Gabriel I, the fifty-seventh patriarch of Alexandria (910–921), and Anba Yuannis IV, the twenty-fifth patriarch of Antioch (902–922). The door is made of forty-two panels arranged in seven horizontal rows and six vertical ones. The panels of the uppermost row represent, from left to right, St. Dioscorus, patriarch of Alexandria; St. Mark, the Evangelist and first bishop of Alexandria; Christ; the Holy Virgin; St. Severus I, patriarch of Antioch; and St. Ignatius, bishop of Antioch. These representations confirm that the monks of the monastery of the Syrians had equal respect for and fidelity to the Coptic and Syrian patriarchates.

The sanctuary is square and surmounted by a high cupola. In the center, under a canopy from the nineteenth century, is the altar from the tenth century, made of black stone instead of the white marble which is the Copts' usual choice. The stucco friezes decorating the walls are most interesting; they go back to the beginning of the tenth century and bear a striking resemblance to the stucco reliefs of Muslim workmanship. In Samarra, the Abbasid capital situated north of Baghdad, one can find rigorously identical stucco decorations. The taste for this sort of ornamentation was in all likelihood brought to Egypt by Ibn Tulun when he was sent there as governor in 868; in Cairo, the mosque that bears his name is an extraordinary example of this sort of decoration.

The Chapel of the Forty-Nine Martyrs

This chapel, dating from the tenth century, is attached to the north side of the church of the Holy Virgin, and access is through the court at the north entrance of the church. It is dedicated to the forty-nine martyrs from the monastery of St. Macarius, who were massacred in 444 during the bloody raid of the Berber plunderers against the monasteries of Scetis. Anba Christodulus, the abun of Ethiopia in the beginning of the seventeenth century, is buried in the chapel.

The Refectory

The ancient refectory, no longer in use, is located west of the church of the Holy Virgin. It is nearly rectangular and its main axis is occupied by a masonry table flanked by two rows of seats also in masonry. Near the east wall there is a large stone pulpit used for the reading of sacred texts and saints' lives during the common meal. The east wall is longer than the west one, and the room is roofed with a vast cupola in which small windows are opened to admit light.

The Church of St. Mary (al-Sitt Mariam)

The church of St. Mary was given this name to distinguish it from the principal church, also dedicated to the Holy Virgin. Its structure dates from the ninth century and, with the exception of the cupola surmounting

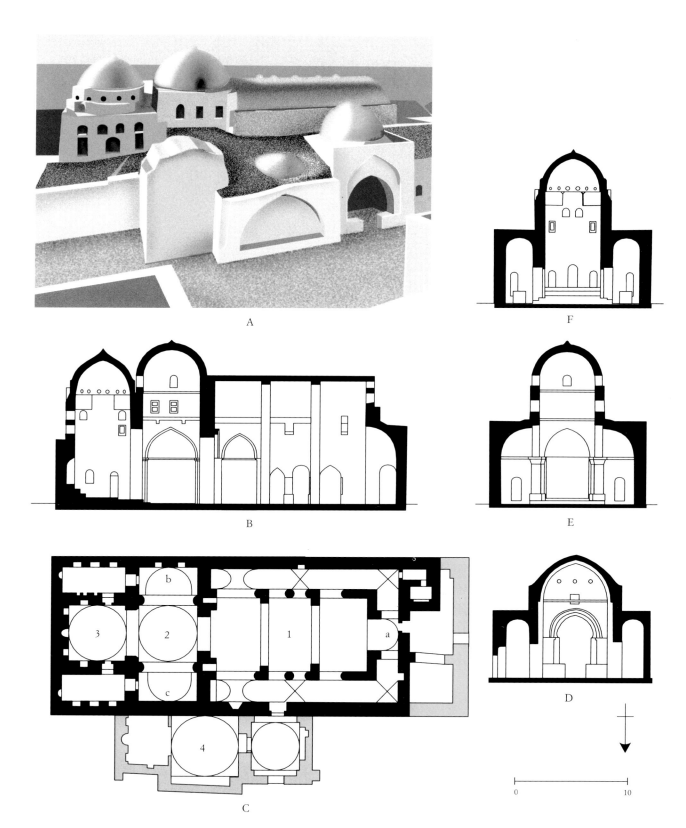

A

F

B

E

C

D

44. Monastery of the Syrians. Church of the Holy Virgin (al-Adra).
A. Isometric view, B. Longitudinal section, C. Plan, D. Cross section of the nave,
E. Cross section of the choir, F. Cross section of the sanctuaries.
1. Nave, 2. Choir, 3. Sanctuary, 4. Chapel of the Forty-Nine Martyrs.
Wall paintings: a. Annunciation, b. Annunciation and nativity, c. Dormition of the
Holy Virgin.

the main sanctuary, exactly reproduces the typology of monastic churches in Tur Abdin. The body of the church comprises the *naos* (a nave), the *khurus,* and the triple sanctuary.

One enters the nave from the south side through a portico whose level is three steps lower than the present level of the monastery courtyard. Three more steps connect the portico with the nave of the church. This nave has a rectangular plan and—a feature characteristic of the churches in Mesopotamia—is transverse in relation to the main east-west axis. The barrel vault, divided into three bays by arches resting on consoles, also reveals its Mesopotamian origin. Near the west end, the floor contains the marble *laqqan.* A large central door and two smaller side doors lead to the choir; the middle door of inlaid woodwork can be dated between the fourteenth and fifteenth centuries. The space serving as choir is also rectangular and transverse in relation to the principal axis; it is roofed with a barrel vault divided into three parts like that over the nave. The iconostasis of the sanctuary, made of dark inlaid wood, probably dates from the fifteenth century.

The Church of Sts. Honnos and Marutha

The little church dedicated to Sts. Honnos and Marutha, no longer used, is attached to the east wall of the church of St. Mary. It dates from the beginning of the fifteenth century, a time when the monks from the ruined monastery of St. John Kama took refuge in the monastery of the Syrians.

The Church of St. John the Little

The church dedicated to St. John the Little, close to the northeast corner of the enclosure wall, is in ruins today. Up to the end of the nineteenth century, it was occupied by Ethiopian monks who had taken refuge in the monastery of the Syrians after their own monastery had fallen into ruins. Indeed, an Ethiopian monas-

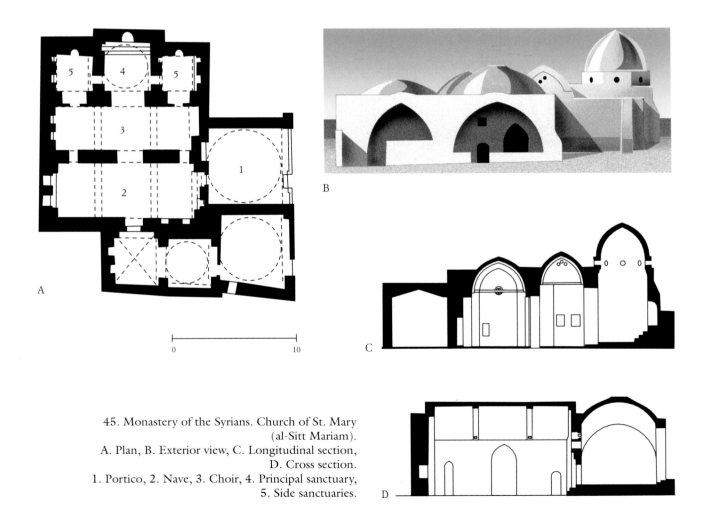

45. Monastery of the Syrians. Church of St. Mary
(al-Sitt Mariam).
A. Plan, B. Exterior view, C. Longitudinal section,
D. Cross section.
1. Portico, 2. Nave, 3. Choir, 4. Principal sanctuary,
5. Side sanctuaries.

tic community lived in the desert of Scetis as early as the twelfth century and occupied the monastery of St. Elisha. When this fell into ruins, the community was received by the monastery of the Holy Virgin of St. John the Little; this in turn had to be abandoned because of its precarious state, and the few remaining Ethiopian monks were welcomed into the monastery of the Syrians.

THE MONASTERY OF AL-BARAMUS
(DEIR AL-BARAMUS)

Historical Information

Macarius and the Two Young Strangers

The monastery of al-Baramus was very probably the first monastery established in Wadi al-Natrun. Indeed, it occupies the place where Macarius the Great settled in 340 (perhaps even around 330) to devote himself to monastic life. The Arabic name al-Baramus derives from the Coptic Pa-Romeos which means "belonging to the Romans." The origin of this name is uncertain and several traditions exist on this point. According to the most widespread, Macarius received two Roman youths, the "young strangers" coming from faraway lands, who in due course became monks in the saint's community. When they prematurely died a few days apart, Macarius consecrated their cell by building a chapel he called "cell of the Romans." The identity of the two youths is also the object of discussion. The most likely interpretation is that they were the illegitimate sons of the emperor Valentinianus I (364–375); their names were Maximus and Domitian and they would have come to Egypt and Scetis after having visited the holy places in Palestine. According to others, the two "young strangers" received by Macarius and later on venerated by the monks of Scetis were not necessarily of Roman origin: the name of the place, "belonging to the Romans," could be due to the fact that a Roman monk named Arsenius settled in Scetis in 394 and became the abbot of the community. Among other positions, Arsenius had been the tutor of Arcadius and Honorius, the emperor Theodosius' sons, who in their turn became emperors; according to this interpretation, this bit of history would explain the confusion and the identification of the two "young strangers" as "Romans."

Sackings and Devastation

The original monastery of al-Baramus, called Old Baramus, was located north of the present one and underwent the same trials as the other monasteries of Scetis at the hands of desert pillagers. Abbot Arsenius himself witnessed the devastating raids of 407 and 410 and both times succeeded in taking flight. The first time, he came back to rebuild the cells and other parts of the monastery that had been destroyed, but the second time, he preferred to withdraw to Troe, the Cairo neighborhood called Tura today, where he died and where a monastery dedicated to him was subsequently established.

One of the martyrs of the first raid was St. Moses the Black, called thus because, being an Ethiopian, he had dark skin. Before becoming a monk and a priest, Moses had led the life of a brigand and committed many crimes. He repented his life of wrongdoing and retired to Scetis where the examples of Sts. Macarius and Isidore led him to a high degree of asceticism and holiness. Having foreseen the attack of the Massic Berber tribes, he urged his disciples to leave the monastic buildings of al-Baramus and take refuge in a safer place. As for him, he remained in al-Baramus with seven other monks in order that the words from the Gospel might be fulfilled, "All who take the sword will perish by the sword" (Matt 26:52).

The present monastery of al-Baramus was established in the sixth century as a counterpart of Old Baramus. Like the other monasteries of Scetis, it also suffered damage and destruction inflicted by Berbers in 810 and 870. In 1047, upon the death of the patriarch Shenuda II, a monk from al-Baramus, Anba Christodulus, was elected patriarch; his brother Yakub (Jacob) replaced him as abbot of al-Baramus and proved to be a man of great holiness and miraculous powers.

Visitors from the Fifteenth to the Twentieth Centuries

During the first half of the fifteenth century, the Arab historian al-Maqrizi visited the monastery and identified it as the monastery of St. Moses the Black; he found it inhabited by only a few monks, like six other monasteries, but he mentions it only at the seventy-sixth place in the list of eighty-six monasteries he cites. In the course of the seventeenth century, two monks of al-Baramus were elected patriarchs: Anba Matthew III in 1631, as the 100th patriarch, and Anba Matthew IV in 1660, as the 102nd patriarch.

The French consul Coppin visited the monastery and described it in 1638 as the "fourth monastery" in the desert of "St. Macarius Bahr al-Malamah" (the Arabic means "sea of reproaches"). According to the monks of the time, this name came from a legend: when the sea still bathed the monastery walls, St. Macarius, having seen a pirate ship approaching, prayed to heaven for help; the waters of the sea suddenly withdrew, and at the same time the pirates and their ship were turned to stone in an instant. Later on, in 1692, another French visitor, De Maillet, visited the monastery and was told the same legend by the monks; he therefore calls the place in his description "Valley of Bahr bila Ma" (the Arabic means "sea without water").

According to the information supplied by later visitors, al-Baramus had twelve monks in 1712, nine in 1799, seven on 1842, twenty in 1881, thirty in 1905, thirty-five in 1937, twenty in 1960, and forty-six in 1970. Today, the monastery is inhabited by some fifty monks.

The Monastery Buildings

The Walls
The monastery is surrounded by massive walls in stone covered with a thick layer of plaster; their height varies between ten and eleven meters and their width is about two meters. They probably were constructed at the end of the ninth century, except the west side, still standing today, which is perhaps somewhat later. A covered walkway along the full length of the walls enabled the monks to keep a close watch and prepare a better defense in the centuries when the Berbers from the desert conducted frequent raids.

Today's entrance to the monastery is on the east side whereas formerly the principal entrance was on the north. The latter comprised an exterior door and an interior one connected by a corridor six meters long and roofed with a barrel vault; this complex structure was purely defensive.

The Church of the Holy Virgin (al-Adra)
The main church of the monastery is dedicated to the Holy Virgin, and its present structure dates from the sixth or seventh century. It has a *naos* containing a nave and two side aisles, the nave being roofed with a barrel vault and receiving light through windows placed on the south and north sides. Arches resting on strong pillars separate it from the side aisles, also roofed with barrel vaults. The usual marble *laqqan* is embedded in the floor at the west end of the nave. A finely carved wooden pulpit stands against the northeast corner of the

46. Plan of the monastery of al-Baramus.
1. Main entrance, 2. Tower,
3. Church of the Holy Virgin,
4. Ancient refectory,
5. Church of St. John the Baptist,
6. Guesthouse, 7. Cells, 8. Garden,
9. Secondary entrance.

north aisle; the priest used it to explain the Scriptures to catechumens before baptism. At the west end of the south aisle, one can see a column with a Corinthian capital which is called "St. Arsenius' column" because, as tradition has it, the saint was accustomed to stop by it and pray.

On the south wall of the nave, there are precious wall paintings, recently discovered and going back to the thirteenth century. A cycle devoted to Christ represents, from east to west, the annunciation, the visitation, the nativity, Jesus' baptism, an unidentified scene with two jars on a table (probably the wedding at Cana), and Jesus' entry into Jerusalem. In the space between two columns is a painting of the archangel Michael. Pentecost is represented on the north wall of the same nave, but the other scenes of the christological cycle on the north wall have disappeared.

From the nave, one enters the *khurus*, set crosswise in relation to it and roofed with a barrel vault; it is reserved for the baptized. Near its north wall, is the small wooden reliquary of Sts. Moses the Black and Isidore. A finely carved wooden door dating from the Fatimid period opens onto the main sanctuary *(haykal)* under whose altar are preserved the relics of Sts. Maximus and Domitian, the venerated protectors of the monastery. In the wall of the iconostasis are embedded five stone crosses which probably go back to the early centuries of the Christian era. The east wall of the middle sanctuary is decorated with wall paintings dating back to the thirteenth century and representing the sacrifice of Abraham (on the left), the enthroned Christ and the Holy Virgin and Child (in the middle niche), and the encounter of Melchizedek with Abraham (on the right). Three apostles are represented under the left and right scene. On the east wall of the south sanctuary, a fragment of a wall painting from the same period shows six saints: Paul of Thebes, Anthony the Great, Macarius the Great led by a cherub, John, Maximus, and Domitian. Eight saints are represented on the south wall of the same sanctuary: from left to right, three that are not identifiable, then Sts. Pachomius, Moses the Black, Barsum the Syrian, Paphnutius, and Onophrius.

Chapels and Baptistery

From the church of the Holy Virgin, one has access to two chapels respectively dedicated to St. Theodore Stratelates (general, from the Greek) and St. George. That of Theodore Stratelates (al-Amir Tadrus) is attached to the north aisle and probably dates from the fourteenth century while that of St. George (Mari Girgis) is located at the west end of the same aisle and dates from the twelfth or thirteenth century. Near this second chapel is a square room which served as a baptistery and still has its stone font.

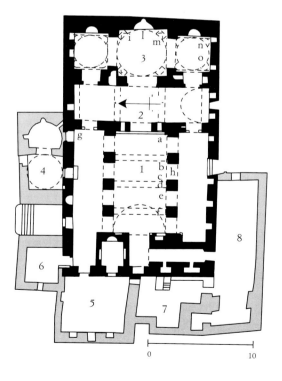

47. Monastery of al-Baramus. Church of the Holy Virgin. *Above:* exterior view. *Left:* plan.
1. Nave, 2. Choir, 3. Sanctuaries, 4. Chapel of St. Theodore Stratelates, 5. Chapel of St. George, 6. Baptistery, 7. Oil press, 8. Refectory.
Wall paintings: a. Annunciation, b. Visitation, c. Nativity, d. Baptism of Christ, e. The wedding at Cana, f. Entry into Jerusalem, g. Pentecost, h. The archangel Michael, i. The sacrifice of Abraham, j. Christ enthroned and the Holy Virgin and Child, k. Abraham and Melchizedek, l. Six holy ascetics, m. Eight holy ascetics (among whom are Pachomius, Moses the Black, Barsum the Syrian, Paphnutius, and Onophrius).

The Refectory

The refectory is on the south side of the church of the Holy Virgin, parallel to its nave. It is rectangular and measures about eleven meters in length and four in width. Two transverse arches divide it into three sections surmounted by three cupolas with circular openings at the top which give a satisfying and atmospheric lighting. A long stone table runs the length of the room; in the northeast corner, there is the stone pulpit from which the reading of the holy Scriptures was proclaimed during the agape after the liturgy. Today, the monks use this refectory only for the feasts peculiar to the Coptic liturgical year. Near the refectory are two rooms for the storing and preparation of food.

The Tower

The tower *(qasr)* probably goes back to the ninth century and for the monks was the ultimate defensive bastion against the attacks and raids of the desert pillagers. Its architecture is typical of Egypt's Coptic monasteries. The entrance is on the second floor on the south side; a small drawbridge, raised in case of danger, would leave the monks enclosed in the tower and completely isolated from the outside. Inside the fortress, everything was organized so that the whole monastic community might remain there for a lengthy period until all danger from enemy attack had ceased. The first floor was a storehouse for food supplies and had a well; the second was the lodgings of the besieged monks; the third had a chapel dedicated to St. Michael which the monks still use today.

The Church of St. John the Baptist

The church of St. John the Baptist was built in the eastern part of the monastery at the end of the nineteenth century by the patriarch Cyril V in the place where the old church dedicated to Sts. Apollo and Abib (Phib) had stood. The south sanctuary of the church has been transformed into a library containing numerous manuscripts and old books written in Coptic, Greek, Arabic, and Hebrew, treating of theological, liturgical, historical, and artistic matters.

Cairo and Its Vicinity

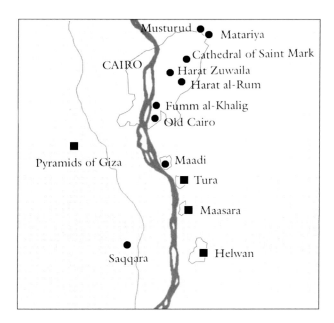

Old Cairo

The district of Old Cairo (Masr al-Qadima in Arabic) is located in the south part of the city, on the right bank of the Nile opposite the island of Roda. This area was already inhabited at the time of the pharaohs and was called Kheri-Aha (place of the battle) because the mythological tradition held that this place had been the scene of a combat between the gods Horus and Seth. In the Greek period, the place took the name Babylon and kept it during the Roman occupation, but its use was gradually discontinued after the Arab conquest. There are many Coptic churches in Old Cairo, both inside the fortress of Babylon and in its immediate surroundings.

The Fortress of Babylon

Historical Information

The district called Qasr al-Shama (Palace of the Candles) occupies the area of the ancient fortress of Babylon, a citadel built by the Romans, with towers and bastions and crisscrossed by interesting narrow streets. According to the historian Diodorus Siculus, this fortress goes back to the nineteenth century B.C.E., when Pharaoh Sesostris, of the twelfth dynasty, after defeating the Babylonians at the end of an especially cruel war, took the prisoners into Egypt to make slaves of them. But the prisoners rebelled and built fortifications to defend the area where they resided, which from then on was named Babylon. However, according to the Coptic historian John, bishop of Nikiou in the seventh century, Nebuchadnezzar, king of Babylon, built this fortress when he occupied Egypt in the second half of the sixth century B.C.E. Modern historians are agreed that the name Babylon (Babalyun in Arabic) derives from the Egyptian Pr-Hapi-n-Iwnw (Nile house of Heliopolis) whose pronunciation was very similar to that of Babylon. It is therefore likely that a nilometer, a gauge for measuring the height of the Nile, especially during flood season, was erected on that spot.

Although partially in ruins, the fortifications that are still extant date from the period of the Roman occupation. Indeed, the Romans used to build fortified citadels on the frontiers of the empire in order to defend it against possible enemy attacks and rebellions by local populations. The Roman fortress of Babylon was constructed by the emperor Diocletian (284–305). The Roman garrison, five thousand strong, resided inside the citadel; it covered almost three hectares and possessed all that was necessary not only for its defense (towers, fortifications, ditches, stores of ammunition) but for the daily needs of its occupants (barracks, infirmaries, stables, cisterns, mills, warehouses, temples—replaced by churches in due course) so that their complete autonomy was insured.

The ruins of two large towers (one of which houses a Greek Orthodox church dedicated to St. George) still exist where the west walls stood. The Nile (which today is four hundred meters away) used to flow at the foot of these walls and the boats were moored in a small port whose vestiges have been discovered between the two towers. The bases of these towers are about six meters below the present level of the ground because of the great quantity of rubbish and rubble accumulated through time. Built of polished stones and baked bricks set in an alternating series of five rows of stone and three of brick, the towers measure about twenty meters in height and thirty meters in diameter while the exterior walls are three meters thick.

The remains of the two south bastions over which the Hanging Church was erected are especially interesting. They flanked the principal gate to the fortress, whose structure is still visible. The bastions and south gate are accessible through the garden of the old wing of the Coptic Museum, by means of a staircase that leads to the original ground level. Under the Hanging Church, there is the old entrance atrium to the fortress of Babylon, whose walls have niches which used to contain statues. Superposed columns and stone elements occupy part of this space; these structures were probably constructed in later times to make it possible to build the church above. The church architects were probably satisfied at first with using superposed columns to support the floor, but later on it proved necessary to reinforce this system by adding stone pillars connected by brick arches. One of the bastions still has a mill and an oven as well as a vaulted room where grain was stored.

Up to the seventh century, the citadel represented the core of Byzantine Egypt's military organization. In 641, after a seven month siege, the Arabs took the fortress, and their military chief, Amr ibn al-As, made his triumphal entry into it. Adjacent to the east of the fortress was a heavily populated center where Amr ibn al-As had established his camp during the siege; this camp became the regular quarters of the garrison and little by little merged with the existing settlement. Thus was born the city which the Arabs called Misr (Egypt), according to their custom of giving to the capitals of their new provinces the name of the province itself, or al-Fustat, from the Latin military term *fossatum*, designating a camp with a ditch. The fortress of Babylon was later on given back to the Copts, who became its sole occupants and began to restore the churches. Although the churches of Old Cairo differ from one another in their architecture and dimensions, they all share one characteristic, which in any case is found in Coptic churches in general: an exterior structure singularly simple

48. Old Cairo. Illustration from Michel Jullien, *L'Égypte—Souvenirs bibliques et chrétiens* (1891).
1. St. Mercurius district, 2. Aqueduct, 3. Mosque of Amr ibn al-As, 4. Armenian monastery, 5. Maronite monastery, 6. Church of St. Sergius, 7. Church of the Holy Virgin al-Muallaqa, 8. Church of St. George, 9. Church of St. Barbara, 10. Roman Gate.

and devoid of ornamentation to the point that at times they are indistinguishable from the surrounding houses made of brick and covered with plaster.

The Monastery of St. George (Deir al-Banat)

The origin of the monastery of St. George, called Deir al-Banat in Arabic, is obscure, but it is probable that its foundation goes back to the seventh or eighth century. Today the monastery is home to some thirty women religious; only the chapel dedicated to St. George and the large room with an anteroom offer any historical and artistic interest. The former, originally a palace from the Mamluk period (1250–1517), was transformed into a church probably in the fourteenth or fifteenth century. The latter is high-ceilinged and separated from the chapel, where St. George's icon is venerated, by a double door of a surprising height (seven meters) and decorated with animal figures. The nuns in charge of the chapel offer for the veneration of the faithful an iron collar which according to tradition was used to hold prisoners before their martyrdom.

The Church of St. George

The church dedicated to St. George is a recent edifice built in the nineteenth century on the ruins of the old church which burned down. The original church of St. George was considered one of the most beautiful and richest in the fortress of Babylon. There is nothing particular to mention about the present structure. It cannot be earlier than the Mamluk period (1250–1517) since it belongs to the four-pillar type of building, which consists of a number of bays of approximately the same size, usually emphasized by cupolas, with the central dome higher and supported by four pillars. Its three sanctuaries are separated from the body of the church by an iconostasis. What remains from the ancient edifice is limited to what is called the wedding hall (Qaʿat al-ʿIrsan in Arabic). This rectangular hall dates from the thirteenth century and measures fifteen meters in length and twelve meters in width; its central part is lower than its lateral parts. The south wall is notable because of high windows made of wood with inlays in ivory and ebony. The walls and ceiling show the traces of wall paintings and fine stucco decorations.

The Church of St. Sergius (Abu Sarga)

This church is at the center of Old Cairo. Its entrance is located in a narrow paved street which delimits its east side. The level of the church is about four meters lower than the present ground level. The church is dedicated to St. Sergius, whom tradition associates with St. Bacchus: Sergius was the servant of Bacchus, the saddler at the emperor Maximian's court. Both were Christians and endured martyrdom together on October 1, 296, in Syria—where the remains of the church dedicated to them are still extant, not far from their place of martyrdom. Among Eastern Christians, they are the object of a particularly fervent cult and devotion.

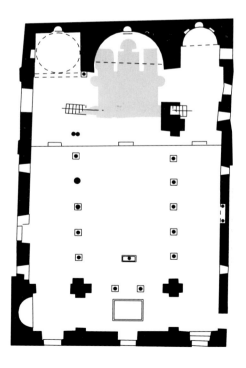
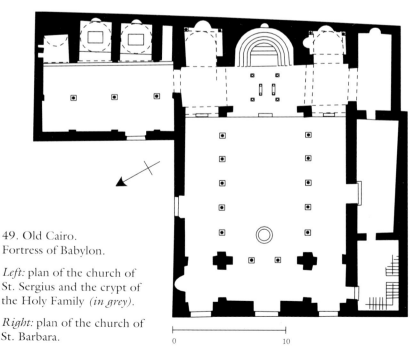

49. Old Cairo. Fortress of Babylon.

Left: plan of the church of St. Sergius and the crypt of the Holy Family *(in grey).*

Right: plan of the church of St. Barbara.

0   10

107

The church of St. Sergius is the oldest in Cairo. It was erected on the spot where, according to a very ancient tradition, the Holy Family took refuge during its flight into Egypt. According to Eutychius (877–940), the Melkite patriarch of Alexandria, the church was built by Athanasius, secretary to abd al-Aziz ibn Marwan, the governor of Egypt (689–704). The original building has been submitted to several restorations and partial reconstructions: the first one took place in the eighth century, after the fire ordered by the Omayyad caliph Marwan ibn Mohammed; the second during the Fatimid period, in the tenth and eleventh centuries. The church has a basilican plan with a *naos* (a nave, two side aisles, and a western return aisle), and three sanctuaries. In the center of the return aisle is a large Epiphany basin; the baptismal font, above which one can discern ancient wall paintings, is located on the north side of the return aisle.

Two pillars and two columns separate the return aisle from the nave. Also, the two side aisles are separated from the nave by two series of five columns. These twelve (eleven of marble and one of pink granite) columns surmounted by Corinthian capitals are the oldest remains of the original church. They may have been recycled material taken from earlier buildings of the fourth or fifth century. Traces of painted figures—probably the apostles—are visible on the columns which support a wooden architrave surmounted by arches. These arches carry the upper gallery, which was reserved for women and is crowned by ten columns with Corinthian capitals.

The ceiling of the edifice is made of wood; it is gabled and has rafters over the nave and flat over the upper gallery. The marble pulpit resting on twelve small columns is merely a copy of that in the church of St. Barbara. The remains of the original pulpit, in rosewood with inlays of ivory and ebony, are preserved in the Coptic Museum. The center iconostasis, dating from the twelfth and the thirteenth centuries, is especially precious and rich in inlays of ivory and ebony. To the left and right of the two smaller doors opening onto the middle sanctuary, there are panels, probably from the tenth century, representing the Last Supper and nativity on the left and three equestrian saints on the right. It is likely that the iconostases of the south and north sanctuaries date from the Turkish period; their inlays of ivory and ebony are in the shapes of crosses, stars, and flowers.

A ciborium resting on four columns rises above the altar of the middle sanctuary *(haykal)*. A bench (synthronon) in the shape of a semi-circle dominates the apse, whose south and north walls are decorated with badly damaged wall paintings which represent respectively Sts. Sergius and Bacchus and the Holy Virgin and Child. Two staircases lead to the crypt, which was excavated at the place where the Holy Family would have sojourned. This crypt is under the middle sanctuary, about six meters beneath the level of the main church. About six meters long and five meters wide, it is a very small church with a nave and two side aisles separated from the nave by two ranks of marble columns, four on the north and five on the south. In the southeast corner there is a small room which probably served as a baptistery.

The Church of St. Barbara (Sitt Barbara)
This church is in the east section of the Babylon fortress, against the Roman walls. Originally it was dedicated to Sts. Cyrus and John (Abu Qir and Abu Yuhanna). Cyrus was a native of Damanhur, a city in the delta; he and his friend, the priest John, decided to appear before the governor of the province in order to make their Christian faith known to him. Having heard them, the governor commanded that they be pierced with arrows, burned in a furnace, tied to horses and dragged to a neighboring town. These orders were carried out, but the two men remained miraculously unharmed. Therefore, the governor had them beheaded. The church was subsequently dedicated to St. Barbara when the relics of this martyr were transferred there. The daughter of a rich pagan, she was born in Nicomedia in Asia Minor in the beginning of the third century. Origen instructed her and she became a convert to Christianity; against her father's will, she refused to get married in order to devote herself entirely to God. At her father's instigation, the Roman governor Marcianus submitted her to torture which she courageously endured to death.

The church is a sister building to that of Sts. Sergius and Bacchus and, like the latter, built by the governor Abd al-Aziz ibn Marwan's secretary Athanasius. It was restored later on in the course of the eleventh century to the condition in which one can see it today. The edifice has a basilican plan with the nave separated from the two side aisles by ten marble columns (five on either side) and with a triple sanctuary. Two pillars and two marble columns separate the western return aisle from the nave. The columns have Corinthian capitals (with the exception of one which has palm leaves) and support a wooden architrave on which rest a series of arches; these in turn support the upper gallery.

On the northeast side of the nave, there is a beautiful marble pulpit supported by ten columns. A wooden iconostasis from the thirteenth century, with inlays in ivory and ebony representing floral designs, divides the middle nave from the middle sanctuary. Above the iconostasis there are nine icons representing Christ, the Holy Virgin, John the Baptist, the archangels Michael and Gabriel, and the four evangelists. The main altar is behind the iconostasis and surmounted by a ciborium resting on four marble columns. A semicircular syn-thronon with seven steps adorned with colorful marbles delineates the perimeter of the apse. The Coptic Museum keeps some very precious objects coming from the church of St. Barbara, including the original iconostasis from the Fatimid period (tenth century) and a large double door from the sixth century.

On the north side of the north sanctuary, a door opens into the church dedicated to Sts. Cyrus and John. Nearly square, it comprises a nave, separated lengthwise by three columns, two sanctuaries, and a room used as a baptistery. The reliquary of Sts. Cyrus and John is kept on the south side of the church next to the entrance.

The Synagogue of Ben Ezra

The synagogue is located in a garden a very short distance from the church of St. Barbara. Originally it was dedicated to the archangel Michael and probably dates from the eighth century. But an ancient Hebrew tradi-tion records that, before the Christian church, a synagogue had occupied this space since the time of Moses; it would have been destroyed by the Romans and then given to the Christian community by the Arabs. At the end of the ninth century, the patriarch Michael III returned the church to the Jews so that the money from the sale might help him pay the heavy taxes levied by the governor Ahmad ibn Tulun. In 1115, the synagogue was entirely renovated under the direction of the Jerusalem rabbi Ibrahim Ben Ezra. However, it is possible that the synagogue is named after Ezra the scribe, who, we are told, transcribed a Torah scroll possess-ing magical powers and deposited it among the archives of the Jewish community of that synagogue.

The inside has two aisles separated from the nave by two ranks of columns. In the center of the nave, there is the bema, a marble pulpit from which the holy books were read. Towards the end of the nineteenth century, at the time of excavations in the perimeter of the synagogue, many manuscripts were recovered which are important as Hebrew literary archives *(genizah)* from the medieval period.

The Church of the Holy Virgin (al-Muallaqa)

Although dedicated to the Virgin Mary (Sitt Mariam), the church is better known as the Hanging Church (al-Muallaqa in Arabic) because it was built over the two south bastions of the Babylon fortress, which were the watchtowers at the main entrance. The biography of Patriarch Yusab (Joseph, 831–849) provides the earliest reference to the church. About 840, due to his conflict with the patriarch Anba Yusab, the governor Ali ibn Yahia the Armenian partially destroyed it. Later on, it was transformed into a mosque, but in the tenth century it was restored and consecrated anew. In the eleventh century the building was chosen as the residence of the Coptic patriarchate when it was transferred from Alexandria to Cairo, and it became a center of study in theology, philosophy, science, and law.

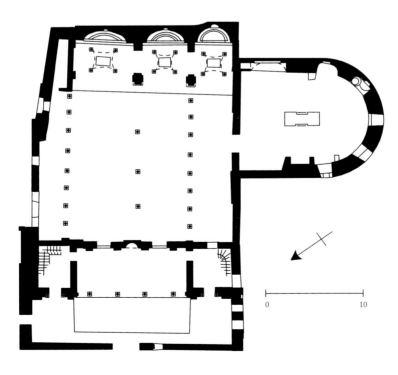

50. Old Cairo.
Fortress of Babylon.
Plan of the church of the Holy Virgin (al-Muallaqa).

109

Like the other churches of Old Cairo, the church of the Holy Virgin has a basilican plan but does not have cupolas; this particularity is due to the "hanging" position of the church, built over two ancient bastions, and to the consequent impossibility of building the foundations and supports necessary to withstand the weight and dynamic thrust of a cupola. In front of the church there is a courtyard; serving as a narthex, a portico decorated with ceramics representing geometrical designs opens onto the east side of the courtyard. The inside of the church comprises a vast nave separated from two side aisles by two ranks of eight columns; in addition, the nave is divided in two by three columns. The columns are made of white marble, except one which is made of black basalt, and have Corinthian capitals. In all likelihood they came from pagan buildings and very probably were formerly painted with the figures of apostles, saints, and martyrs; only one of them still has its decoration representing an archangel.

In the nave, against a column, there is a magnificent marble pulpit dating from the eleventh century but with older elements. It rests on fifteen small graceful columns arranged in pairs, except for one standing by itself; the columns of a pair are identical but each pair is different from the others. They probably represent Christ alone in front, the twelve apostles, and the two evangelists Luke and Mark. The marble panels of the pulpit are decorated with mosaic motifs and bas-reliefs representing crosses, shells, and wreaths of flowers.

At the east end of the nave and aisles, three iconostases made of cedar mark off the three sanctuaries; their small finely carved panels have inlays of ivory and ebony. The middle iconostasis, the most precious, dates from the thirteenth century. Its uppermost part bears icons: the enthroned Christ in the center; the Holy Virgin, the archangel Gabriel and St. Peter on the left; St. John the Baptist, the archangel Michael, and St. Paul on the right. Behind the iconostasis is the principal sanctuary (*haykal*), dedicated to the Holy Virgin; in the center is a marble altar surmounted by a wooden baldachin held on four columns. The side sanctuaries, to the left and right of the principal one, are respectively dedicated to St. George and St. John the Baptist. The uppermost part of the iconostasis of the sanctuary of St. George is adorned with a series of icons depicting the saint's martyrdom; the uppermost part of the iconostasis of the sanctuary of St. John the Baptist has seven icons showing the saint's imprisonment and beheading.

From the south aisle, one has access to the little church dedicated to the Ethiopian king and saint, Takla Haymanut. The door separating it from the principal church is one of the finest examples of medieval Coptic decorative art. Made of cedar, it has very precious ivory decorations. The church of Takla Haymanut is the oldest part of the complex and over the east bastion of the gate. In the sanctuary, one can see two particularly interesting though rather damaged wall paintings. They date from the twelfth or thirteenth century and represent respectively Christ with the twenty-four elders of Revelation and the nativity. Near the sanctuary, in a

51. Wooden lintel from the 5th–6th centuries originally in the church of the Holy Virgin (al-Muallaqa), now kept in the Coptic Museum of Cairo. Detail of the scene of Jesus' entry into Jerusalem.

niche carved out of the wall, there is a stone baptismal font decorated with undulating motifs, the hiero-glyphic symbol for water. A small staircase leads to the upper story where there is a square chapel whose ceiling rests on four wooden columns; it is dedicated to St. Mark.

The South District

About one kilometer south of the Babylon fortress, in one of the poorest neighborhoods of Cairo, there are several churches which were erected in a very early period and now are part of monastic complexes.

The Church of the Holy Virgin of Babylon al-Darag

Dedicated to the Holy Virgin, this church is inside the monastery called Babylon al-Darag, that is to say, Babylon of the Steps. This name might come from the fact that, from the beginning, the level of the church and monastery was lower than the surrounding area and that one had to go down a staircase to reach it. According to an ancient tradition, Babylon al-Darag is one of the places where the Holy Family sojourned during its flight to Egypt. Although it is without a doubt one of the oldest churches in Cairo, it has kept only a few parts of its original architecture. Its nearly square plan comprises a narthex, a nave with two side aisles, and triple sanctuary; four ancient marble columns with beautiful capitals separate the nave from the small side aisles. The narthex contains two baptismal fonts. The three sanctuaries are dedicated to St. George (north), the Holy Virgin (middle), and the archangel Michael (south).

The Monastery of St. Theodore

The monastery of St. Theodore (Deir Tadrus) is next to that of Babylon al-Darag. Its enclosure wall was probably built between the tenth and twelfth centuries; the present two churches within it, dating from the fourteenth century, are dedicated to St. Theodore and to Sts. Cyrus and John. The church of the holy martyr Theodore, roofed with cupolas, has a narthex, a middle nave with two side aisles, and three sanctuaries. The middle cupola is decorated with four stucco crosses in relief; the columns, with richly carved capitals, which divide it from the side aisles.

Little is left from the earliest structure of the church dedicated to the martyrs of Damanhur, Cyrus and John (Abu Qir and Yuhanna). Its present plan differs from the strict traditional plans since the south aisle is slightly shorter than the nave, but this particularity is perhaps due to the important renovations made in the course of the seventeenth and eighteenth centuries.

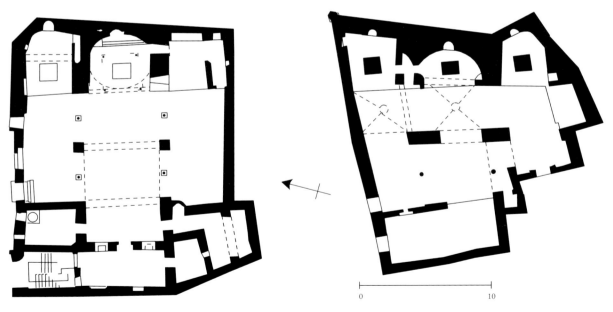

52. Old Cairo. South district.
Plan of the church of the Holy Virgin of Babylon al-Darag *(left)* and the church of Sts. Cyrus and John *(right)*.

The Church of Michael the Archangel

The church dedicated to the archangel Michael (al-Malak al-Qibli) stands about five hundred meters south of the monastery of St. Theodore. It was built at the time of the caliph al-Hakim bi-Amr Allah Abu Ali al-Mansur (996–1021), but almost nothing has survived from the original construction because the edifice underwent a great deal of rebuilding and remodeling in the course of centuries. The church has always been a very popular place of pilgrimage for the Copts, who have a particular devotion to the archangel Michael because he is credited with having the power to regulate the floods of the Nile.

The District of St. Mercurius

The monastery of St. Mercurius (Deir Abu al-Seifein) stands less than one kilometer north of the Babylon fortress near the Amr mosque. This Coptic neighborhood, surrounded by high walls, owes its name to the ancient women's monastery called Deir al-Banat, and to the largest of the three churches which are still in existence today. The other two churches are dedicated to St. Shenute (Anba Shenuda in Arabic) and the Holy Virgin (al-Adra al-Damshiriya). Formerly, the Nile flowed near the east wall of the neighborhood; today its bed lies some four hundred meters to the west.

The Church of St. Mercurius

The church was founded probably in the seventh century and dedicated to St. Mercurius, a Roman officer belonging to a noble family, who underwent martyrdom for having vigorously defended the Christian religion. According to an old tradition, an angel appeared to him and gave him a second sword (whence his name Abu al-Seifein, "the one with the two swords") as a symbol of his energy in the defense and diffusion of Christianity. Iconography represents St. Mercurius in his armor, on horseback, and with two swords drawn and crossed above his head as he tramples on the emperor Julian the Apostate. His body is said to have been brought from Palestine to Old Cairo in the fifteenth century.

The edifice suffered from fires and destruction in the course of the eighth century and what was left of it was used to store sugarcane. At the end of the tenth century, it was rebuilt by the patriarch Anba Abraham the Syrian with the authorization of the Fatimid caliph al-Muizz li-din Allah. Damaged again by fire in 1168 during a riot, it was restored in 1175; at that time the marble columns dividing the nave from the side aisles were replaced by massive pillars. The nave has a gable roof supported by wooden rafters; in contrast, the choir and sanctuary are roofed with a large cupola. In the east part of the nave, there is a precious marble ambo decorated with mosaics and mother-of-pearl and supported by graceful small columns.

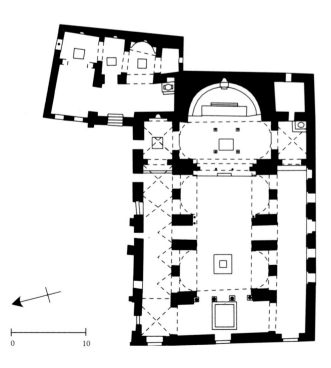

53. Old Cairo, district of St. Mercurius. Plan of the church of St. Mercurius (Abu Seifein).

0   10

32. Old Cairo. Walls of the fortress of
Babylon and the church of the Holy Virgin
(al-Muallaqa).

33. Old Cairo. Interior of the church of
St. Barbara in the fortress of Babylon.

34, 35. Old Cairo, district of St. Mercurius.
Church of St. Mercurius, apse and a detail
of the wall painting.

36, 37. Church of St. Mercurius. Details of
the paintings decorating the wooden
ciborium in the church of St. Mercurius.

Preceding pages:
38, 39. Church of St. Mercurius.
Representations of the Holy Virgin and
Child and of Christ painted on the columns
flanking the door of the iconostasis.

40. Saqqara. Monastery of St. Jeremiah.
Ruins of the main church (7th century).

41. Saqqara. Monastery of St. Jeremiah.
Ruins of the monastic complex (7th
century).

Following pages:
42. Coptic Museum of Cairo. Detail of a
painting from the monastery of St. Jeremiah
(7th century) in Saqqara representing
Sts. Apollo and Pamun.

43. Coptic Museum of Cairo. Sixth century
capital from the monastery of St. Jeremiah
in Saqqara.

44. Cairo, neighborhood of Fumm
al-Khalig. Church of St. Menas.

45. Region of Beni Suef, formerly called
Pispir. Deir al-Maimun, where St. Anthony
lived as an anchorite for several years.

Following pages:
46. Al-Fayyum. Monastery of St. Gabriel
(Deir al-Malak Ghubriyal), on the slopes of
Gebel al-Naqlun, founded in the 6th
century, a prestigious center where many
anchorites gathered in the early centuries of
Christianity.

47. Al-Fayyum. Monastery of the Holy
Virgin (Deir al-Hammam).

The iconostasis of the middle sanctuary is made of ebony with inlays of ivory in the shape of crosses and floral designs. Its door is flanked by two Corinthian columns on which the images of Christ and the Holy Virgin are painted (thirteenth–fourteenth centuries). At the center of the sanctuary, the altar is surmounted by a magnificently painted wooden ciborium resting on four marble columns. Behind the altar, a platform with steps (synthronon), decorated with white and blue ceramic, delineates the wall of the apse.

The church of St. Mercurius has the singular privilege of possessing very rare icons, dating from different periods between the fourteenth and eighteenth centuries. From the north aisle, a staircase leads to a small room, dark and dank, where Anba Barsum the Naked lived for more than twenty-five years between the end of the thirteenth century and beginning of the fourteenth. On September 10, the saint's feast day, the liturgy is celebrated there and many pilgrims coming from faraway attend it, trusting in the miraculous virtue of Anba Barsum's relics.

Also from the north aisle, a door opens onto a courtyard, adjacent to which is a chapel dedicated to the holy martyr Jacob (James). It contains especially precious iconostases and wooden decorations which are elegant and refined. On the right of the chapel there is a small baptistery with a stone font, called the caliph's baptistery. Indeed, according to legend, the caliph al-Muizz li-din Allah became a convert to Christianity and was baptized here in the strictest secrecy.

The Church of St. Shenute (Anba Shenuda)

This church is next to that of St. Mercurius—its entrance portal is on the same street, a mere twenty meters to the south. In the fifth century, Shenute was the renowned abbot of the White Monastery, established near Sohag in middle Egypt. Passionate and violent, he was the very model of the authoritarian and despotic archimandrite who led the monks with fanatic vigor.

The foundation of the church goes back probably to the eighth century. Having suffered many raids and many destructive attacks, it was repeatedly restored and its architecture was modified little by little. The present building dates from the first half of the fourteenth century, when Anba Benjamin renovated the interior of the church. Lying about two meters below today's street level, the edifice is thirty-five meters long and fifteen meters wide. It has a basilican plan with the north and south side aisles being separated from the nave by two series of five marble columns topped by Corinthian capitals. On the northeast side of the nave there is a magnificent wooden pulpit resting on eight small columns also made of wood and embellished by floral motifs with ivory inlays.

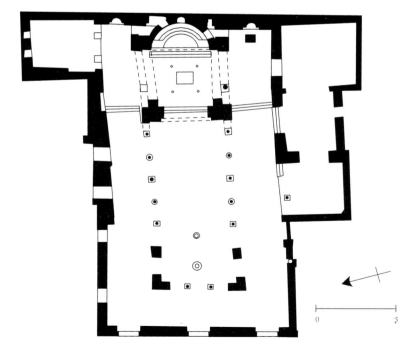
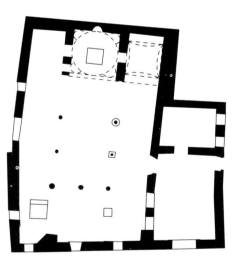

54. Old Cairo, district of St. Mercurius. Plan of the church of St. Shenute *(left)* and the church of the Holy Virgin (al-Damshiriya) *(right)*.

The middle sanctuary is dedicated to St. Shenute, the north one to the Holy Virgin, and the south one to the archangel Michael. The iconostasis of the main sanctuary is made of cedar adorned with ivory inlays in geometrical and cruciform shapes. Behind the iconostasis the altar is surmounted by a wooden ciborium supported on four marble columns. The iconostasis of the south sanctuary, which previously was that of the middle sanctuary, shows outstanding ivory inlays dating from the fifteenth century.

The church of St. Shenute has numerous icons, the majority of which date from the eighteenth century. In the north aisle, one sees those of the Holy Virgin and Sts. Anthony and Paul; in the south, those of the archangels Michael and Gabriel, St. Shenute, Anba Abraham, Sts. Dimiana, Constantine, and Helena, as well as Jesus' baptism, crucifixion, and resurrection.

The Church of the Holy Virgin (al-Damshiriya)
The church of the Holy Virgin is better known under the name of al-Damshiriya, after the name of the city of Damshir, the place of origin of the Coptic dignitary who restored the edifice during the eighteenth century. Built probably in the seventh century, the church was destroyed in 785 on the orders of the governor Ali ibn Sulaiman al-Abbas. During the caliphate of Harun al-Rashid (786–809), the following governor, Musa ibn Isa, promised the Copts to rebuild all that his predecessor had demolished. The renovations that were executed from the eighteenth century on did not fundamentally alter the original structure. The plan is basilican with a narthex, nave with two side aisles, and three sanctuaries; the nave is separated from the aisles by three columns and from the narthex by one column. The seven marble columns are different in their characteristics and dimensions; above the capitals, masonry pillars accent the verticality of the architecture and the harmony of the spaces.

The three sanctuaries *(haykal),* placed to the east as is customary, are divided from the nave and aisles by wooden iconostases. The middle one, decorated with cruciform ivory motifs and surmounted by icons, is the most precious. A high cupola dominates the main altar. The walls of the nave, aisles, and narthex are adorned with numerous icons dating from the eighteenth and nineteenth centuries.

OTHER CHURCHES OF CAIRO

The Church of St. Menas at Fumm al-Khalig
The church dedicated to St. Menas (Mari Mina) is located in the neighborhood of Fumm al-Khalig, about two and a half kilometers north of Old Cairo, inside the walls of the monastery of the same name. As we have seen, among the many traditions concerning this holy martyr, the most trustworthy reports that Menas was

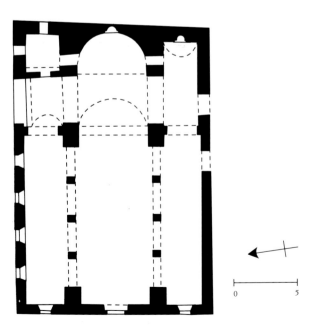

55. Cairo, Fumm al-Khalig. Plan of the church of St. Menas.

Egyptian, a native of Nicopolis in Mareotis (Maryut). An officer in the Roman army, he endured martyrdom in Egypt or Libya in 296 under the emperor Diocletian for having energetically and passionately defended the Christian faith. The name Menas is typically Egyptian since its origin goes back to the pharaoh Menes, who unified upper and lower Egypt around 2900 B.C.E. and founded the city of Memphis.

St. Menas is always represented clad in tunic and chlamys and at prayer between two kneeling camels in accordance with the legend telling of the tribune Athanasius, a pious man, who after Menas' dreadful martyrdom decided to take his remains to Egypt with himself and his retinue. After a long sea crossing, Athanasius and his men landed in Mareotis, loaded the relics on a camel and began to cross the desert. But suddenly the camel stopped and obstinately refused to walk on. They loaded the relics on several other camels who just as obstinately refused to move. Judging that this was a divine sign, Athanasius buried the relics on that spot which became a place of popular devotion. Some seventy kilometers southwest of Alexandria, in the locality of Abu Mina, one can still see the ruins of the complex built in the fifth century on the saint's place of burial and one of the most important centers of pilgrimage in Eastern Christianity down to the end of the ninth century.

The church of St. Menas at Fumm al-Khalig was founded in the eighth century and demolished, rebuilt, and restored several times in the course of its history. After its destruction a few years earlier under the caliph Hisham ibn Abd al-Malik ibn Marwan, it was rebuilt a few years later by the patriarch Theodore, then restored in 1180 under the patriarch John VI. During the eleventh century, the wing corresponding to the north aisle was ceded to the Armenian community which had grown considerably because of the immigration into Egypt of many Armenians oppressed in their own country by Turkish invaders. Separated from the nave by a masonry wall, this wing remained the Armenians' property until 1926, when it was returned to the Copts; thus, the church was restored to its original plan.

Twenty meters long and fifteen meters wide, the edifice has a narthex, a nave, two side aisles, and three sanctuaries. Each of the two side aisles is divided from the nave by three masonry pillars; the ceiling is a barrel vault. On the north side of the nave, there is a fine marble pulpit resting on twelve small pillars. The main sanctuary, dedicated to St. Menas, possesses a wooden iconostasis with ivory and ebony inlays in the shape of crosses. On the south side, to the right of the iconostasis of the south sanctuary, a door opens onto a vaulted corridor which ends at the east in a room used as a baptistery. Farther south is the small church dedicated to St. Behnam.

The Churches of Harat Zuwaila

In the neighborhood of al-Qurunfish in the Fatimid section of Cairo, there remain the ruins of an old monastery and some important churches. These ruins occupy the place where according to tradition the Holy Family sojourned and where a women's monastery is established today. One of the churches is dedicated to the Holy Virgin, another to St. Mercurius (Abu al-Seifein), and the third to St. George.

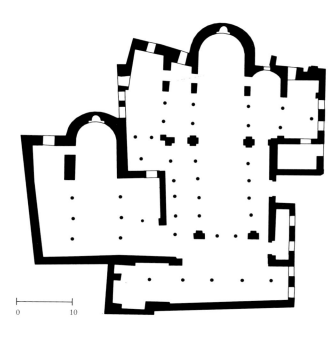

56. Cairo, Harat Zuwaila. Plan of the church of the Holy Virgin and the adjacent church of St. Mercurius.

The oldest and largest is that of the Holy Virgin. Although founded in the tenth century, it is mentioned for the first time only at the beginning of the twelfth, on the occasion of the consecration of the new bishop of Cairo under Macarius' patriarchate (1102–1128). It was destroyed a first time in 1321 and when rebuilt had the honor of being the see of the Coptic patriarchate until 1660. In the course of the centuries, it was often remodeled and restored, with the result that the fourteenth century structure has been notably altered. It comprises a narthex, a *naos* (a nave with two side aisles), a *khurus* (choir), and three sanctuaries *(haykal)*. The nave is separated from the aisles and narthex by reused columns with Corinthian capitals. Against the north columns stands a most beautiful marble ambo resting on four small graceful cabled columns; its wooden lectern suggests the shape of an eagle. The middle sanctuary is separated from the nave by a wooden iconostasis finely worked with ivory inlays and crowned by thirteen icons representing the Holy Virgin and the apostles. The door of the sanctuary dates from the Fatimid period and is made of ivory panels engraved with scenes of birds and other animals.

The church of St. Mercurius (Abu al-Seifein) dates from 1773. It flanks the south side of the church of the Holy Virgin and communicates with it, while the church dedicated to St. George, the smallest of the three, is on its upper story.

The Churches of Harat al-Rum

In the neighborhood of al-Ghuriya there is a women's monastery dedicated to St. Theodore, and within its perimeter stand a church dedicated to the Holy Virgin and another to St. George. The church of the Holy Virgin was probably built in the tenth century but was destroyed and rebuilt or restored several times, and it served as the see of the Coptic patriarchate from 1660 to 1799. The present building dates from the beginning of the nineteenth century and is composed of a narthex, a nave separated from the two side aisles by pillars, and a triple sanctuary; its roof has twelve cupolas. In the interior, one can see a precious wooden iconostasis decorated with refined ivory inlays. From the north aisle, one enters the chapel dedicated to St. Theodore, the warrior saint who became a martyr under Diocletian and to whom miraculous cures are attributed. The church of St. George, where relics of the martyr are venerated, has a structure similar to that of the church of the Holy Virgin.

The Cathedral of St. Mark

The cathedral of St. Mark is located in the quarter of Abbasiya in the modern north area of Cairo. It is a recent edifice of monumental dimensions and is at once the see of the Coptic patriarchate and the majestic reliquary containing St. Mark's remains. These were removed from the basilica in Venice and given to Patriarch Cyril VI by Pope Paul VI on the occasion of the nineteenth centennial of the saint's death.

PLACES OF PILGRIMAGE

In the vicinity of Cairo, a few traditional places of pilgrimage are associated with the itinerary which, according to tradition, the Holy Family followed when it had to flee to Egypt.

Musturud and Matariya

Musturud is located in the northeast suburbs of Cairo, on the site of ancient Heliopolis. The place where the Holy Family is thought to have taken refuge and a well whose water is regarded as miraculous are venerated in the crypt of an ancient church. Pilgrims from the Coptic world come here, particularly in August during the days preceding the feast of the assumption of the Holy Virgin.

The memory of the passage of the Holy Family is also recalled in the nearby locality of Matariya. Here, pilgrims venerate the twisted trunk of the tree whose dense branches miraculously bent in order to hide the child Jesus, thus protecting him from the soldiers dispatched by Herod. The Christian legend of the tree of Matariya probably derives from the worship of the sacred tree of Heliopolis, under which the child Horus was nursed. Today's sycamore, unfortunately withered, was planted in 1672 on the spot where the original tree had stood; when the tree died, its branches were collected and preserved by the Franciscans. The place had been recently relandscaped and is the goal of pilgrims from all over the world.

The Church of the Holy Virgin at Maadi
Some ten kilometers south of Cairo, on the banks of the Nile and in a particularly atmospheric landscape, stands a church dedicated to the Holy Virgin; its foundation goes back to a very ancient period although its present structure with three cupolas is as recent as the eighteenth century. According to tradition, the Holy Family sojourned in this place and took a boat from here to reach upper Egypt by going upstream on the Nile. The southwest corner of the church shelters a sacred well whose water quenched the Holy Family's thirst and is regarded as miraculous.

SAQQARA

Saqqara, about fifteen kilometers south of the Pyramids of Giza and about thirty kilometers from Cairo, is the largest necropolis in Egypt and the one that covers the greatest part of its history, from the first dynasty (3000 B.C.E.) to the Coptic period. Within its vast enclosure, the remains of the monastery of St. Jeremiah (Deir Apa Jeremiah) have been unearthed; it was built in the sixth century and abandoned probably around the middle of the ninth.

The Monastery of St. Jeremiah (Deir Apa Jeremiah)

The ruins of the monastery of St. Jeremiah are in the south part of the excavations of Saqqara, about five hundred meters from the Step Pyramid built by the pharaoh Djoser. Conducted between 1906 and 1910 by the English archaeologist James E. Quibell, a first campaign of excavations freed a surface of eighteen thousand square meters from the sand and brought to light a vast church, a funerary building, a refectory, monastic cells, and other buildings. A great quantity of decorative elements, architectural fragments (columns, capitals, friezes), and wall paintings were taken from the site and today are kept in the Coptic Museum in Cairo. Thereafter, the site was somewhat neglected by archaeologists until 1970 when new explorations were conducted by the German archaeologist Peter Grossmann. The sixty years of abeyance between 1910 and 1970, interrupted only by the limited diggings in the 1970s, have resulted in a return of the sand over the area of the monastery; in spite of this, it offers an especially evocative spectacle to the onlooker's eyes.

Historical Information
The history of the monastery is associated with Anastasius I, who was emperor from 491 to 518. The historian-monk John of Nikiou speaks indeed of a certain Jeremiah, a native of Alexandria and the abbot of a monastery close to Memphis, who was known to this emperor. In another source, his *De situ Terrae Sacrae (The Site of*

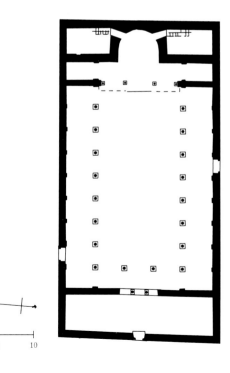

57. Saqqara, Monastery of St. Jeremiah.
Plan of the main church (7th century).

0   10

the Holy Land), written about 520–530, the monk Theodosius mentions the existence of two monasteries in the vicinity of Memphis, one dedicated to St. Apollo and the other to St. Jeremiah. The attribution of the monastery to St. Jeremiah is supported by many inscriptions naming and images representing this holy abbot and often associating him with another abbot named Enoch which were recovered during the excavations.

It is probable that the birth and development of the monastery followed the usual process: an anchorite must have settled alone in this desert spot on the margin of fertile lands and made his rudimentary dwelling out of one of the tombs from the pharaonic period in the necropolis of Saqqara. Some time later, the ascetic's reputation for holiness and his charisma probably attracted a few disciples, then more numerous ones, to such an extent that a stable community came into existence and it became necessary to provide adequate buildings for religious purposes and daily life.

The first phase of the construction goes back to the middle of the sixth century. Its aim was to establish the essential facilities a community needed to live. In the seventh century, a second phase of construction was intended to give dignity and prestige to the monastery. At that time, the main church was enlarged: fine free-stone was used and decorated with small friezes and painted decorations. In addition, a large refectory was built and a funerary building from the pharaonic period was transformed into one for the monks.

The monastery of St. Jeremiah is one of the rare examples of ancient Egyptian cenobitic complexes that have been recovered by archaeologists. Here, the monks did not live a completely anchoritic life—ascetical solitude or groups of anchorites settled in separate and independent lodgings as in Kellia (the Cells)—they led a common life in vast edifices designed for it. Each monk had his own cell to which he had access through a common antechamber. In view of the needs of a large community, the monastery possessed—besides the religious edifices—buildings necessary for daily life: refectories, warehouses, stables, cisterns, ovens to bake bread, oil presses, and artisans' shops. The whole complex was surrounded by high defensive walls, some vestiges of which survive in the south section. The archaeological discoveries (tombs, inscriptions, painted figures) attest that the monastic complex had an area intended for women religious.

It is very probable that the monastery was abandoned around the middle of the ninth century for reasons which remain unknown to us and about which neither historical sources nor archaeological discoveries tell us anything.

The Main Church

It is located in the central area of the monastery. Only the limestone floor and the bases of the columns and of the exterior walls remain. Spared in the raids that followed the abandonment of the monastery, a few columns lie on the ground. Archaeologists' research has shown that a first church was built about the middle of the sixth century; made of unbaked bricks, it was of very modest size (twenty-one meters by twelve) in

58. Saqqara, Monastery of St. Jeremiah. Capital with painted decorations (6th century).

Facing page:
59. Saqqara, Monastery of St. Jeremiah. Detail of the stone ambo (6th–8th centuries), kept in the Coptic Museum of Cairo. The Coptic inscription around the shell reads: Father, Son, and Holy Spirit, Amen.

comparison to the later building, dating from the seventh century, whose vestiges can still be seen today. This second edifice was an especially significant and prestigious achievement. It is made of limestone blocks certainly taken from the sumptuous constructions of late antiquity which stood right there; the monks demolished them in their search for precious building material. With these recycled resources, the monastery artisans especially skilled in stonecutting masterfully succeeded in adapting this recycled material for the realization of an edifice of unerring elegance and great decorative richness.

The church measures thirty-nine meters in length and twenty meters in width. The west side of the building had a rectangular narthex giving access through a wide portal to the *naos,* comprising a nave, two side aisles, and a western return aisle. Eighteen columns separated the nave from the aisles; their Corinthian capitals, richly adorned with floral motifs, are preserved in the Coptic Museum in Cairo. Some of the capitals are decorated with vine branches and clusters of grapes sinuously intertwined. Pilasters, corresponding to the interior columns, imparted the same rhythm to the exterior walls. Curiously, the columns corresponding to the entrance doors on the west and south are different from the others: those placed opposite the main entrance (on the west), and which are still lying on the ground, were made of pink granite whereas those of the south entrance were made of marble.

The sanctuary area of the church was made of one rectangular bay, probably preceded by four small slender columns; the apse on the east and two rooms on the north and south sides opened onto the sanctuary area. From the apse area, two staircases led to two other rooms larger than the preceding ones and situated at a lower level.

The interior of the church was richly decorated with paintings on the walls, the columns, and the semicircular apse. At the time of the excavations conducted by Quibell, the greatest part of the painted decorations had already disappeared; there remained only fragments representing saints on the columns, friezes with ducks, draperies, and geometrical designs.

The Funerary Chapel

A building whose vestiges are still visible and which was very probably the funerary chapel of St. Jeremiah, the monastery's founder, and of other illustrious monks stood in the west part of the monastery. The excavations conducted by Grossmann have shown that this building was not used for liturgical functions. Furthermore, the homogenous character of its construction suggests that, built before the foundation of the monastery at the end of antiquity, probably under the Roman Empire, it had already served funerary purposes. Therefore, it was probably reused by the monks with some minimal remodeling to serve a similar end. Its basilican plan has a nave, two side aisles, and a return aisle on its west side; on the east side, a triumphal arch gave access to the funerary chamber, whose walls were covered with precious marble plaques.

The Refectory and Adjacent Buildings

The great refectory of the monastery was located some thirty meters north of the main church. It was a rectangular room whose roof was supported by a twofold rank of columns arranged along the main north-south axis. On the south side one had access to a spacious room, probably serving for the monks' meetings, where the splendid limestone seat of the abbot was found and is now preserved in the Coptic Museum in Cairo. From the east side of the refectory one had access to a square chapel with an apse to the east. Four marble columns, whose bases are still visible, supported its roof.

North of the refectory was a courtyard, which the archaeologists called "courtyard of the octagons," and a rectangular room divided in two by a line of columns; this was probably the infirmary. All the rooms we have mentioned were embellished by paintings whose traces Quibell found during the excavations of 1906–1910. Those of the refectory must have been particularly rich in references to biblical episodes—among which was the sacrifice of Isaac, today in the Coptic Museum in Cairo.

The Monastic Cells

The monastic cells unearthed by excavations were distributed over the whole area of the monastery and were rectangular and made of unbaked bricks. There were windows high on the walls to admit both light and air. The east walls of the cells are especially interesting; in the Coptic Museum one can see small semi-circular apses with a vault in the shape of a quarter-sphere. Originally, these niches were decorated with paintings representing the enthroned Christ or the Holy Virgin with the Child on her knees and were framed with architectural motifs made of small columns or pilasters adorned with capitals. The niches had a sacred function and were used by the monks for their personal devotions. To the left and right of the principal niche, one sometimes finds smaller niches where containers and various objects for daily use could be kept and where the oil lamps could be placed.

Al-Fayyum and the Region of Beni Suef

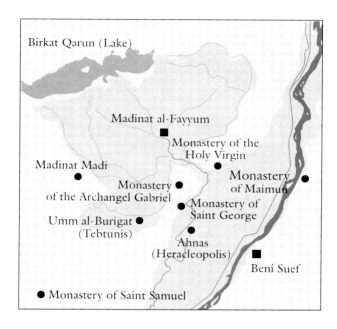

Al-Fayyum

Al-Fayyum is a large natural depression in the western Egyptian desert. Although similar to other depressions in the country, such as Qattara, al-Fayyum is different because of its exceptional fertility, due to the sediment brought by the waters of the Nile which reach it through Bahr Yusuf (Joseph's Canal) and to a soil particularly rich in alluvium. The fertile area covers an area of about four thousand square kilometers. Entirely below sea level, the northern part of the depression is partially occupied by Lake Birkat Qarun, called Moeris in antiquity. Its surface is two hundred and fourteen square kilometers; it is about fifty meters below sea level, and its maximum depth is eight meters.

The name al-Fayyum dates from the Coptic period and derives from the term *pa-yom*, which simply means "the sea." Formerly, the region had been called She-resi, which in ancient Egyptian means "south lake," then Arsinoe, the name of the sister and wife of Ptolemy II Philadelphus. No river flows into Birkat Qarun since the waters of the Bahr Yusuf diverge into several rivulets in the depression of al-Fayyum, and the lake does not give rise to any streams. It was much larger in antiquity; archaeological discoveries and hydrological analyses have enabled us to establish that at the time of the twelfth dynasty (2000–1785 B.C.E.), the lake covered an area eight times greater than it does now and was about twenty meters below sea level. Little by little, because of climatic variations and changes in the level of the Nile and its bed, the surface of the lake diminished and reached today's dimension which has been stable for several centuries. Populated in the past by many crocodiles, its waters are now brackish because of the strong seasonal evaporation which, however, is compensated by the constant seepage of subterranean waters.

The desert stretches surrounding the fertile depression were sought after by Christian ascetics as early as the end of the third century, during Diocletian's persecutions. By the beginning of the fifth century, these regions were already occupied by hundreds of hermitages and monastic centers where an anchoritic spirit, as fervent as it was rigorous, reigned. According to tradition, St. Anthony visited these places during the first half of the fourth century, gathering followers and inspiring them with the monastic ideal. The oldest monastery of the region is probably the one dedicated to the archangel Gabriel on the slopes of Gebel al-Naqlun. Tradition has it that it was founded in the fourth century, and its story has often been linked with that of the monastery of St. Samuel on Gebel al-Qalamun, which became the most prestigious monastery in the region from the seventh century on.

The Monastery of the Archangel Gabriel (Deir al-Malak Ghubriyal, Deir al-Naqlun)

The monastery of the archangel Gabriel (Deir al-Malak Ghubriyal) is located at the edge of the fertile plain on a limestone rock on the slope of Gebel al-Naqlun, which is a series of arid hills in which the first ascetics of al-Fayyum settled; this is the reason why the monastery was originally called Deir al-Naqlun. The monastery is about fifteen kilometers from Madinat al-Fayyum and about three kilometers from the village of Qalamshah.

Of modest dimensions, the monastic complex occupies only part of the original settlement. This latter comprised not only the large monastic center, the vestiges of which are right against the walls of the modern monastery, between it and the mountain, but also one hundred or so hermitages scattered on the heights of Gebel al-Naqlun. It is still possible today to find these hermitages in the hollows and caves the ascetics used for shelter: traces of walls in dry stone or unbaked brick as well as pottery fragments attest that these places were once occupied by venerable inhabitants.

Archaeological research conducted within the perimeter of the present monastery and the hermitages of the *gebel* have shown the close relation existing between the two. From its foundation, probably during the second half of the fifth century, the monastic complex included both a certain number of hermitages built among the rocks and a church and auxiliary buildings built on the rocky terrace below the upper reaches of the *gebel*. A legend, devoid of any archaeological and historical confirmation, places the foundation of the monastery in the fourth century. There are numerous texts written on papyrus recovered on the site; written in Greek, Coptic, and Arabic, they attest to the great vitality of the monastery until the thirteenth century. The reasons for its decline from that time on are not known with any certainty, although the excavations have been able to show that at the end of the thirteenth century, a violent fire devastated the monastery, perhaps beyond any hope of repair.

All that remains of the ancient center today are a part of the walls, the church dedicated to the archangel Gabriel, and a few additional buildings. One can date the foundation of the church from the tenth–eleventh centuries; it comprises a narthex on the west, a *naos* (a nave and two side aisles), a *khurus* (choir), and a triple sanctuary. The nave is separated from the side aisles by two ranks of three columns with precious Corinthian capitals; these columns certainly belonged to an older church. On the south side of the nave is the *laqqan*. The central part of the *khurus* is roofed with a cupola; the side sanctuaries, to the north and south, are rectangular while the middle one is semi-circular and adorned with small decorative columns. The narthex and *khurus* are certainly from a later date and occupy spaces which were formerly part of the nave. In the 1990s, beautiful wall paintings from the eleventh century, representing the Holy Virgin and Child, apostles, and saints, were found in the church. In the monastery area, archaeologists have identified the vestiges of a massive tower and of a church constructed on its ruins in the tenth–eleventh centuries.

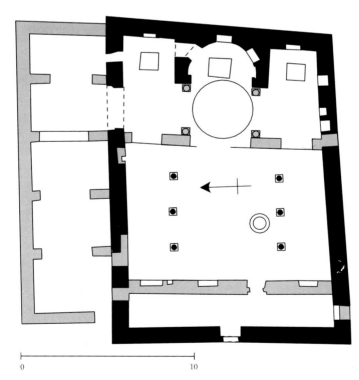

60. Al-Fayyum. Monastery of the archangel Gabriel (Deir al-Naqlun). Plan of the church. *In black:* original building (10th–11th centuries). *In grey:* later building.

0   10

On feast days, and especially on the feast of the archangel Gabriel, the Christians of the vicinity come in pilgrimage to the monastery and sometimes stay there for a few days, lodging in the older monastic buildings which have been turned into a guest house.

The Monastery of the Holy Virgin (Deir al-Hammam)
Also called Deir al-Hammam because of its proximity to the village of the same name, or monastery of the martyr Isaac (Deir Abu Ishaq), the monastery of the Holy Virgin is located about three kilometers from the pyramid of al-Lahun. It was partially rebuilt during the nineteenth century and extensively renovated in the recent past. The only original constructions that have survived to our day are the walls of the church, the floor of which is a few meters below the present courtyard. This edifice has been the object of important restoration and remodeling in the course of its history; however, it is of ancient construction since documents discovered there date from the eighth century. Today, the building possesses a *naos* (a nave and two side aisles), separated from the three sanctuaries by a *khurus* (choir); two cupolas cover the nave.

The Monastery of St. George (Deir Mari Girgis)
The monastery dedicated to St. George is situated in the village of Sidmant al-Gebel, seven kilometers north of Ihnasia al-Medina. The only ancient building still standing is the church, whose original plan with a nave and two side aisles has been submitted to extensive modifications and repairs in the course of time. Three cupolas supported by pillars and columns cover the nave. Here and there one can still see architectural elements dating from the seventh–eighth centuries.

Ahnas-Heracleopolis (Ihnasia al-Medina)
The village of Ihnasia al-Medina is about fifteen kilometers west of Beni Suef. Its name comes from the ancient *Henen-nesut*—the principal town of the twentieth nome of Egypt—transformed into the Coptic Ahnas. The most venerated deity in the town was Harsaphes, who had a ram's head and was identified with the Greek god Heracles, to whom the town owed its name, Heracleopolis (Heracleopolis Magna).

Among the ruins of the ancient town, one can discern the vestiges of a road flanked by colonnades, of shafts of columns, and of friezes going back to the fifth and sixth centuries. The presence of a sizeable Christian community and of numerous churches is confirmed by literary sources from the fourth to seventh centuries. Particularly precious architectural fragments are kept in the Coptic Museum in Cairo.

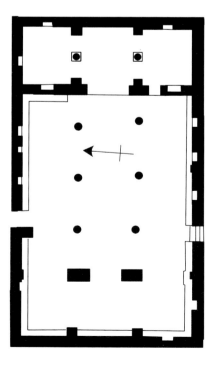

61. Al-Fayyum, Umm al-Burigat
(Tebtunis).
Plan of a church (7th century).

The Churches of Umm al-Burigat (Tebtunis)

Umm al-Burigat stands on the site of ancient Tebtunis, southwest of al-Fayyum. Established under the twentieth dynasty (twelfth–eleventh centuries B.C.E.), the city enjoyed a great prosperity during the Ptolemaic and Roman periods because of a temple dedicated to the crocodile-god Sebek. Among the ruins of the city, the vestiges of three churches have been unearthed; they have a basilican plan and are built in a somewhat rudimentary fashion with recycled materials. They have no apses; their sanctuaries are rectangular and in all likelihood date from the seventh century. One of these churches presents two unusual features: the first, on the west side of the nave, consists in two transverse brick pillars behind which there is a return aisle linking the south and north aisles. The second, unique in Egypt, is a passage with a double arch formed by means of the central column separating the middle sanctuary from each of the side sanctuaries. The feature—windows with arcatures—serving as a link between the two side sanctuaries and their respective aisles is also unusual.

The Churches of Madinat Madi (Narmuthis)

The ruins of the ancient city of Madinat Madi, the Greek Narmuthis, are found some ten kilometers west of the town of Itsa, near the village of Abu Gandir. The city was founded during the Middle Kingdom and endowed with sacred edifices about 1800 B.C.E. by the pharaohs of the twelfth dynasty, Amenemhet III and his son Amenemhet IV.

In the southeast section of the city, an Italian archaeological expedition has discovered the vestiges of many churches going back to the fifth and sixth centuries. Only the traces of the exterior walls and some fragments of columns remain. The diversity of architectural elements leads the experts to think that materials and parts from previous buildings were reused. These churches have now three, now five, and even, for one church, seven aisles. This, however, does not mean that they were important; their provincial architecture, characterized by aisles of equal and moderate dimensions, had not yet assimilated the traditional model of a nave and two side aisles, with the nave being larger and more prestigious.

The Monastery of Maimun (Deir al-Maimun)

This monastery is not located in the region of al-Fayyum but is very near it, on the right bank of the Nile, some thirty kilometers north of Beni Suef. It stands on the place where, according to tradition, St. Anthony came in about 285, at the age of thirty-five. He lived there a few years before definitively settling in the Eastern Desert, where the great monastery which bears his name stands today.

In his *Life of St. Anthony* (12.3), St. Athanasius describes Anthony's arrival in this region as follows: "Strengthened in his purpose more and more, he went steadily on to the mountain. On the other side of the

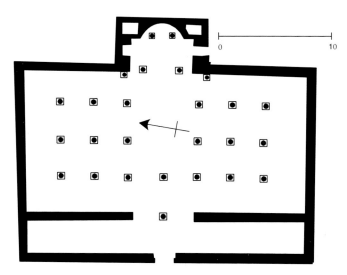

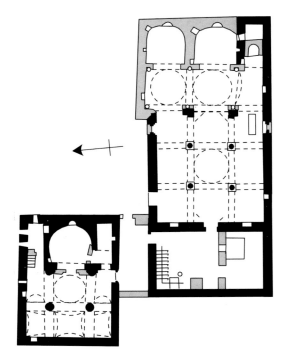

Above: 62. Al-Fayyum, Madinat Madi (Narmuthis).
Plan of the church with seven aisles
(5th–6th centuries).

Right: 63. Region of Beni Suef, Deir al-Maimun.
Plan of the churches of St. Anthony and St. Mercurius.

140

river he discovered a fort which had been deserted for so long that it was full of reptiles; he crossed over and settled there" (Athanasius, 116). In his *Lausiac History* (21.1), Palladius calls the place Pispir, and situates it between the city of Babylon (today's Cairo) and that of Heracleopolis (today's Ihnasia al-Medina). From antiquity to modern times, this place has been the point of departure for camel caravans headed into the desert and carrying merchandise and pilgrims toward the Red Sea to the monastery of St. Anthony.

Today, the former monastic complex is occupied by a village. However, two churches still exist, the larger one dedicated to St. Anthony, the smaller and older, to St. Mercurius (Abu al-Seifein). In the south aisle of the church of St. Anthony, one can see an open tomb hollowed out of the rock, which according to tradition the saint used as a bed. The present structure is the result of modifications to the original basilican plan. In contrast, the church of St. Mercurius has kept its original structure with a central cupola resting on four columns.

The Monastery of St. Samuel (Deir Anba Samwil)

The monastery of St. Samuel is located about fifty-five kilometers from the small town of Maghagha in the Western Desert, in a region called al-Qalamun. Although outside the depression of al-Fayyum, this monastery historically belongs to the monastic complexes of this region.

Samuel did not found the monastery but reorganized it in the middle of the seventh century by adding all the buildings necessary for monastic life, establishing a model of organization and life for the monks of the community. The origin of the monastery is to be assigned probably to the fifth century, when anchorites began to gather in one place in order to help one another materially and spiritually and to have a church in which they could participate together in liturgical celebrations.

In the course of the first half of the seventh century, the monastery was abandoned because of the severe harassment inflicted by the Melchite patriarch Cyrus. When Heraclius, the emperor of Byzantium, defeated the Persians and reconquered Egypt in 629, he appointed the Georgian Cyrus—who had been a bishop in Colchis—Melchite patriarch of Alexandria and *dux augustalis* (august leader) of Egypt. During the years when Cyrus exercised the twofold power of religious and secular leader (631–641), he tried by all possible means, including violence, to convert the Monophysites to the orthodoxy defined at the Council of Chalcedon. The bishops were expelled from their sees and the monks from their monasteries.

Samuel was born in the delta region, near Pelhip, a village close to Fuwa. Early on he left his village in order to withdraw into solitude, first in the desertic mountains of al-Qalamun, then, at the age of eighteen, in the desert of Scetis (Wadi al-Natrun) where he became a disciple of Agatho. In 631, when the patriarch Cyrus began to harshly repress Monophysitism, the monasteries of Scetis were the first to suffer his violent attacks. Samuel had to flee this place and with a few confreres took refuge in al-Fayyum, in the monastery of

64. Al-Fayyum, Umm al-Burigat (Tebtunis). Detail of a wall painting from the 11th century representing Adam and Eve in the Garden of Eden, before *(right)* and after *(left)* their sin.

al-Naqlun. But even there he knew only a brief respite because Cyrus' persecutions reached also into al-Fayyum. A resolute defender of Monophysitism, Samuel was arrested, tortured, then freed under condition that he leave the place. He then withdrew to an abandoned chapel in Wadi al-Muwaylih, south of al-Fayyum. Even so, his misfortunes were not at an end, for he was captured by Berber pillagers who made him a slave. After three years in bondage, Samuel was released by his guards, who had attempted by all possible means to convert him to sun worship. He earned his freedom as a reward for having miraculously cured the wife of one of his jailers. He returned to the desert of al-Qalamun where, with the help of his many disciples, he undertook to rebuild the ancient monastery where he lived another fifty-seven years to the age of ninety-six; it was then named after him.

At Samuel's death, the monastery had 120 monks. But it had to be abandoned during the ninth century because of the Bedouins' violent attacks, destructive raids, and ravages. Rapidly reoccupied by the monks, the monastery was provided with powerful fortifications described by the historian Abu Salih, who visited it in the beginning of the thirteenth century. There were strong walls, four towers, a large church dedicated to the Holy Virgin, twelve chapels, an abundant spring, extensive vegetable gardens, and vast orchards.

With its three hundred monks, the monastery of St. Samuel was regarded at the time of Abu Salih as one of the most important in Egypt. In the following centuries, it underwent a slow and sad decline and finally was completely forsaken at the end of the sixteenth or beginning of the seventeenth century. This decline is also attested by the historian Maqrizi, who, upon visiting the monastery in the beginning of the fifteenth century, found only two of the four towers described by Abu Salih and noticed that the produce of the gardens and palm trees were now harvested by the Bedouins because the number of monks had so seriously dwindled.

Among the travelers who found the monastery deserted, we must mention the learned Belzoni from Italy, Wilkinson from England, and Schweinfurth from Germany, who came to the site in 1819, 1832, and 1886 respectively. Having been abandoned close to three hundred years, the monastery was occupied anew in 1897 and completely restored by ten monks from the monastery of al-Baramus in Wadi al-Natrun under the direction of the abuna Ishaq. These eleven monks had left the Wadi al-Natrun because of clashes over disciplinary matters and had been excommunicated by the patriarch; however, this penalty was lifted five years later. Abuna Ishaq lived there for almost forty years devoting himself with the utmost fervor to the spiritual and material renewal of the monastery.

The monastery of St. Samuel has three churches. The church of the Holy Virgin was built in 1958 on the ruins of the medieval church mentioned by Abu Salih and preserves St. Samuel's relics. The church called the catacomb-church is on the ground floor of the only extant ancient tower and probably goes back to the seventh century. It comprises a narthex, a small nave, and a rectangular sanctuary. On the upper story of the tower is the church dedicated to St. Samuel, built about 1940 by the abuna Ibrahim, the successor of Abuna Ishaq.

Around the monastery, the vestiges of ancient buildings attest to the presence of religious communities from the early centuries of Christianity. The cave in which St. Samuel lived is about five kilometers east of the monastery, near the summit of Gebel al-Qalamun.

The Eastern Desert

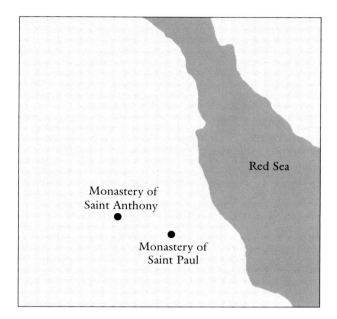

The monasteries of St. Anthony and St. Paul, dedicated respectively to the founder and the originator of Christian anchoritism in Egypt, stand in the Eastern Desert, the vast desertic band separating the Nile from the Red Sea, near the southern Gebel al-Galala (Gebel al-Galala al-Qibliya) close to the Gulf of Suez. One can reach the monastery of St. Anthony by taking a detour from the road connecting the Nile valley, near Beni Suef, and the Gulf of Suez at Ras Zafarana. Beginning thirty-three kilometers from Ras Zafarana, this detour of fifteen kilometers leads to the monastery. As the crow flies, the monastery of St. Paul is close to the monastery of St. Anthony, but being on the other slope of the desert massif of Gebel al-Galala, it can be reached only by the road running along the coast of the Red Sea; at an intersection twenty-five kilometers south of Ras Zafarana, a detour of thirteen kilometers leads to the monastery.

THE MONASTERY OF ST. ANTHONY
(DEIR ANBA ANTUNIUS)

Historical Information

Saint Anthony
The renown of St. Anthony, a holy monk, a worker of miracles and wonders, is due to his contemporary and biographer Athanasius, patriarch of Alexandria, a pillar of Christian history. In his *Vita Antonii (Life of Anthony)*, Athanasius intends to give the Christian world a perfect example of monastic life, which is simultaneously proposed as a model to imitate and interpreted within a vaster project of Christian society in which all forms of ecclesial life find place.

Anthony was born about 250 in middle Egypt to a rural family of some means. When hardly twenty years old, he decided to leave behind the comfortable life to which he seemed destined and disposed of his own possessions. He first retired to the edge of his town, then into a forsaken necropolis, there devoting his life to asceticism and subjecting himself to an iron discipline and the harshest deprivations. At thirty-five, desiring to withdraw to a more isolated place, he settled in an abandoned fortress in a desert location called Pispir (today, Deir al-Maimun) not far from the east bank of the Nile and there spent twenty years of anchoritic life together with some disciples. But since his reputation as a holy monk was attracting a multitude of visitors who disturbed his solitude, he resolved to take refuge in a more inaccessible place and, joining a Bedouin caravan, he went deep into the Eastern Desert. As Athanasius narrates (*Life of Anthony* 49.7–50.1): "He traveled with them three days and three nights, until he came to a very high hill, at the foot of which was water, very clear, and sweet, and very cold. Beyond, there was level ground and a few wild date palms. Anthony, moved by God, as it were, was delighted with the place" (Athanasius, 180). He loved the place so much that he dwelled there, in a rigorous ascetical solitude, for fifty years until his death in 356 at the age of 105. During this period, he remained in contact with the disciples he had left in Pispir—either they came to see him or he went to see them—as well as with the highest authorities of the church of Alexandria, which he helped very efficaciously in its controversy with the Arians, a fact that increased his reputation of holiness even more.

Although Anthony was not the originator of Christian monasticism, he rightly gained the title of founding father. The extraordinary influence and undeniable fascination his person exerted, further enhanced by the work of his biographer Athanasius, marked the beginning of a movement which spread throughout the whole Christian world.

The Foundation of the Monastery

The foundation of the monastery of St. Anthony goes back to the years that followed the saint's death. The sources agree that the first constructions of the monastic nucleus date from the time of the emperor Julian the Apostate (361–363). St. Anthony's disciples built the communal center at the foot of the mountain where he spent the last part of his ascetical life.

In all probability, the original buildings were extremely poor and pared down to the essentials: a church, a refectory, a few additional spaces such as a kitchen and a storeroom for food supplies. The early monks lived separately in the caves of the surrounding mountains and gathered in the church area only to celebrate the Eucharist and the common meal (the agape) on Sundays and other feasts of the liturgical year. It was not until later—probably in the second half of the fifth century—that the anchorites began to form closer bonds among themselves by building their cells within the communal center. This evolution had several interrelated causes: the need to defend themselves against the incursions of the Bedouins, the possibility for the younger monks to have spiritual guides and for the older monks and the sick to receive proper care. However, the rule of the Antonians remained rigorously semi-anchoritic, the communal activities limited to liturgical celebrations, the agape, and mutual help in providing for material and spiritual needs.

In the course of the fifth century, the monastery of St. Anthony became a refuge for the ascetics of the desert of Scetis in lower Egypt forced to abandon their hermitages because of the violent and destructive raids which the Berber pillagers of that region conducted with particular frequency and ferocity. Many illustrious monks thus found asylum in the monastery of St. Anthony, among them St. John the Little, who remained there until his death.

65. Monastery of St. Anthony. Overall view from Michel Jullien,
Voyage dans le Désert de la Basse Thébaïde (1884).

144

Preceding pages:
48. Monastery of St. Anthony. The
defensive tower and the church dedicated
to the saint.

49. View of the monastery of St. Anthony
on the slopes of the mountain where the
saint lived in ascetic solitude for almost fifty
years until his death in 356.

50, 51. Monastery of St. Anthony. Church
of St. Anthony (interior and
exterior).

52, 53. Church of St. Anthony. Details of the
cycle of wall paintings from 1232–1233
representing warrior saints on horseback and
their martyries.

54, 55. Monastery of St. Anthony. Wall paintings in the chapel of the Apocalypse (1232–1233): enthroned Christ blessing (left) and St. John the Baptist (right).

Preceding pages:
56, 57. Monastery of St. Anthony. Details
of wall paintings in the chapel of the
Apocalypse with the symbols of the
evangelists.

58. Church of St. Anthony. Cupola over
the main sanctuary.

59. View of the monastery of St. Paul,
founded in the 5th century in the place
where the holy anchorite had retired.

60. Monastery of St. Paul. The defensive
tower and the church erected over the cave
where the saint lived in solitude until his
death in about 340.

Following pages:
61. Monastery of St. Paul. View of the
interior of the monastery of St. Paul.

62. Monastery of St. Paul. Ancient
refectory.

Monophysites and Melchites

After the Council of Chalcedon, held in 451, the patriarchate of Alexandria did not accept its dogmatic definitions and opposed the orthodox doctrine, adopted at the imperial court of Byzantium and thus called Melchite (from *melik,* "king," hence *melkita,* "of the king"). Indeed, the Coptic world remained faithful to the Monophysite doctrine of Abbot Eutyches. He upheld the thesis according to which the two natures of Christ, the human and the divine, became at the incarnation one nature, the divine nature. The Dyophysite doctrine (from *dyos,* "two") was opposed to the Monophysite (from *monos,* "one," and *physis,* "nature"); supported by the patriarch of Constantinople and promulgated at Chalcedon, it holds that the natures of Christ are two, the human and the divine, both perfect and indivisible but distinct. During the seventh and eighth centuries, the monastery of St. Anthony was occupied by Melchite monks as ancient manuscripts indicate by mentioning their close bonds with the Melchite patriarchate of Alexandria. The Ethiopian Synaxarion narrates that in 790 a few Monophysite monks from the monastery of St. Macarius in Scetis succeeded in secretly entering the monastery of St. Anthony by being disguised as Bedouins and in taking the body of St. John the Little to bring it back to Scetis even though it was carefully guarded by the Melchite monks of the monastery.

In the course of the eleventh century, the monastery suffered the painful effects of a serious epidemic of plague, which had spread throughout the whole of Egypt, and also destructive raids by the Mamluk Turks under the command of Nasr al-Dawla. Extensive restorations were made a century or so later by the Coptic monks who, after several changes of fortune, had come back to occupy their monastery.

Center of Coptic Worship

The thirteenth and fourteenth centuries were the most brilliant period of the monastery of St. Anthony, and the arts and literature then knew an extraordinary efflorescence. It is to this period that one can ascribe the paintings of the church of St. Anthony (1232–1233) and the enlargement of the library, and its enrichment with numerous texts, religious, scientific, and literary in character. At the same time, many copies and translations were also made and many searches for ancient manuscripts conducted. Among the most important works achieved, one must mention the monk Simeon's translation into Ethiopian of the Ethiopian Synaxarion, the book of saints of the Ethiopian Church, whose original accounts were written in Arabic. In the fifteenth century, the monastery of St. Anthony had the honor of seeing its abbot, John, chosen to represent the Coptic Church at the Council of Florence (1438–1445), an event of enormous theological importance since it was an attempt to effect the union of the Latin Church of Rome with the Eastern Churches—the Byzantine Church of Constantinople and the Monophysite churches of Egypt, Ethiopia, Syria, and Armenia.

The golden age of the monastery of St. Anthony was interrupted at the end of the fifteenth century when the Bedouins of the surrounding desert—many of whom were working at the monastery—attacked it, killed all the monks, and wreaked havoc in the buildings. The church of St. Anthony was turned into a kitchen and the manuscripts served to feed the fire used for cooking. Some years later, the monastery was restored under the patriarchate of Gabriel VII (1525–1568), who sent twenty monks from the monastery of the Syrians in Wadi al-Natrun to revive monastic life and tradition. In the course of the seventeenth century, the Franciscans concluded an agreement with the monastery of St. Anthony: in exchange for the yearly payment of about forty scudi (about forty dollars), two or three Franciscans could reside in the monastery in order to learn Arabic and so prepare themselves for their missionary ministry in the East.

Throughout the centuries, the monastery of St. Anthony has always played a very important role in the history of the Coptic Church. Among other proofs, this is confirmed by the large number of patriarchs who received their religious formation there. In three hundred years, from the seventeenth to the nineteenth century, twelve Antonian monks were elected patriarch, thus determining the destiny of the Coptic Church. Today, the monastery is home to a few dozen monks. However, some of them do not reside there permanently; they exercise their ministry in the churches of the region of Beni Suef.

The Monastic Buildings

The Walls

Today, the monastery of St. Anthony is surrounded by an enclosure of about one kilometer, which contains around sixty thousand square meters for the buildings and cultivated areas. The present enclosure is but the latest enlargement of the monastery, effected in 1854 on the initiative of the patriarch Cyril IV. The story of the building of the walls is indeed quite complex and reflects the major events of the monastery's history.

The oldest walls probably correspond to the limit of the most important monastic buildings, that is, the church dedicated to St. Anthony, the refectory, and the tower; this first enclosure goes back to medieval times. Another major enlargement of the enclosure was certainly done before the time of the Armenian church historian Abu Salih, who described around 1200 the monastery as "surrounded by fortified walls within which there is a large garden with palm trees, apple trees, pear trees, pomegranates, as well as other plants and various vegetables, and three springs of water which, flowing in all seasons, irrigate the garden and satisfy the monks' needs." The last phase of construction dates from 1854 and has given the enclosure its present configuration. The walls are between ten and twelve meters high and are surmounted by a covered way along their full length.

The Tower

The tower is without doubt one of the oldest edifices in the monastery and has kept its original structure despite several restorations and remodelings. As is usual in Coptic monasteries, one enters the tower on the second floor by a drawbridge which once lifted completely isolated the building from the exterior world and enabled the monks to defend themselves against the incursions and destructive plunder of the Bedouins. The ground floor is reserved for the storage of foodstuff and has a well. The second floor comprises several rooms used by the monks as cells during sieges and other dangerous periods. The third and last floor is occupied by a chapel dedicated to the archangel Michael, the traditional defender of Coptic monasteries.

The Church of St. Anthony

The church of St. Anthony is the oldest in the monastery. Its foundation surely goes back to the original settlement of the saint's disciples. The present structure is much more recent and in all likelihood dates from the twelfth or beginning of the thirteenth century. It has a *naos* comprising a single nave, a *khurus* (choir), and a triple sanctuary. The nave is divided into two bays roofed with cupolas and separated by a large arch. The church is entirely decorated with wall paintings and, in spite of partial losses, this cycle of paintings is the most complete which has come down to us from the Coptic pictorial universe. In these paintings one can detect the hand of two different artists: the greater part is the work of Master Theodore, who, as an inscription indicates, decorated the whole interior in the years 1232–1233; only certain parts are the work of another painter active during the first half of the fourteenth century.

In the western bay, reserved for the laity, Theodore has represented the warrior saints, among them Claudius, Menas, Theodore, George, and Victor. Some are painted on horseback, in military garb, their respective

66. Monastery of St. Anthony. Entrance of the monastery with the ancient pulley system, from Michel Jullien, *Voyage dans le Désert de la Basse-Thébaïde* (1884).

162

martyrdoms shown in the background. On the south side, one has access to the chapel dedicated to the four living creatures of the book of Revelation (the lion, ox, eagle, and human being), appearing in a program dominated by the figure of Christ between the Holy Virgin and St. John the Baptist. In contrast, Theodore has represented in the eastern bay of the nave the enthroned Holy Virgin and Child and the most renowned ascetics in Egypt: Pachomius, Arsenius, Pshoi (Bishoi in Arabic), Samuel, Isaac, Anthony, Paul, the three Macarii, Maximus and Domitian, Moses the Black, Pisentius, and Shenute (Shenuda in Arabic). Three steps lead to the *khurus,* south of which is the tomb of St. Anthony. The *khurus* is a very small room with a barrel vault whose lower part Theodore decorated with paintings of prophets and saints (among whom are Sts. Mercurius and George in armor and on horseback); the upper part, with two themes related to the resurrection of Christ (the holy women at the sepulchre and Christ's encounter with the two Marys) is the work of the fourteenth century master whose style is inspired by traditional Byzantine art, whereas Theodore's manner is a perfect example of medieval Coptic iconography.

The three sanctuaries facing the *khurus* are dedicated to St. Anthony (center), St. Athanasius (south), and the evangelist Mark (north). In the cupola of the central sanctuary, Christ Pantocrator (Lord of the Universe) appears surrounded by angels. Four scenes from the Old Testament are painted above the altar: the purification of Isaiah's lips by the seraph, the meeting of Melchizedek and Abraham, the sacrifice of Isaac by Abraham, and the sacrifice of Jephthah's daughter. These four scenes symbolize the function of the sanctuary: the celebration of the Eucharist, which recalls and makes present the sacrifice of Christ. By joining the Old Testament prophecies with their realization by Christ, Theodore places the emphasis on the continuity of the divine plan through the connection between the Old and New Testaments. The apse is decorated as usual with a painting of Christ enthroned in the concha and the Holy Virgin and Child enthroned below, while the other walls represent patriarchs, prophets, and saints.

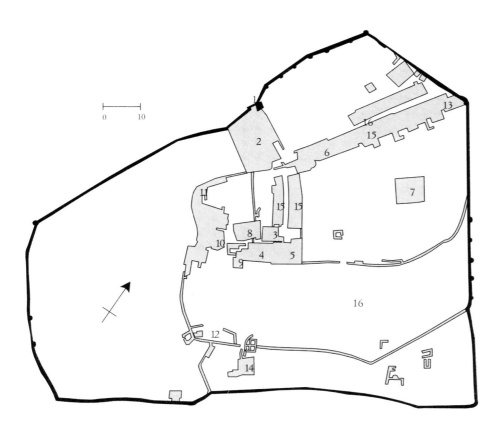

67. Monastery of St. Anthony.
Plan. 1. Entrance, 2. Guesthouse, 3. Tower, 4. Church of St. Anthony,
5. Church of the Holy Apostles, 6. Church of St. Anthony and
St. Paul, 7. Church of St. Mark, 8. Ancient refectory, 9. Kitchen,
10. Mill, 11. Oven, 12. Oil press, 13. Library, 14. Spring of
St. Anthony, 15. Cells, 16. Gardens.

The Church of the Holy Apostles

The church of the Holy Apostles, also called the church of Sts. Peter and Paul, is the "summer" church where the liturgy is celebrated from April to October. Its foundation is ancient but its present architecture dates from the reconstruction of 1772. As is customary, it has three sanctuaries; these are dedicated to the Holy Virgin (north), the apostles (middle), and St. Anthony (south). Twelve cupolas cover the church, three over the sanctuaries and nine over the nave.

The Refectory and the Church of the Holy Virgin

The refectory and the church of the Holy Virgin are within a massive edifice, used also as a warehouse for food supplies, connected to the tower by a drawbridge. On the ground floor is the old refectory, which underwent substantial restorations in 1560–1570 but is no longer in use. It is rectangular and roofed with a barrel vault, and a large stone table occupies the principal axis of the room.

The church dedicated to the Holy Virgin is on the second floor of the building; it has one nave and one sanctuary roofed with four cupolas. The wooden iconostasis, decorated with ivory inlays and cruciform figures, is especially precious. This church takes on a particular significance in the month of August, for the offices are celebrated there during the fifteen days of fast preceding the feast of the Assumption.

The Church of St. Mark

The church of St. Mark is located in the large palm grove of the monastery. It is dedicated to the ascetic Mark, who lived in the fourth century and was a disciple of Anthony. This church was probably built in the fifteenth century on the spot where Mark's cell had stood, but its present structure is the result of a radical remodeling in 1766. Twelve cupolas cover the church, which has a nave, two side aisles, and three sanctuaries. The middle sanctuary is dedicated to the ascetic Mark, the north to St. Theodore (Tadrus), and the south to

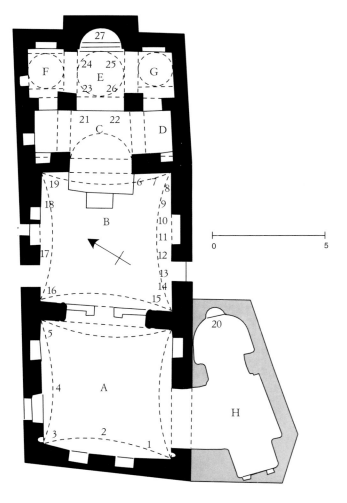

68. Monastery of St. Anthony. Church of St. Anthony. A. Nave, west bay, B. Nave, east bay, C. Choir, D. Tomb of St. Anthony, E. Sanctuary of St. Anthony, F. Sanctuary of St. Mark, G. Sanctuary of St. Athanasius, H. Chapel of the Four Living Creatures of Revelation. Wall paintings:
1. Sts. Claudius and Victor
2. St. Menas
3. St. Theodore
4. St. George
5. St. Phoibammon
6. St. Anthony
7. St. Paul the Anchorite
8. St. Isaac
9. St. Paul
10. St. Samuel
11. St. Pshoi
12. St. John the Little
13. St. Sisoes
14. St. Arsenius
15. St. Barsum the Syrian
16. St. Pisentius
17. Sts. Maximus and Domitian
18. The three Sts. Macarius
19. The Holy Virgin
20. Christ between the Holy Virgin and St. John the Baptist
21. The holy women at the tomb
22. The meeting of Christ and the two Marys
23. The purifying of Isaiah's lips
24. The encounter between Melchizedek and Abraham
25. The sacrifice of Abraham
26. The sacrifice of Jephthah's daughter
27. Christ enthroned and the Holy Virgin and Child

164

St. Mercurius (Abu al-Seifein). In the course of the centuries, the church has been a center of pilgrimage and has even attracted desert Bedouins because of the miraculous cures and wonders attributed to the relics of the holy monk, which are still kept in this church.

The Church of Sts. Anthony and Paul

The church of Sts. Anthony and Paul was built in the beginning of the twentieth century and serves the pilgrims who come to the monastery in greater and greater numbers. It has five cupolas and five steeples.

The Spring of St. Anthony

The spring named for St. Anthony flows near the south side of the enclosure, supplying the monastery's needs at the rate of one hundred cubic meters per day. Its temperature is almost constant at twenty-three degrees Celsius and has a sweetish taste despite its rather high concentration of chlorides. The composition of mineral salts has probably changed in the course of time because in the seventeenth century some visitors noticed a rather strong salinity due to a high proportion of nitrates. For instance, here is what Johann Michael Wansleben says, after visiting the monastery in 1672 during a mission to Ethiopia on behalf of the Duke of Saxony, "The monks drink it but it is not wholesome, especially for those who are not used to it; the nitrates which the water contains cause blisters on the skin and an itch as I myself have experienced." Not far from the spring, one can see an oil press and two millstones for grinding wheat which date from medieval times.

The Cave of St. Anthony

The cave where Anthony spent his years of ascetical solitude and where he died in 356 is in the mountain rising behind the monastery and about three hundred meters above it at the place where the cliff becomes steeper. To ascend from the monastery to the cave, one follows a path made for this purpose, and in the more precipitous passages the walking is made easier by wooden steps. After a hike of an hour or so, one arrives at the cave through an excavated passage from which the eyes embrace the desert plain spreading at the foot of the mountain. Some three meters under the hollowed out passage is a "terrace" where Anthony used to spend the hours devoted to manual labor weaving baskets from palm leaves. A narrow gallery about ten meters long leads to the interior of the cave in which Anthony had installed his cot and sought shelter from the weather and animals.

69. Entrance to St. Anthony's cave, where the saint lived an ascetic life, on the mountain situated behind the monastery.

Historical Information

St. Paul of Thebes

The monastery probably goes back to the fifth century and its foundation is linked with the memory of the great saint and anchorite Paul of Thebes, who lived there in a cave for almost eighty years. What we know of his life we owe to St. Jerome, who in his *Vita Pauli (Life of Paul)*, written between 375 and 380, depicts him as the first monk (Prologue, 1): "[Some] claim that Anthony was the founder of this mode of life. . . . They are right in part; not so much that he holds precedence in time as that all others were inspired by him. In truth, Amathas and Macarius, disciples of Anthony . . . affirm even to this day that a certain Paul of Thebes was the originator of the practice" (Jerome, 225).

Paul was born in 228 to a rich family living in the lower Thebaid. Having lost his parents at the age of sixteen, he decided to renounce his inheritance and consecrate his life to God. The terrible persecutions of Decius and Valerian in the years 249–260 led him to withdraw into the wilderness of the Eastern Desert where he lived until the age of one hundred and thirteen. Clothed with a tunic made of plaited palm leaves, he had for his food just half a loaf of bread which a raven brought him every day. Jerome narrates that one day it was revealed to Anthony that someone holier than he lived in the desert. Setting out to find him, Anthony met Paul and, attracted by his holiness, had a friendly conversation with him. When it was evening, the raven came as usual bringing food to Paul, but this time there was a whole loaf, half for Paul, half for Anthony. When Paul felt that death was near, he asked his friend Anthony to fetch the cloak which the patriarch Athanasius had given him. Anthony went to his hermitage and, taking this cloak, returned to Paul's cave. When he arrived, he saw angels carrying the soul of the holy ascetic to heaven, and entering the cave, he saw Paul's body. Two lions approached and dug the grave into which Anthony placed the body wrapped in the cloak. Anthony kept with particular devotion the tunic of palm leaves which from then on he wore for the solemn offices of Easter and Pentecost.

The Monastery

The monastery of St. Paul is mentioned in the travel narrative of Antoninus Martyr, a native of Placentia, who went to visit the saint's tomb in the years 560–570. Throughout the centuries, the monastery has always been spoken of in tandem with that of St. Anthony, for it is generally considered subordinate to the latter.

70. Monastery of St. Paul. Overall view from Michel Jullien,
Voyage dans le Désert de la Basse-Thébaïde (1884).

Ancient written sources seem to indicate that the monastery was originally occupied by Melchite monks, then, after various events, by Egyptian and Syrian monks. The presence of Syrian monks is again mentioned in the first half of the fifteenth century, but their trace disappears from the following century on.

Medieval historians and travelers also gave the monastery of St. Paul (Deir Anba Bula) the name Deir al-Numur (Monastery of the Tigers), probably because of the wildness of the place. Like that of St. Anthony, the monastery of St. Paul suffered from the Bedouin incursions. The one of 1484 was especially destructive: many monks were massacred, the library put to the torch, and the treasures devastated. The restoration of the monastery and the renewal of monastic life were undertaken with the support of the patriarch Gabriel VII, who sent ten monks from the monastery of the Syrians in Wadi al-Natrun. Unfortunately, in the second half of the sixteenth century, the monastery was attacked and ransacked twice and the monks were finally forced to leave.

After a long period of desolation which lasted 119 years, the monastery became the object of the solicitude of John XVI, who in 1701 promoted an extensive program of reconstruction and had the place occupied anew by a group of monks from the monastery of St. Anthony. Modern buildings have recently been erected to provide lodgings for the flocks of pilgrims who come more and more often to visit the saint's tomb. Despite their undeniable usefulness, these new edifices, attached to the walls, have been detrimental to the poetry and unity of the medieval monastic complex.

The Monastic Buildings

The Walls

High defensive walls surround the monastic buildings. As in the case of the monastery of St. Anthony, the history of the construction of the enclosure of the monastery of St. Paul is rather complex and corresponds to its major historical phases. A considerable enlargement was done at the beginning of the eighteenth century on the initiative of the patriarch John XVI. The definitive enclosure as it is today was completed in the course of the nineteenth century and includes the spring, the cisterns, and other areas used as courtyards, gardens, and monastic buildings (cells and refectory). On the east side, next to the main entrance, one can see the ancient hoist used in the past to haul up merchandise and lift visitors into the monastery.

The Tower

The ancient tower *(qasr)* rises alongside the church of St. Paul. Entered as usual by means of a drawbridge, it was the last defensive bastion against the desert plunderers' raids. In the past, the ground floor served as a

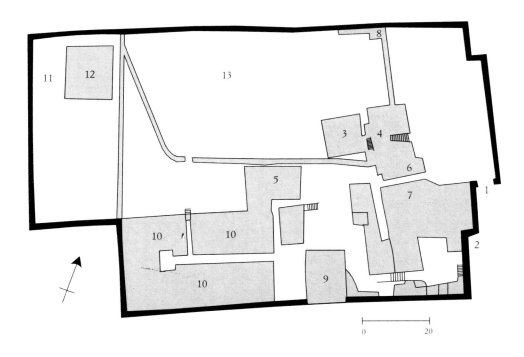

71. Monastery of St. Paul. Approximate plan. 1. Entrance, 2. Pulley, 3. Tower, 4. Churches of St. Paul and St. Mercurius, 5. Church of St. Michael, 6. Ancient refectory, 7. Ancient mill, 8. Oil press, 9. Guesthouse, 10. Cells, 11. Spring of St. Paul, 12. Cistern, 13. Gardens.

cemetery for the monks; the second floor was a storeroom for the food reserves which insured the monks' subsistence during the periods of siege. The third floor was divided into cells for the monks and also contains a chapel dedicated to the Holy Virgin, with a sanctuary roofed with a wooden cupola. This dedication to the Holy Virgin runs contrary to the custom in Coptic monasteries of dedicating the chapel on the highest story to the archangel Michael; but the latter is already the titular saint of the large church situated in the center of the monastery.

The Church of St. Paul

This church is three meters beneath the present level of the monastery. The south part, the oldest, is hollowed out of the cave in which, according to tradition, St. Paul lived in solitude for almost eighty years. In all likelihood its transformation into a church goes back to the fifth century, which one surmises is the period in which the monastery was founded. The north part is more recent and dates from the medieval period.

One has access to the church by a staircase attached to the walls of a chapel roofed with a cupola decorated with wall paintings representing the equestrian figures of Sts. Apater and his sister Irene, Isidore, Apa Iskhirun, James, and Julius. They were painted in 1713 by a monk of this monastery and probably reproduce a similar iconography, older and lost to us. The church proper comprises one nave in the center and three sanctuaries dedicated to the twenty-four elders of Revelation (north), St. Anthony (center), and St. Paul (south). The central and south sanctuaries and the part of the nave facing them are excavated in the rock, whereas the remainder of the building (to the north) is constructed of masonry.

The paintings on the walls of the cave also date from the renovation of the decor in 1713. They portray biblical subjects such as the archangels Michael, Gabriel, and Raphael, as well as the angel and Daniel's three companions Hananiah, Mishael, and Azariah, respectively called Shadrach, Meshach, and Abednego by the officer of King Nebuchadnezzar (Dan 3:10-26). Wall paintings in very poor condition, dating from the first half of the fourteenth century, are preserved in the middle sanctuary dedicated to St. Anthony. It is still possible to identify representations of Christ enthroned, the annunciation, St. John the Baptist, angels, and archangels.

Located in the south side of the nave is a marble shrine where St. Paul's body is kept. However, there is a tradition that the saint's relics were transported to Constantinople in 1240 and from there to Venice in 1381. An urn that contains remains which are deemed to be those of St. Paul of Thebes is in the church of St. Julian in Venice. Recently an examination and an analysis of these relics have shown that they are fragments

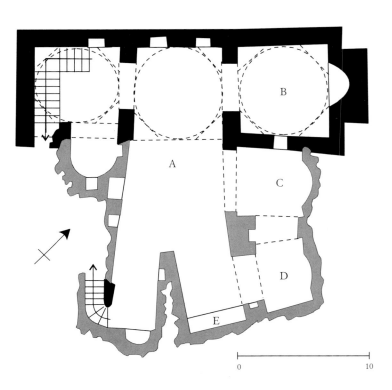

72. Monastery of St. Paul.
Plan of the cave and the church of St. Paul.
A. Nave, B. Sanctuary of the twenty-four elders
of Revelation, C. Sanctuary of St. Anthony,
D. Sanctuary of St. Paul, E. Tomb of St. Paul.

of the legs of a very old man (over eighty) who lived between the first century C.E. and the first half of the fourth century. These results fully confirm the thesis that the Venice relics are St. Paul's even though the almost complete body of the saint rests in the Egyptian monastery which bears his name.

The Church of St. Mercurius
The church of St. Mercurius (Abu al-Seifein) is located above Paul's cave to which it is connected by the original staircase leading to the subterranean church. It dates from the end of the eighteenth century and does not possess any particularly interesting elements, with the exception of its precious iconostasis inlaid with ivory and mother-of-pearl. As we have seen, St. Mercurius is traditionally represented on horseback with two swords (*seifein* in Arabic), the one symbolizing his function as an officer in the Roman army, the second, his defense of the Christian faith. The human figure trampled by the horse represents Julian the Apostate, who, according to an ancient tradition, was killed during his military campaign against the Persians not by an enemy's lance but by Mercurius'. Thus was punished the last unrelenting adversary of Christianity and the fervent defender of paganism.

The Church of St. Michael
The church dedicated to the archangel Michael (al-Malak) is used for the daily liturgy because the space available inside the subterranean church of St. Paul, the true spiritual center of the monastery, is too small. Built in 1777, the building is roofed with twelve cupolas and has two sanctuaries: the north one is dedicated to St. Michael and the south one to St. John the Baptist.

The Refectory and the Mill
The ancient refectory, situated in the east wing of the monastery, goes back to medieval times and is no longer used. A barrel vault covers the main axis of the room, which is occupied by a heavy masonry table whose west end is fashioned into a lectern from which the sacred texts and the lives of the saints and martyrs were read during the community meal. On the west side of the narrow passage through which one enters the refectory, there are two rooms used as mills in the past. The big stone millstone was set into motion by gigantic wooden gears turned by draft animals.

73. Church of St. Paul. Cupola over the entrance to the church, decorated in 1713 with figures of warrior saints.

The Spring of St. Paul

A spring named for St. Paul is in the north wing of the monastery and still supplies the monks a part of the water they need for drinking, cooling, washing, and irrigating the vegetable and other gardens at the rate of four cubic meters of water per day. A second spring exists some hundred meters away to the south of the monastery. It is called the Pool of Miriam, after the sister of Moses and Aaron, who according to tradition washed there during the Exodus.

The Region of al-Minya

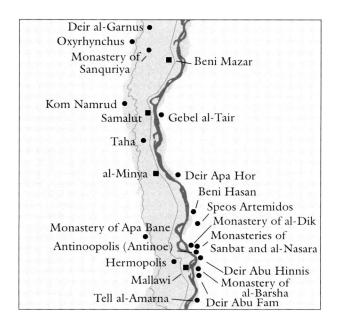

OXYRHYNCHUS AND ITS VICINITY

Oxyrhynchus

The ruins of the city of Oxyrhynchus lie near the present village of al-Bahnasa seventeen kilometers west of Beni Mazar, on the banks of the Bahr Yusuf. The first campaigns of excavations conducted between 1896 and 1907 by English and Italian archaeologists aimed chiefly at discovering papyri, and they did succeed in recovering several thousand documents written in Greek and Arabic which are extraordinary and incomparable testimonies to the life and economy of Egypt during the first centuries of our era. The discovery of these papyri at the end of systematic searches was the consequence of some chance findings near what must have been the dump of the ancient city and from which the farmers of the vicinity extracted fertilizer *(sebakh)* for their fields. It was only in 1922 and 1930 that studies on the topography and architecture of the city were undertaken. But even today, although there are excavations in progress, there are no plans for an archaeological campaign aiming at a methodical and complete unearthing of the city.

The city played an interesting role in Egyptian mythology and was the main city of the nineteenth nome during the dynastic period; its name then was Per-meged. The name Oxyrhynchus was given it during the Roman period because of the local worship of a fish of the Nile called by that name.

Oxyrhynchus occupied an area two kilometers long and eight hundred meters wide surrounded by a high wall with five gates. Its main streets were flanked by colonnades and the city had many public buildings and places of worship. Among the public edifices mentioned in the papyri or whose traces have been discovered, one can cite the theater, which could seat eleven thousand spectators and also serve for mass events on the occasion of special feasts whether religious or civil; the hippodrome, where the traditional chariot races took place; four public baths, which fulfilled a need for the low and middle classes since running water was not available in their homes and supplied a convenient meeting place for the wealthier classes. There was also a gymnasium, which was the center of the cultural life of the city during the Hellenistic and Roman periods, and two small ports on the Bahr Yusuf. It is very probable that Oxyrhynchus also had barracks since it supported military garrisons on several occasions during the Roman and Byzantine periods. The places of worship were many during the Ptolemaic and Roman periods: experts identified Egyptian temples to Serapis, Zeus-Amon, Hera-Isis, Atargatis-Bethynnis, Osiris; Greek temples to Demeter, Dionysius, Hermes, Apollo, the goddess Fortune; and Roman temples to Jupiter Capitolinus and Mars.

At the time of its peak development, the city may have had over thirty thousand inhabitants. From the fourth century on, it became one of the leading centers of Egyptian Christianity: scores of churches and monasteries were erected—to the point that according to the anonymous author of the *History of the Egyptian Monks (Historia Monachorum in Aegypto)* the number of monks reached several thousand. These figures are certainly exaggerated, but they are an indication of a strong concentration of monks in the city. The *History of the Egyptian Monks* (5.1-4) describes it in these terms: "The city is so full of monasteries that the very walls resound with the voices of monks. Other monasteries encircle it outside, so that the outer city forms another town alongside the inner. The temples and capitols of the city were bursting with monks; every quarter of the city was inhabited by them. Indeed, since the city is large, it has twelve churches where the people assemble. As for the monks, they have their own oratories in each monastery. The monks were almost in a majority over the secular inhabitants, since they reside everywhere right up to the entrances, and even in the gate towers. In fact there are said to be five thousand monks within the walls and as many again outside, and there is no hour of the day or night when they do not offer acts of worship to God. Moreover, not one of the city's inhabitants is a heretic or a pagan. On the contrary, all the citizens as a body are believers and catechumens, so that the bishop is able to bless the people publicly in the street" (*Desert Fathers,* 67).

The ancient city covered both the area, now become a desert, west of al-Bahnasa, and that of the village itself. In the streets of the latter, one can easily recognize fragments of decorations coming from Christian edifices: capitals, friezes, and shafts of columns. The mosque also utilized Corinthian and composite columns and capitals that had belonged to Christian churches.

The Monastery of al-Sanquriya (Deir al-Sanquriya)

The monastery of al-Sanquriya is located about fifteen kilometers from the little town of Beni Mazar. Although the present buildings are rather recent, the foundation of the monastery probably goes back to the fourth or fifth century, which was the time of the greatest splendor of Oxyrhynchus. The monastery church dates from medieval times but has kept some ancient elements: the four columns at the center of the nave and those of the portico situated near the northwest corner of the building were part of the ancient church.

The Monastery of al-Garnus (Deir al-Garnus)

Deir al-Garnus stands a few kilometers west of the little town of Aba al-Waqf and some ten kilometers from the road connecting Maghagha with Beni Mazar. A church from the nineteenth century is all that is left from an ancient monastery dedicated to the Holy Virgin. On its west side, one can see a well from which, according to tradition, the Holy Family drew water in the course of its journey through Egypt. In the courtyard are many architectural fragments from an older church, including columns and capitals from the sixth century.

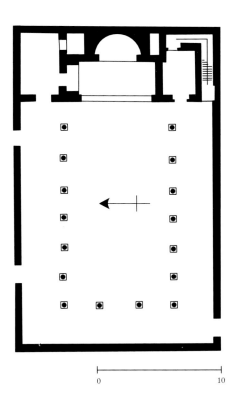

74. Kom Namrud.
Plan of the church of the
monastic complex
(end of 6th century).

0   10

The locality is a place of pilgrimage in honor of the Holy Family; according to tradition, the Holy Virgin of al-Garnus protects children against snake and scorpion bites.

Kom Namrud

About twenty-seven kilometers northwest of the town of Samalut, near the village of Shusha, the vestiges of a large monastic center have been discovered; it is very likely that it depended upon the vast establishment of Oxyrhynchus. The center had a large church with a nave and two side aisles, dating from the end of the sixth century; its floor, the bases of its columns as well as a few shafts and capitals are still visible. These columns had different dimensions and shapes which suggests that they came from earlier edifices. The church measured thirty meters in length and seventeen in width and had two entrances on the north side. The side aisles were connected by a return aisle on the west. The sanctuary area had an apse and was flanked by two small rooms, each with storage space.

In the area surrounding the church, numerous architecturally identical hermitages have been identified. Originally, each of them had a rectangular plan with a courtyard surrounded by a high wall, and three rooms against the east wall of the enclosure, two of which had a prayer niche in the east wall. Little by little, these hermitages were modified by the addition of new rooms and new courtyards. This evolution is similar to that of Kellia (the Cells), where the original hermitage, sheltering one elder and one disciple, was enlarged to allow more and more anchorites to gather together.

The monastic settlement of Kom Namrud is a representative example of the anchoritic formula between anchoritism and cenobitism, found also in Kellia, in the beginnings of Scetis, and at Deir al-Naqlun. While leading the anchoritic life in their own hermitages or in the company of one confrere at the most, the monks convened in one church to celebrate the liturgy and availed themselves of communal buildings for other purposes such as the care of the elderly and sick.

The Church of St. Menas in Taha

The church dedicated to St. Menas (Mari Mina) stands in the city of Taha, midway between Samalut and Minya and a few kilometers west of the main road running along the Nile. In the past, Taha was an important bishopric. The present church dates from the seventeenth–eighteenth centuries but has preserved vestiges and interesting fragments from the ancient paleo-Christian edifice. Also worthy of note are the two marble columns with their capitals in the west part of the building and the large Epiphany basin in the northwest corner, into which the faithful plunged themselves during the celebrations organized on the feast of the Epiphany. The circular basin is decorated with a flowerlike design with eight lobes.

THE MONASTERY OF APA BANE
(DEIR ABU FANA)

Historical Information

The monastery of Apa Bane (Deir Abu Fana) is found in the Eastern Desert, on the edge of the fertile plain, twelve kilometers west of Itlidim and about three from Qasr Hur. The ancient sources (*History of the Egyptian Monks [Historia Monachorum in Aegypto]*, *Sayings of the Fathers [Apophtegmata Patrum]*, Palladius' *Lausiac History [Historia Lausiaca]*, Sozomen's *Church History [Historia Ecclesiastica]*, and others) mention a certain Benus or Banus (Bes) who lived in the region of Deir Abu Fana and can be identified with Apa Bane, who, according to the *History of the Egyptian Monks* (4.1), "surpassed everyone in meekness. The brothers who lived round about him assured us that he had never sworn an oath, had never told a lie, had never been angry with anyone, and had never scolded anyone. For he lived a life of the utmost stillness, and his manner was serene, since he had attained the angelic state" (*Desert Fathers*, 66).

According to the old texts, Apa Bane came from a well-to-do family of Memphis. Having withdrawn to live the life of an anchorite, he spent eighteen years in rigorous asceticism, constantly standing in a dark cell without eating any food prepared by human hands. Even during his hours of sleep he remained standing with his chest leaning against a wall built for this purpose. Bane was accustomed to pray with his hands lifted toward heaven in an Eastern attitude associating prayer with water. He had the gift of clairvoyance, particularly in the case of the death of the emperor Theodosius I in 395.

Apa Bane's remains were discovered in 1992 in a tomb located under the floor of the funerary church of the monastery and their study has yielded especially interesting results. Analyses have confirmed in a surprising way and explained what the historical sources reported. Bane died at about forty from a disease contracted in his youth: his spine was completely calcified which limited his mobility and practically made him unable to lie down. This explains why he was shut-in for eighteen years and why he remained standing even during the hours of sleep. This incapacity also explains the name he was given: *bane* means date palm in Coptic. The deformation and rigidity of the spine suggested the comparison with a palm tree that withstands the wind of the desert. This infirmity was not regarded as a disease but as trial sent by God to Bane and accepted by him, a trial giving him the opportunity to live a particular kind of ascetical life.

The announcement of Theodosius' death and the fact that Bane died shortly afterward allow us to place his birth around 355 and his death around 395. His reputation and the miracles which happened at his tomb contributed to the prosperity of the monastery, which in the fifth century acquired exceptional splendor and prestige. But by the beginning of the seventh century, the monastery was deserted and in ruins. The causes of such a demise are not known with any certainty, but one may surmise that it was the result of an epidemic which rapidly wiped out the community or, more plausibly, the result of changes in the climate. Indeed, the archaeological studies have shown that from the sixth century on, the buildings were progressively invaded by sand and that the monks desperately struggled against this by erecting appropriate structures. But all was in vain and they had to gradually abandon the monastery. Only the high part, on the hill where the "sanctuary-church" stands, is still extant; around it a small monastery still existed in the Middle Ages, as attested by historical accounts from the thirteenth to fifteenth centuries.

The Churches and the Archaeological Area

The monastery was built on different levels in a hilly region; these have been leveled out owing to the progressive advance of the sand. The sanctuary-church, dedicated to Apa Bane, is the only building not overcome by sand and is surrounded by high brick walls erected as a barrier against it. The original building goes back to the sixth century, but it was partially transformed in the Middle Ages when a small monastic community settled there. The entrance is on the north side. The plan consists of a nave, two side aisles, and a sanctuary area similar to a triconch and flanked by two additional rooms which were subdivided into four by the construction of partitions. The nave is separated from the aisles by two ranks of five columns. An eleventh column placed in the middle of the west side delineates a return aisle between the other two. Except for the column at the southwest corner, the columns are not those of the original building.

The triconch of the sanctuary area is simplified since the side apses are not semi-circular but rectangular and thus are less deep than the main apse. The latter is decorated with fine niches and small columns. The vault is adorned with a large cross richly embellished with carefully executed geometrical motifs dating from the twelfth–thirteenth centuries. It is the symbol of the monastery, which is sometimes called Deir al-Salib in Arabic, Monastery of the Cross. The same motifs are repeated several times on the interior walls of the church: beautiful wall paintings from the high Middle Ages represent crosses, each one different in shape and decoration.

A recent Austrian archaeological campaign has partially brought to light the rest of the monastic complex, which lies north of the hill. Among the most interesting buildings, one which could be called a funerary church, a vast room for the ritual of water, and a refectory have been identified. The church has a basilican plan comprising a nave, two side aisles, a return aisle on the west side, and a sanctuary which has an apse, niches, and adjacent rooms on three sides. The entrance was on the south side through a narthex placed on the west side, from which a staircase gave access to the upper galleries. The building goes back to the sixth century and is an enlargement of a previous chapel erected at the end of the fourth or the beginning of the fifth century, in all likelihood to shelter the body of Apa Bane. The funerary purpose of the church was recently confirmed when the tomb of Apa Bane and those of other abbots of the monastery were discovered under the nave floor. The original chapel probably comprised only one nave and one apse. When the church was constructed, the foundations of the chapel walls were used as stylobates.

On the south side of the church archaeologists discovered a large room closely connected with the funerary church; in it they have identified the remains of a fountain. It is probable that this room was intended to be used in the rituals of prayer and funerals inspired by the Eastern veneration of water which historical sources have attributed to Apa Bane, as we have seen. Along the east side of the fountain room and connected with it, the remains of a refectory have been identified; it is a rectangular space about fifteen meters long where the table for the meals is still visible.

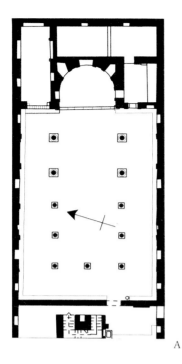
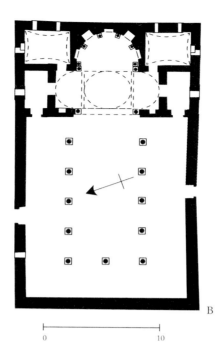

A

B

C

75. Monastery of Apa Bane.
A. Plan of the funerary church
(6th century).
B. Plan of the "sanctuary-church"
(6th century).
C. Representation of the cross in
the "sanctuary-church."
D. Ruins of the funerary church.

D

Hermopolis Magna

The ruins of the city of Hermopolis (Hermopolis Magna), today called al-Ashmunein, lie about ten kilometers northwest of Mallawi. Previously the city was called Khmun, "city of eight," because of the group of eight primordial deities preceding the creation. Indeed, according to tradition, it is here that the sun rose for the first time and the world was created. It was the main city of the fifteenth nome of Upper Egypt and the principal center of the worship of Thot, the god of healing and wisdom, the patron of scribes, represented under the form of an ibis or baboon. In the Greco-Roman period, the city was named Hermopolis, the city of Hermes, because of the association between Thot and Hermes, and it became an important center of pilgrimage. Its prosperity was due to the prestige of this deity, adopted here as Hermes Trismegistus (Hermes three times great) by Greeks and Egyptians alike.

The Great Basilica

The imposing vestiges of a great basilica from the Christian period have come down to us; its dimensions (sixty-six meters long and forty-six wide at the transept) prove that it was certainly the episcopal church of the city. Constructed during the first half of the fifth century, probably between 410 and 440, over the remains of a temple dating from the era of Ptolemy III (247–222 B.C.E.), the basilica belongs to the type of church with a nave, two side aisles, a western return aisle, as well as a transept. The nave is lined with granite columns which are crowned with precious Corinthian capitals and separate it from the aisles. In addition, the colonnades of the side aisles encircle the triconch transept and frame the altar placed before the apse, in the center

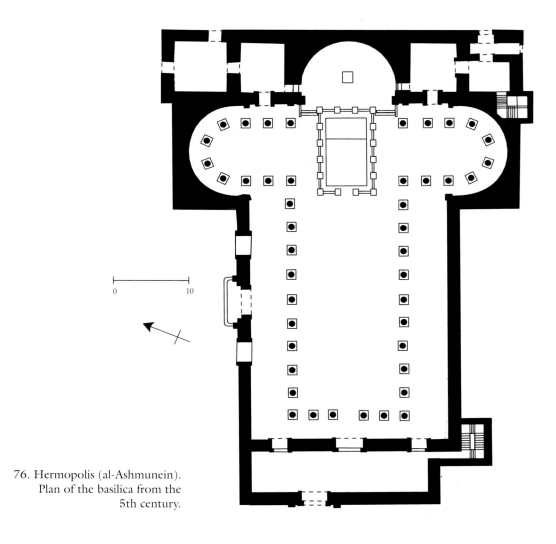

76. Hermopolis (al-Ashmunein).
Plan of the basilica from the
5th century.

of the transept. The circular form of the transepts' extremities must have given the building an especially awe-inspiring aspect, and it was the sole known example of this type in Egypt until the recent discovery of the basilica of al-Hawariya in Mareotis, west of Alexandria.

The church complex had two great portals: through the first one, at the west end, one went from the atrium into the basilica through a narthex; the second, on the north side, was an impressive entrance preceded by a propylaeum with four columns. Another propylaeum with four columns marked the entrance to the great atrium leading to the basilica. The number of rooms built against the church is surprising; the one in the northeast corner has a baptismal font.

South of the great basilica, near the temple of Ramses II, the ruins of another church have been identified; it is smaller than the great basilica but has a similar architectural structure.

ANTINOOPOLIS AND ITS VICINITY

Antinoopolis (Antinoe—Ansina)

The ruins of the city of Antinoe (Antinoopolis in Latin and Ansina in Arabic) occupy a large area along the east bank of the Nile, opposite the town of al-Roda, north of Mallawi. The city was founded in 130 by the emperor Hadrian in memory of his favorite, Antinous, who had drowned here while bathing in the Nile. At the time, the place was not completely desertic; archaeological excavations have unearthed the remains of temples going back to the time of Amenophis IV and Ramses II, as well as tombs from the New Kingdom. Hadrian's intention was to build a large, rich city in which the administrative control of upper Egypt would have been concentrated.

Inhabited by a population primarily Greek and Roman, Antinoopolis rapidly became the capital of the Thebaid and kept this title throughout the whole Roman period. The emperor Diocletian promoted it to the

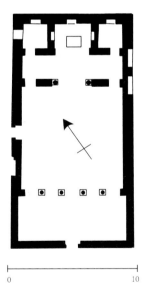

0   10

77. Antinoopolis (Antinoe).
Plan and presbytery of a church from the 6th century discovered in the west part of the city. View of the triumphal arch, from *Description de l'Égypte* (1809).

177

rank of metropolis, and from the fourth century on, it became an important episcopal see, rich in churches and monasteries both inside the city and in its immediate vicinity. In the first years of the fourth century, many Christians underwent martyrdom there. Among them, St. Colluthus, a physician martyred in 304 or 308, and the protector of the city, was the object of a particular devotion. In his *Lausiac History* (58.1; 59.1), Palladius offers an interesting piece of information on the city: "I spent four years in Antinoe in the Thebaid and in that time I gained a knowledge of the monasteries there. About twelve hundred men dwell around the city living by the toil of their hands and practicing asceticism to a high degree. Among them there are also anchorites who have confined themselves in rocky caves. . . . In the town of Antinoë are twelve monasteries of women" (Palladius, 140, 141).

The decline of the city began with the Arab conquest in 641. But it is still mentioned in the tenth century, when Severus of Antioch cites "the Ansina bishopric" in his writings, and at the end of the twelfth century, when the traveler Ibn Gubayr describes the town existing then and states that the ancient Greek city had been destroyed by Saladin. The last mention of Antinoopolis dates from the fourteenth century. The ruins of the city are near the village of Sheikh Ibada, between the Nile and the rocky foothills of the desert. Antinoopolis was surrounded by brick walls and presented all the characteristics of Roman urbanism: a chessboard plan, porticoes with columns, triumphal arches, baths, amphitheater, hippodrome, temples, and later on churches and monasteries. Until the beginning of the nineteenth century, the ruins of the city had remained almost intact, but under Muhammad Ali (1872–1925) the most valuable building materials were used in the construction of a large sugar refinery. Today, only traces remain from the theater, the temples, the circus, the hippodrome, and the other palatial edifices the city contained. In contrast, one can still see extensive and evocative vestiges of the brick buildings.

The area of Antinoopolis has been for a long time the object of research and excavations conducted under Italian auspices. These excavations have revealed numerous churches, some of which were part of monastic complexes. One of the most interesting is the church discovered near the south cemetery. It is furnished with an apse encircled by a concentric series of columns and has a nave with four side aisles quite distinctive in appearance: the outer aisles are very narrow and served only as ambulatories; the intermediary aisles are almost twice as wide, whereas the nave is narrower than the intermediary aisles. The edifice probably dates from the fourth century and represents the Egyptian architectural tradition of that time, subsequently abandoned. Another church from the fourth century was discovered in the vicinity of the north cemetery; it has a basilican plan with a nave and two aisles. The city still has the traces of churches with simply a nave or with two and

78. Antinoopolis (Antinoe).
Ruins of a building made of unbaked brick.

four aisles, as well as the vestiges of a square church with an apse. This last belonged to a sizeable monastic community of which some ten rooms containing ten beds apiece have been found. In the west section, near the cliff that separates the high plateau from the bed of the Nile, archaeologists have discovered a church from the sixth century with a choir and a triple sanctuary and with considerable remains of painted decorations; it too was part of a monastery.

The Monastery of al-Dik (Deir al-Dik)

The vestiges of the monastery of al-Dik are about four kilometers north of Antinoopolis, in the desert stretches at the foot of the rocky escarpment. Entirely built of unbaked bricks, the complex was surrounded by a high enclosure and its rectangular church had one nave (with four bays) and one sanctuary. The surrounding mountains are honeycombed with caves anchorites occupied in the past.

The Monasteries of Sanbat and al-Nasara (Deir Sanbat and Deir al-Nasara)

The ruins of the monasteries of Sanbat and al-Nasara lie two kilometers north of Antinoopolis, in the desert area along the lower rocky escarpments. These monasteries comprised rooms made in the natural caves of the cliff and adapted by the anchorites, as well as buildings of unbaked brick erected at the foot of the mountain for communal activities and for the care of the elderly and sick monks.

The Church of Abbot John (Deir Abu Hinnis)

The village of Deir Abu Hinnis is located two kilometers south of the ruins of Antinoopolis. The church, dedicated to an uncertainly identified saint named John (Abu Hinnis), is at the center of the village. It probably goes back to the end of the fifth century. Its original plan in all likelihood comprised only one nave, a narthex, and a single sanctuary with an apse and two small rooms on either side. The building was profoundly transformed when the original wood roof was replaced with cupolas; at that time, the nave was divided into three parts by the insertion of masonry pillars to withstand the thrust of the cupolas. In both longitudinal walls, three rectangular niches were hollowed out; they are adorned with little pilasters having Corinthian capitals. The semi-circular apse is also decorated with three niches in the same style.

In the mountain east of the village, a church hewn from the rock goes back to the early Christian centuries. Its walls are covered with ancient wall paintings, unfortunately very degraded. According to certain opinions, this church could be the *martyrion* (martyry, "martyr-church") of St. Colluthus.

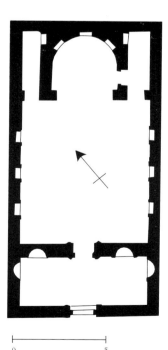

79. Deir Abu Hinnis. Church of St. John the Abbot. Plan of the original church from the end of the 5th century and detail of a niche.

179

The Church of the Monastery of al-Barsha (Deir al-Barsha)

The village of al-Barsha is on the bank of the Nile, opposite Mallawi, a few kilometers south of Antinoe. Its church is dedicated to St. Pshoi (Bishoi in Arabic), the founder of the homonymous monastery of Wadi al-Natrun (the former Scetis), who, according to tradition, fled from Scetis in 407 because of a furious attack by the Bedouins and took refuge in the region of Antinoe where he died in 417. The present structure of the church, modern for the greater part, has preserved elements which can be dated from the twelfth or thirteenth century; the semi-circular central apse, the rectangular room located north of the apse, the *khurus,* and the pillars of the nave belonged to the original building. On the north side, a staircase leads to a chapel above the sanctuaries of the church. Dedicated to St. Pshoi, the chapel is made of a transverse *khurus* and three sanctuaries; the walls and arcades are painted with interesting geometrical motifs.

In the mountains close to the village, there remain many stone houses going back to the period of the pharaohs as well as tombs dating chiefly from the Twelfth Dynasty (2000–1785 B.C.E.), which the anchorites used in the early Christian centuries. The walls show red cruciform motifs and inscriptions in the Coptic language.

ANCHORITIC SETTLEMENTS AND ROCK CHURCHES ON THE EAST BANK OF THE NILE

In middle Egypt, the right bank of the Nile offers a much less lush vegetation than does the left. For long stretches, the desert reaches almost to the bank of the river; only strips a few hundred meters long where irrigation is possible are suitable for cultivation. The cliff which separates the river valley from the high plateau and follows the winding course of the Nile has recesses and natural caves. As a consequence, it has been used from very ancient times to build necropolises and rock temples. Among the necropolises of greatest renown in the region, one must mention that of Beni Hasan, the most important burial ground of the Middle Empire, and that of al-Amarna, the fabulous capital of the "heretical" pharaoh of the Eighteenth Dynasty, Amenophis IV. One can attribute to the same dynasty, and more precisely to Queen Hatshepsut, the rock temple which the Greeks called Speos Artemidos (Grotto of Artemis).

In the course of the fourth and fifth centuries, when the monastic phenomenon knew an astonishing expansion, a great number of the natural caves and of those which under the pharaohs had been made into the tombs of notables or into temples became a safe refuge for Christian ascetics, whether they wanted to live in

80. Gebel al-Tair.
View of the "monastery of the pulley," from Girolamo Segato,
Atlante Monumentale dell' Alto e Basso Egitto (1837).

180

solitude or lead the contemplative life in small groups. Furthermore, many caves and rock temples were transformed into churches used by the colonies of ascetics or the surrounding Christian communities.

The Church of the Holy Virgin of Gebel al-Tair
The church of the Holy Virgin (Deir al-Adra) stands on the right bank of the Nile, some forty kilometers north of the Minya bridge. The building is among the dwellings of Gebel al-Tair, on top of a rocky cliff from which one has a broad view of the valley of the Nile, fields carefully cultivated by the farmers, and lush palm tree groves.

The spot bears several names which derive from different traditions and legends. The Arabic name Gebel al-Tair means "mountain of the birds" because of the thousands of birds that live and nest in the cliff. The place is also called Gebel al-Kaff, "mountain of the hand." This name comes from a legend according to which the Holy Family, during its wanderings in Egypt, was passing by this place in a small boat headed up stream when suddenly the Holy Virgin noticed an enormous rock coming loose from the mountain and about to fall on the boat and its occupants; the child Jesus promptly intervened and stopped the rock by extending his hand. The shape of the hand remained miraculously imprinted on the rock, and in 1168, during his campaign in Egypt, Amaury, the sovereign of Jerusalem, removed the part of the rock bearing the imprint and took it with him to Syria.

While being dedicated to the Holy Virgin (al-Adra), the church is also called Deir al-Baqara, an Arabic name meaning "monastery of the pulley," because formerly one entered the monastery from the base of the cliff up a crevice in the rock by means of a pulley. According to tradition, this church was founded in the fourth century by the empress Helena in memory of the passage of the Holy Family. From the outside, the building looks like a massive modern construction with a steeple in the northeast corner. In fact, the ancient building was carved in its entirety from the rock. In 1938, works of remodeling and restoration removed the original stone roof in order to make the church taller and create a second level; moreover, extra rooms were added on the south and west sides. The original edifice was probably a tomb from late Roman antiquity which was transformed into a church only in the seventh century; its structure is indeed comparable to that of the funerary monuments of Roman Egypt.

The church has a *naos* (a nave with two side aisles and western return aisle) and three sanctuaries; the small side aisles and western return aisle are separated from the nave by ten columns hewn from the rock. On the south side, the baptismal font has been carved in a column. On a higher level than the nave, the area in front of the middle sanctuary serves as a *khurus;* two columns surmounted by precious Corinthian capitals delineate

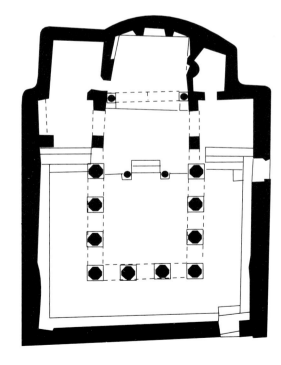

81. Gebel al-Tair.
Plan of the church of the Holy
Virgin (Deir al-Adra).

0   5

181

this space, which prolongs the nave. The sanctuary behind the iconostasis is also hewn from the rock and decorated with small pilasters and niches. The small room to the south of the sanctuary was the ancient entrance to the church; tradition reports that the Holy Family stayed there for a brief time. Above the west entrance, friezes from ancient Christian edifices in the area present motifs drawn from the vegetal and animal realms. Among them is one of particular interest: it shows seven human figures, each one inside a niche and holding a book in the left hand; it is probably a representation of seven apostles, part of a larger composition the rest of which is now lost.

The church of the Holy Virgin is the goal of a pilgrimage during the great Marian feasts; hundreds of Coptic pilgrims, including entire families, converge from the whole of Christian Egypt. Traditionally, it is here that the Copts of the vicinity have their children baptized; to fill this need, a vast building has recently been constructed next to the church; it contains seven baptismal fonts allowing a great number of children to be rapidly baptized.

The Church of St. Hor (Deir Apa Hor)

The church of St. Hor (Deir Apa Hor) is located four kilometers south of al-Minya in the village of Deir Sawada on the east bank of the Nile. It is entirely hewn from the rock and probably was originally a pagan temple later transformed into a Christian church. The nave has a rectangular plan and in the center a square area roofed with a cupola. On the east side there are two sanctuaries. From the north sanctuary one has access to a square room which was certainly part of the pagan temple. Along the south wall a series of compartments were used as burial places in the past. A second, dedicated to St. Dimiana, has been erected above the first.

The Tombs of Beni Hasan

The necropolis of Beni Hasan is situated on the east bank of the Nile opposite Abu Qurqas. It is the most important Middle Kingdom necropolis in the region lying between Memphis and Asyut. It contains thirty-nine large tombs where the nobles from the sixteenth nome of upper Egypt who lived under the Eleventh and the Twelfth Dynasties (2130–1785 B.C.E.) are buried. During the paleo-Christian era, some communities of anchorites dwelt in these tombs, at times adapting them to the demands of their mode of life. Here and there, one can see inscriptions in red and representations of the cross. One of these tombs (no. 28) served as a church for the monastic community.

Speos Artemidos

The temple which the Greeks called Speos Artemidos (Grotto of Artemis) is about one kilometer south of the necropolis of Beni Hasan. It is a rock temple founded by Queen Hatshepsut (1505–1484 B.C.E.) and

82. Gebel al-Tair. Church of the Holy Virgin.
Detail of a frieze representing the apostles and capital.

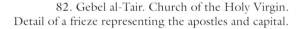

83. *Top of page:* Abu Fam. Rock-hewn necropolis.

Center of page: Tell al-Amarna, the capital of the heretical pharaoh Amenophis IV. Necropolis used by anchorites of the first Christian centuries.

Bottom of page: Tell al-Amarna. Rock-hewn tomb converted into a church.

dedicated to the lioness-headed goddess Sekhmet, whom the Greeks subsequently identified with Artemis. In the course of the fifth century, this temple was transformed into a church by some colonies of anchorites who had settled in the tombs and caves in the surroundings. On the south wall of the portico, one can see many graffiti and inscriptions in Coptic. By walking two kilometers in the wadi adjacent to the temple, one reaches a place named Valley of the Anchorites in homage to the many anchorites who lived in the neighboring caves during the fifth and sixth centuries.

The Monastery of the Soldier (Deir Abu Fam)

The anchoritic complex of Abu Fam or Bifam (Bifam is a variant of Phoibammon) is located about four kilometers south of the village of al-Barsha. The place is also called al-Sheikh Said after the Muslim saint who is buried there. Christian anchorites made use of the tombs carved into the steep rocky walls under the Sixth Dynasty (2350–2180 B.C.E.) to receive the mummies of the governors of the fifteenth nome of upper Egypt. Two tombs have been modified to serve as churches; one of them (no. 25) has a semi-circular apse on the east whose structure is accented by two pilasters with Corinthian capitals supporting an arch.

The Necropolis of Tell al-Amarna

Located on the east bank of the Nile and called Akhetaton in the ancient Egyptian language, Tell al-Amarna was made the capital of Egypt, the royal residence and center of the new worship of Aton (the sun) by the "heretical" pharaoh Amenophis IV (1353–1335 B.C.E.). The city was abandoned some fifteen years after its foundation, upon the pharaoh's death and the return to the worship of the ancient gods. Today only unimpressive ruins are left. The pharaonic necropolis is on the desertic cliff east of the city. In the first Christian centuries, the tombs were occupied by anchorites who made them their dwellings. One of these tombs, that of Prince Penehsi, was used as a church; to this end, a rectangular room with an apse and oriented to the east was hewn from the rock in the north part of the tomb.

63. Base of a column of the prestigious city of Oxyrhynchus, one of the most important centers of Egyptian Christianity.

64. A view of the Nile from Gebel al-Tair.

65. Gebel al-Tair. Church of the Holy Virgin (Deir al-Adra), also called "monastery of the pulley" because in the past one entered it from the bottom of the cliff by means of a pulley.

66. Gebel al-Tair. Church of the Holy Virgin (Deir al-Adra) (7th century). Interior view.

67. Deir Abu Fana (monastery of Apa
Bane). Funerary church of the monastic
complex.

68. Antinoopolis. Ruins of the city founded
by the emperor Hadrian in 130 in homage
to his favorite Antinous; in the background,
the village of Deir Abu Hinnis.

69. Hermopolis. The impressive vestiges of the basilica erected during the first half of the 5th century according to the plan of a church with a nave, two side aisles, and a transept.

70. Bawit. Monastery of St. Apollo. Ruins of the prestigious monastery founded in the 4th century, abandoned in the course of the 10th, and now largely covered by desert sand.

The Region of Asyut

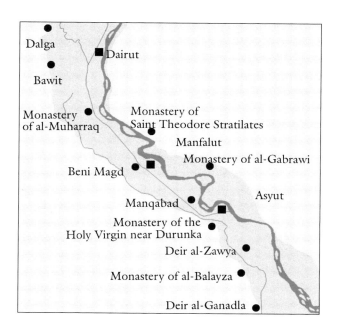

THE MONASTERY OF ST. APOLLO IN BAWIT
(DEIR ABU ABULLU)

Historical Information

The vestiges of the ancient monastery of Bawit are on the west bank of the Nile, in the desertic area facing the fertile plain, some fifteen kilometers from Dairut. The name of this place probably comes from the Coptic term *auht* which means "assembly," "congregation," and also "monastery."

The first monastic settlement was the work of the monk Apollo in the second half of the fourth century, probably between 385 and 390. The anonymous compiler of the *History of the Egyptian Monks* (8.1-5, 7, 18) knew him personally and speaks of him in these terms: "We visited another holy man, named Apollo, in the territory of Hermopolis. . . . Now we saw this man, who had hermitages under him in the desert at the foot of the mountain, and was the father of five hundred monks. He was renowned in the Thebaid and great works were ascribed to him, and the Lord performed many wonders through him, and a multitude of signs were accomplished at his hands. Since from childhood he had given proof of great ascesis, at the end of his life he received the following grace: when he was eighty years old he established on his own a great monastery of five hundred perfect men, almost all of them with the power to work miracles. When he was fifteen years old, he withdrew from the world and spent forty years in the desert, scrupulously practicing every virtue. Then he seemed to hear the voice of God saying to him, 'Apollo, Apollo, through you I will destroy the wisdom of the wise men of Egypt, and I will bring to nothing the understanding of the prudent pagans' (cf. Is. 29:14). And together with these you will also destroy the wise men of Babylon for me, and you will banish all worship of demons. And now make your way to the inhabited region, for you will bear me "a peculiar people, zealous of good works".' (Tit. 2.14). . . . He set off for the inhabited region. . . . and for a while he lived in the neighbouring desert. He occupied a small cave and dwelt there at the foot of the mountain. His work consisted in offering prayers to God throughout the day, and in bending his knees a hundred times in the night and as many times again in the day. He . . . [was] living in the power of the Spirit and performing signs and wonderful miracles of healing. These were so amazing that they defy description. . . . Many monks flocked to him from every quarter because of his renown; and inspired by his teaching and manner of life, a vast number of people renounced the world. A community of brothers formed itself around him on the mountain, as many as five hundred of them, all sharing a common life and eating at the same table" (*Desert Fathers*, 70–73).

Practically nothing remains from the ancient monastery, but during the sixth century, a new phase of construction began when a community of women, whose name was associated with St. Rachel, settled there. The monastery reached its highest point in the seventh century when the monastic complex counted up to five thousand monks. A slow decline set in after the Arab conquest and the monks gradually abandoned the place. From the tenth century on, the desert sand began to invade the deserted buildings, and today most of them still lie in oblivion.

The Ruins of the Monastery
In the beginning of the twentieth century, French archaeologists conducted excavations in the ruins of the monastery. These have brought to light two churches, some groups of buildings, and part of the walls. The Bawit complex is known the world over because of the abundant architectural and painted decorations that were recovered there and which were divided between the Coptic Museum in Cairo and the Louvre Museum in Paris. Totally abandoned in 1913, the work of research has never been resumed, and it is particularly

84. Bawit. Monastery of St. Apollo. Decorative elements from the wall paintings of the monastery and plan of the south church (6th century).

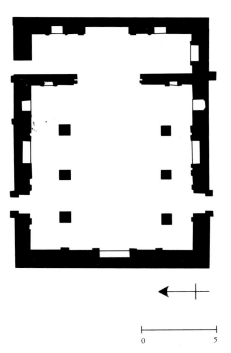

0   5

saddening that the excavations of one of the greatest Egyptian monasteries have not been accompanied by satisfactory written and photographic documentation and have not been the object of any subsequent systematic archaeological campaign. In 1976, a number of wall paintings were found at the site and have been transported to the Coptic Museum; however, no report about the circumstances of their discovery is available.

The monastery occupied an astoundingly large area since it was surrounded by an enclosure about three kilometers in length. Two churches have been discovered at the center, called respectively the north church and the south church. Only the south church has been completely freed from the sand and partially reconstructed, with its rich architectural and painted decorations, in the Louvre Museum. It was built in the sixth century over an earlier edifice from the fourth. The two phases of construction are characterized by different masonry techniques: the older one used freestone while the more recent one used brick faced with recycled stone. The earlier building was probably neither a pagan nor Christian place of worship, while the second presents all the characteristics of a church: a nave with two side aisles, a sanctuary with a niche, and entrances on its south and

85. Bawit. Monastery of St. Apollo.
Wall paintings on the semi-circular vault of a chapel (6th–7th centuries): enthroned Holy Virgin and Child; enthroned Christ; the apostles Bartholomew, Philip, Andrew, and Peter.

north sides. Decorations carved in stone and wood and painted friezes with geometrical, vegetal, and figurative motifs ran along the interior and exterior walls of the building. The north church was near the south church; it dates from the eighth century and like the other is the result of the transformation of a previous building.

THE MONASTERY OF THE HOLY VIRGIN
(DEIR AL-MUHARRAQ)

Historical Information

The monastery of the Holy Virgin, called Deir al-Muharraq, is today the most important in middle and upper Egypt. It rises at the place where, according to tradition, the Holy Family stayed for three years, six months, and ten days until the angel of God appeared to Joseph and told him, "Get up, take the child and his mother, and go to the land of Israel" (Matt 2:20). The name al-Muharraq is interpreted in different ways. According to some, it derives from the Arabic word *maharraq,* which means "to burn," and alludes both to the aridity of the surrounding area and to the local practice of burning the fields to get rid of weeds.

Almost nothing is known about the life and history of the monastery from its origins to the medieval period. A venerated tradition reports that the Holy Virgin appeared to the patriarch Theophilus (384–412) in order to dissuade him from building a church in this holy place. In this way, the future pilgrims could understand the humility of the places chosen by the Holy Family for its stay in Egypt. Dedicated to the Holy Virgin, today's church dates from the twelfth or thirteenth century. It was perhaps at that time that the tradition arose according to which the Holy Family sojourned in this place—and it probably arose as a consequence of an ambitious project of construction inside the monastery. The particularly sacred character of the place would no doubt have encouraged pilgrimages and generated financial support on the part of the Christian communities of Egypt.

In the course of the fourteenth and fifteenth centuries, four abbots of the monastery of al-Muharraq were patriarchs: Gabriel IV (1370–1378), Matthew I (1378–1409), Matthew II (1452–1465), and John XII (1480–1483). At the beginning of the nineteenth century, twenty monks and two hundred laypersons lived there. The population decreased in 1857 and 1871 because some of the monks were transferred to the monastery of al-Baramus in Wadi al-Natrun. At the end of the nineteenth century, the monastery rallied with the arrival of new monks. In 1883, there were eighty of them. At that point, it was the richest and largest monastery in Egypt.

Today some fifty monks live at al-Muharraq, and at the same time a fair number of monks belonging to the monastery exercise their priestly ministry in Christian communities in Egypt and elsewhere. The monastery

86. Monastery of the Holy Virgin (Deir al-Muharraq). The defensive tower, probably from the 8th century, repaired in the 12th.

plays a particularly important role for the Christian church in Egypt because it is a very active center of Coptic culture: its theological seminary, established in 1905 by Qummus Bakhum, has about one hundred students. The cycle of study lasts five years and covers such matters as theology, biblical exegesis, psalmody, as well as Coptic, Arabic, and English languages. Every year at the end of June, close to one hundred thousand pilgrims come to the monastery for the feast of the consecration of the church to the Holy Virgin. On this occasion, the vast monastic complex bursts with life as entire Coptic families converge on the monastery, coming in crammed buses or carts drawn by donkeys or camels. Extensive buildings have recently been erected to lodge them. During this festive period, an average of three thousand children are baptized. In 1988, on the occasion of the yearly pilgrimage, a tragic accident occurred causing the death of forty-seven persons, including twenty-six children, who perished in a fire that occurred in the tents of the pilgrims' camp.

The Church of the Holy Virgin

The church dedicated to the Holy Virgin is at the heart of the monastery among its oldest buildings and is about one meter below the present level of the courtyard. Its construction dates from the twelfth or thirteenth century when a substantial remodeling of the monastery was undertaken. It is highly probable that an earlier church existed going back to the time of the foundation of the monastery; the traditions are more audacious and place its origin around the year 60, that is, in the years immediately following St. Mark's arrival in Egypt.

The entrance to the church is on the north side and has a nave and two side aisles, roofed with cupolas, and one sanctuary with two adjoining rooms to the north and south. According to tradition, the sanctuary marks the place where the Holy Family settled down. The stone top of the altar, dating from 747, is especially interesting. Certainly cut as an altar table, it was subsequently used as a funerary stele. It reverted to its original function when the church was rebuilt in the twelfth or thirteenth century. Flanking the church is another large church dedicated to St. George, erected in 1988 where an earlier church dedicated to Sts. Peter and Paul had stood.

The Tower

The tower *(qasr)* was for the monks the ultimate defensive stronghold against the attacks of the desert looters. The original edifice, probably from the eighth century, was restored and partially rebuilt during the twelfth. It is nearly a square about ten meters on each side and is sixteen and a half meters high. It comprises three levels and, as is usual in Coptic monasteries, is entered on the second floor by means of a drawbridge. The first floor is a warehouse for food supplies; the monks stayed on the second floor during sieges and attacks; the third floor is still occupied by a chapel dedicated to the archangel Michael. Its present structure dates from the restoration conducted under the patriarch Gabriel VII in the middle of the sixteenth century.

The Pachomian Castle

In the vast "exterior" (as it is called) courtyard a modern edifice called the Pachomian Castle represents the richness of al-Muharraq. It is a fine example of the purity and elegance of Eastern architecture at the beginning of the twentieth century. Built by the hegumen Qummus Bakhum (1905–1928), it is the episcopal residence and seat of the monastery library. It has a large hall for audiences as well as sumptuous halls for official events.

OTHER CHURCHES AND MONASTERIES

The Church of the Holy Virgin in Dalga (al-Adra)

The village of Dalga is on the edge of the Western Desert, sixteen kilometers west of Deir Muwas. The church dedicated to the Holy Virgin (al-Adra) stands in the middle of the village. Although it was substantially remodeled in the course of the centuries, the interior of the building has kept a few columns, surmounted by Corinthian capitals, belonging to the original construction from paleo-Christian times. Above the ancient entrance to the church, a bas-relief representing a cross between two gazelles was also part of the original building.

The Church of the Archangel Michael (al-Malak Mikhail)

The church of the archangel Michael (al-Malak Mikhail) in the village of Beni Magd, three kilometers west of Manfalut, is about two meters below the level of the surrounding ground. The present architectural structure dates from the seventeenth century, but the foundation of the church is certainly much older since the historian al-Maqrizi assigns it to the thirteenth century. It has a *naos* (a transverse nave), a *khurus* (choir), and a triple sanctuary. North of the last is a corridor leading to a square room divided into four bays by a central pillar; in the southwest bay is the large Epiphany basin used during the celebrations of the feast.

The Monastery of St. Theodore Stratelates (Deir Amir Tadrus)

The monastery of St. Theodore Stratelates (general, from the Greek; Deir Amir Tadrus), on the east bank of the Nile opposite the village of Beni Shuqeir and north of Manfalut, is located within an ancient abandoned cemetery. Its church was built in the great natural cave which was certainly inhabited before Christian times. It has a choir, a semi-circular sanctuary decorated with niches, and an adjacent room. In the cave, behind the church, one can see the remains of a round Epiphany basin used during the feast's celebrations.

The Monastery of al-Gabrawi

The village of al-Gabrawi is situated eight kilometers south of Abnub on the east bank of the Nile. In the middle of the village, a church dedicated to St. Victor (Mari Buqtur) dates from the eighteenth or nineteenth century. On its north side are the remains of two rows of ancient columns which apparently belonged to a forum within a *castrum* (a fortified Roman camp). At a later time the *castrum* was occupied by monks, who turned the old forum into a church. The surrounding mountains are rich in rock tombs from the pharaonic period; a great number of them were occupied by anchorites in the first Christian centuries, and painted decorations and inscriptions attest to their presence. At the foot of the mountains, there are vestiges of monastic buildings, made of unbaked bricks, which were almost certainly connected with the hermitages in the caves above.

The Churches of Manqabad

A few remains of Christian churches, probably going back to the sixth century, have recently been unearthed about twelve kilometers northwest of Asyut, near the village of Manqabad at the beginning of the road leading to the oasis of al-Kharga. A rectangular enclosure surrounds the ruins of a center which was inhabited during the Roman and Byzantine periods. Perhaps this was originally a *castrum* (a fortified camp) of the late Roman period, subsequently occupied by a monastic community. Here, the remains of three small churches with a basilican plan have been discovered, each with one nave, a choir, and one sanctuary with an apse flanked by two additional rooms.

The Monastery of the Holy Virgin near Durunka (Deir al-Adra)

The monastery of the Holy Virgin near Durunka (Deir al-Adra) is located about ten kilometers south of Asyut and is set midway up the desertic cliff. The whole monastery is visible from afar because of the imposing buildings recently erected to accommodate the thousands of pilgrims who come from all over Egypt to visit

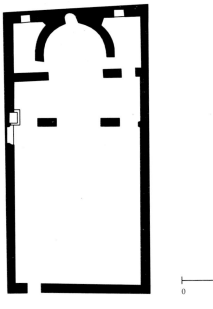

87. Manqabad.
Plan of a church with only one nave, dating from the 6th century.

198

the place where, according to tradition, the Holy Family found refuge after having left al-Muharraq. Protracted celebrations take place in the month of August to commemorate this event. The heart of the monastery is the large cave in which the Holy Family is said to have stayed and which was used as a church from the early centuries of Christianity. Previously the place had probably been exploited as a quarry during the pharaonic period.

In the vicinity of the monastery, one can see the ruins of other monasteries on the mountain, two to the north, Deir al-Izam and Deir al-Muttin, and one to the south, Deir Rifa. In this last one, a church dedicated to St. Theodore Stratelates (al-Amir Tadrus) was established inside a rock temple from the pharaonic period, while another church dedicated to the Holy Virgin (al-Adra) is entirely hewn from the rock.

The Church of St. Athanasius in Deir al-Zawya

The village of Deir al-Zawya is at the edge of the cultivated plain some twenty kilometers southeast of Asyut. It is likely that there once was a monastery in this location; its origin is poorly known but it certainly antedated the Arab conquest. Its existence is attested not only by the church dedicated to St. Athanasius at the center of the village but also by the numerous vestiges of hermitages which have been identified at the foot of the desertic cliff. The complex was probably a semi-anchoritic monastery in which the monks led their individual ascetical life in their hermitages and used the church to celebrate the liturgy together and the other communal buildings for the care of the elderly and sick monks.

The present-day church is not ancient, but it has preserved particularly precious architectural and decorative elements which belonged to the original church and date from the end of the fifth century or beginning of the sixth. Carved niches have been hollowed in the sanctuary walls; the lower part has three niches delimited by a rounded arch adorned with geometrical and floral motifs. The upper part has five smaller niches flanked by little columns with capitals, surmounted by a broken frieze, and decorated on the inside, four with a shell and one with an eagle. A frieze adorned with festoons which form circular medallions containing flowers runs along the sanctuary wall under the five niches. This decorative typology (frieze, shell, festoon which forms medallions containing flowers) is quite similar to that of the White and Red Monasteries of Sohag. The motif of the eagle with extended wings derives from Roman triumphal and funerary iconography and is found elsewhere in the Coptic edifices in the region of Thebes (Dandara, Luxor, Madinat Habu).

The Monastery of al-Balayza (Deir al-Balayza)

The extensive ruins of the monastery of al-Balayza (Deir al-Balayza) on the mountain that dominates the village of the same name lie south of Asyut some ten kilometers from Abu Tig. Its origin probably goes back to the fifth century when a few anchorites made use of quarries from the pharaonic period as places to live their ascetical life. But as early as 620 or thereabouts, Persian invaders ransacked and destroyed it, and it had to be abandoned. The buildings of a cenobitic community of monks have been discovered within a strong brick enclosure: some churches (one hewn out of a rocky cavity and another, with a basilican plan, in the southeast

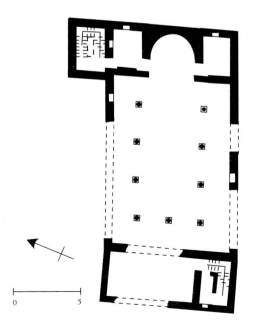

0   5

88. Monastery of al-Balayza. Plan of the main church (probably 6th century).

199

part of the monastery), two refectories, numerous cells, and other rooms. In 1907, interesting papyri, especially concerning the liturgy, were discovered in the ruins of the monastery; one of them mentions Anba Apollo as its founder.

The Monastic Foundations of Deir al-Ganadla

In the vicinity of the village of Deir al-Ganadla, some twenty kilometers south of Asyut, are ruins of ancient monastic foundations. About four kilometers west of the village, one can visit the vestiges of a monastic complex hewn out of a stone quarry from the pharaonic period. Two churches are still extant. The main one, entirely cut from the rock except for its east side, is dedicated to the Holy Virgin and goes back to the first Christian centuries. The walls and ceiling bear traces of interesting wall paintings. The second church, which is much more recent, has nine cupolas which in groups of three cover the transverse nave, choir, and triple sanctuary.

One kilometer north of Deir al-Ganadla is an area named Wadi Sarga (Valley of Sergius), rich in caves and rocky clefts which in the past sheltered Christian anchorites. Some of these caves are decorated with interesting wall paintings which can de dated from the sixth and eighth centuries; the most recognizable represents the Last Supper. A few kilometers farther north, close to the village of Dikran, are ruins of some hermitages which were probably part of five monastic complexes founded by Anba Macrobius in the sixth century. In general, each hermitage has a principal room and some smaller ones for prayer, rest, and possible guests.

The Region of Sohag and Akhmim

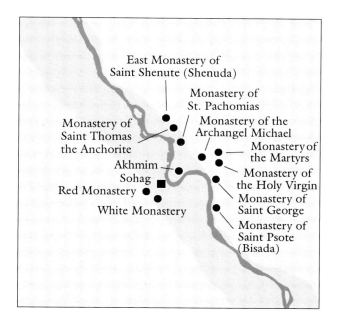

The cities of Sohag and Akhmim in middle Egypt face one another on the left and right banks of the Nile. This region is particularly rich in Coptic vestiges; among the most interesting from the historical and artistic viewpoints are the churches of the ancient and celebrated Red and White Monasteries founded at the end of the fourth century.

The White Monastery (Deir al-Abiad) and the Red Monastery (Deir al-Ahmar) are a few kilometers west of Sohag, at the edge of the desert. The White Monastery, also called the monastery of St. Shenute (Deir Anba Shenuda), is located six kilometers from the town, whereas the Red Monastery, also called the monastery of St. Pshoi (Deir Anba Bishoi), is located in a Coptic village about three and a half kilometers north of the White Monastery.

Furthermore, the territory of ancient Panopolis, today Akhmim, on the east bank of the Nile, is rich in Coptic remains, whether churches or fortified monasteries.

THE WHITE MONASTERY
(DEIR AL-ABIAD—DEIR ANBA SHENUDA)

Abbot Shenute
The extraordinary renown of the White Monastery is due to the life and works of St. Shenute (Shenuda in Arabic), one of the preeminent personalities of Egyptian monasticism. He was born about 348 into a peasant family in a village close to Akhmim (called Panopolis by the Greeks and Shmin by the Copts). At a very young age he embraced monastic life in the community founded by his maternal uncle Apa Pjol at the desert's edge on the west bank of the Nile opposite Akhmim and near the village of Athribis.

At his uncle's death in about 388, Shenute became the abbot of the monastery and contributed vigorously and passionately to its remarkable development. The monastic community founded by Pjol (Bigol in Arabic) under Pachomius' rule rapidly grew due to the arrival of many confreres attracted by Shenute's reputation for holiness. New edifices were constructed, including a large church and buildings for male and female religious. It is estimated that the land belonging to the monastery covered at least fifty square kilometers. Besa, Shenute's successor and biographer, reports that at the time of Shenute four thousand monastics depended on his monastery—two thousand monks and eighteen hundred nuns, some of whom led an anchoritic life in the surrounding caves, all the while keeping in close and constant contact with the White Monastery. Many monks and nuns lived in outbuildings which were in fact agricultural colonies supplying the needs of the whole community.

In the course of his long life, which tradition states lasted 120 years, Shenute's activity focused not only on the discipline and spiritual progress of the monastics but also on the monastery's relations with the ecclesiastical hierarchy and the administrative authorities, the struggle against the residual pockets of paganism, and the formation of a Coptic literary culture. Shenute was a passionate and authoritarian archimandrite who played his part with firmness and vigor. In contrast to Pachomius' well-balanced personality and his humble and benevolent devotion to his task, Shenute had a possessive temperament. Where Pachomius served his own monks, Shenute was their absolute master and lord. Inside the White Monastery, the discipline was particularly unyielding and most rigorously maintained. Shenute's monks were obliged to pronounce an oath at the time of their definitive commitment to monastic life: "I swear before God, in this place consecrated to him—and may the words of my lips be my witnesses—that I do not want to stain my body, I do not want to steal, I do not want to swear falsely, I do not want to lie, I do not want to do evil secretly. If I am not faithful to what I have sworn, I want to be denied the reign of heaven. May God, the witness of this oath, destroy my soul and my body in the fire of hell if I should break my oath."

In the White Monastery there were two liturgical services each day, in the morning and the evening. In contrast, the eucharistic liturgy was celebrated only on Saturday and Sunday. There were two daily meals, at noon and at sunset, even though Shenute preferred that his monks eat but one meal. The diet was especially austere and more strict than that of the Pachomian monasteries: not only were the monks to abstain from wine and meat but also from eggs, cheese, and fish.

Shenute showed an intransigent harshness in his dealings with remaining pagan rituals. He regularly organized punitive expeditions to destroy and burn temples and to knock down idols. On these occasions, his ardor and that of his monks spared the pagans neither blows nor beatings with sticks. On the other hand, he showed himself charitable toward the poor, cared for the sick, and gave hospitality to all who asked for help. In fact, when the Blemmye/Beja tribes invaded the Thebaid, the doors of the White Monastery were opened to succor thousands of fleeing refugees.

Shenute is regarded as a pillar of the Egyptian Church because he contributed to the defense of orthodoxy at the side of Cyril, the patriarch of Alexandria. In 431, at the venerable age of eighty-three, he attended the council of Ephesus, at which the Nestorian doctrine was condemned. Nestorius, the bishop of Constantinople, stressed the difference between the "humanity" and "divinity" of Christ and had opposed the venerated tradition which declared the Holy Virgin to be the Mother of God (Theotokos), proposing to rather call her the Mother of Christ (Christotokos) since she had given birth only to the human component of Christ.

Moreover, Shenute enriched Coptic literature, of which he is a preeminent author. Well versed in Greek philosophy, mythology, and literature, he worked at giving the Coptic tongue the expressive qualities of a genuine literary language. He thus contributed to the cultivation and reinforcement of Egyptian identity, which succeeded in withstanding the Arab invasion and the expansion of Islam. Written in Sahidic Coptic, Shenute's work includes homilies, sermons, letters, and theological treatises, of which unfortunately only fragments have come down to us. Shenute also made the White Monastery into a center of Coptic culture where the monks translated the Fathers of the Church, made the Coptic version of the Bible uniform, and created a large library of religious and literary texts. This multiform activity was a fundamental contribution to the unity of the Coptic Church, especially about the middle of the fifth century, a time when it was separating itself from the Roman and Byzantine Church by adhering to its Monophysite convictions.

The Dark Centuries

At the death of Shenute, Besa, his biographer, succeeded him in the charge of archimandrite. He also had a remarkable personality and wrote many works in Coptic, especially letters and homilies. His successor was Zenobius, disciple and *notarios* (secretary) of Shenute.

We have only sparse and fragmentary information about the history of the monastery in the following centuries. Inscriptions on the wall paintings in the apse of the church shed some light on the end of the eleventh century and beginning of the twelfth; written in Armenian, they attest to the presence of an Armenian monastic community to which we owe not only the wall paintings in the apse but also extensive works of restoration. In 1137, when he was stripped of his powers, the Armenian Tag al-Dawla, a vizier under the caliph al-Hafiz, withdrew to the White Monastery to lead the monastic life. The Armenian presence and the important works of embellishment and restoration undertaken then coincide with a period when the Armenians were particularly influential at the court of the Fatimid caliphs and when Christian churches and monasteries received many donations. The splendor which the monastery knew during the first half of the twelfth century came to an end when soldiers of Shirkuh, the Kurdish general, attacked the monastery in about 1168 and desecrated Shenute's tomb.

In the thirteenth century the historian Abu Salih speaks of a large church able to accommodate one hundred persons and containing the relics of the apostles Simon and Bartholomew. In the course of that century, a considerable work of restoration must have taken place because of severe earthquakes between 1202 and 1260 which shook the monastery buildings. The history of the monastery in the following centuries is almost totally unknown. At some point, it is certain that it was abandoned and occupied by Coptic families. It is only since 1984 that the monastery has had a few monks and that work has been done to remove from the inside of the church the provisional arrangements done rather recently to provide shelter for the families living there. Furthermore, archaeologists have begun excavations which have brought to light the vestiges of ancient monastic buildings west of the church.

The Church of St. Shenute

Since Arab times, the stone used for its construction, an especially light-colored sandstone, gave the church of St. Shenute the name White Monastery (Deir al-Abiad). The mass of the edifice is particularly impressive and its block-like forms recall those of the architecture of pharaonic times, devoid of any exterior decoration but endowed with an extraordinary monumentality in its volume. The exterior walls, slightly slanted, are made of large stone blocks taken from buildings of the pharaonic era in the neighboring city of Athribis. On some of these stones, decorative motifs and hieroglyphs indicate their original destination, for instance, on the west side of the church, the left pillar of the main entrance door and the frieze near the northwest corner; on the south side, the right pillar of the secondary door.

The study of the decorations of these stones and inscriptions has demonstrated that they belonged to edifices dating from periods between the twenty-sixth and twenty-ninth dynasties (664–380 B.C.E.). What led Shenute and his monks to utilize these stones was not only an obvious concern for economy but also the satisfaction of their iconoclastic fury against the remnants of paganism. The foundation of this building goes back to the last years of Shenute's life, as is incontestably confirmed by all his biographies. The experts usually agree to place the date of construction about 440. The rectangular exterior walls are seventy-five meters in length and thirty-seven in width. The interior of the church is a basilica with a nave ending in a triconch sanctuary, two

89. View of the White Monastery, from Girolamo Segato, *Atlante Monumentale dell' Alto e Basso Egitto* (1837).

side aisles, and on the west a return aisle, as well as a narthex, also on the west, and a large rectangular room along the south.

The present entrance is on the south side because the main entrance on the west as well as the secondary ones have been walled up. Originally, the building had six entrance gates: two on the west, two on the south, and two on the north. The entrance leads into a large rectangular hall forty-six meters long and eight meters wide; on the west this space ends in a fine apse with six columns, and on the east in a wall where a door flanked by two graceful niches opens into a square room. It is difficult to determine with any certainty the original function of such a large space. From a strictly architectural viewpoint, one can compare it to the narthex of certain churches of Tur Abdin in northern Mesopotamia, which was similarly placed along the south side. But contrary to the churches of Tur Abdin, the White Monastery also possesses the traditional narthex on the west. It is perhaps more plausible to see this vast room as a gathering place or a refectory in which the monks assembled for the agape after the liturgical celebration. On the sides of the room one can see brick constructions which certainly were not part of the original edifice but which were probably added in the Middle Ages when the wooden roof was replaced by cupolas.

One goes into the church proper through a door facing the entrance. The nave is twelve meters wide, and the side aisles are separated from it by two series of columns which are connected on the west side. Standing on high plinths, these columns differ from one another both in their dimensions and structure: some are monolithic, others have a shaft composed of many drums, still others are made of bricks. This diversity shows in an irrefutable way that, like the capitals and friezes, some of the columns once belonged to older edifices from the Roman period. The colonnades were surmounted by a second order of smaller columns which crowned the upper galleries on three sides. In the original wooden roof, beams placed crosswise in relation to the principal axis supported the floor of the galleries and terraces, while massive rafters supported the gable roof covering the central nave. Given the scarcity of wood in Egypt, it must have been very difficult to procure beams of such length. This is why it was impossible to replace it by the same material when the roof finally collapsed in the Middle Ages, so the builders erected a wall in front of the presbytery in order to form a sort of transept roofed with a cupola, leaving the greater part of the nave open to the sky. At that time, since the number of monks was much smaller than before the Arab invasion, the vast spaces of the church had lost their primary function and could be adapted to other uses such as lodgings for the monks and pilgrims. Consequently, brick partitions were erected which were removed from the original edifice only a few years ago.

In the nave before the door leading to the sanctuary, one can observe traces of the floor of the bema, the area of the church where certain liturgical functions took place. Toward the center of the nave, against the north colonnade, a granite monolith in which five steps have been carved is all that is left from the abbot's chair. On the west side, a door leads to the narthex, whose ends have apses formed by columns disposed in a semi-circle. Behind the south apse, a staircase gave access to the upper galleries. The large room located in the southwest corner of the church complex was rebuilt after its collapse in the beginning of the nineteenth century, a fact that prevents us from knowing what its original structure was. But even today, one can draw water from a well which surely existed when the monastery was founded.

The area of the presbytery of the ancient church, which today is separated from the nave by a high wall, is exceptionally interesting. Its structure is a triconch (or "in trefoil"), characterized by three apses opening on three sides of the rectangle and the fourth side opening onto the nave. The walls of the apses are decorated with niches framed by columns; each apse contains two superposed orders of five niches and six columns. The alternation of niches and columns is not an architectural innovation but continues a Hellenistic tradition. The decoration of the niches, which have a broken tympanum, is especially interesting. The semi-domes of the three apses are decorated with wall paintings executed in the twelfth century by Armenian and Egyptian workshops. The decoration of the main apse (east) represents the vision of Ezekiel with Christ enthroned in the center and in the extremities four medallions depicting the evangelists. The wall painting of the south apse shows a great blue cross which has a piece of red material hanging from its arms and is encircled by a halo held by angels; this principal composition is framed by the images of the Holy Virgin and St. John. The arches of the apses are painted with medallions representing angels, saints, and prophets.

The Other Buildings of the Monastery
West of the large church complex, vestiges of monastic buildings, which were part of the original nucleus of the monastery, have been discovered. There were rooms to receive visitors, cells for the monks, kitchens, and a refectory.

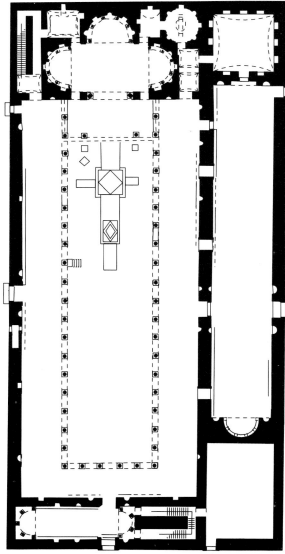

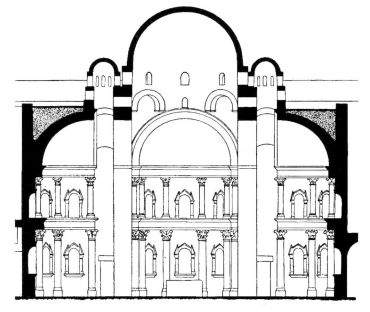

90. White Monastery.

Top of page: apse with columns in the narthex and a decorated niche.

Remainder of page: plan of the church and cross section (middle of 5th century).

0   10

Historical Information

Almost everything about the Red Monastery is unknown. It owes its name to the color of its construction material, red brick, which differentiates it from the White Monastery; however, it architecturally resembles that monastery and is probably contemporaneous with it.

The St. Pshoi (Bishoi in Arabic), to whom the monastery is dedicated, is not to be confused with his homonym from the celebrated monastery in Wadi al-Natrun; he was a contemporary of Apa Pjol, the founder of the White Monastery, and the probable founder of the Red Monastery. In his *Life of Shenute* Besa has this allusion, "The holy apa Pjol and the young man Shenoute went out walking together, and with them also went apa Pšoi [Pshoi] from Mt Psōou. He too was a holy man who walked after godly things" (Besa 9, p. 44). One can therefore identify "Psōou" [Psou] with the Red Monastery.

The fifteenth century Arab historian al-Maqrizi names the monastery but says nothing about its history. Therefore, it is possible that it was closely connected with that of the White Monastery. The Frenchman Dominique Vivant Denon, who visited Egypt during Napoleon's campaign in 1798–1799, states that the monastery had been ransacked and burned down by the Mamluks a few days before his arrival. Today the Red Monastery is not occupied by monks, but its church still serves the Coptic communities of the surrounding villages and the pilgrims who come on the big feasts of the liturgical year.

The Church of St. Pshoi

Built in the second half of the fifth century, the church of St. Pshoi is architecturally similar to that of St. Shenute at the White Monastery. But besides the difference in the building material (brick instead of stone), the church of the Red Monastery is of more modest dimensions (forty-four meters in length and twenty-three in width) and does not have a west narthex; all the other architectural elements are identical: the nave with the small side aisles connected on the west, the upper galleries, the triconch sanctuary, and the large rectangular room on the south side of the edifice. The separation between this room and the church has been destroyed but its place is easily identifiable.

However, a more attentive analysis of this church reveals other particularities that differentiate it from that of St. Shenute. An examination of the portals and columns (bases, shafts, and capitals), for example, shows clearly that they were made for this building; on the contrary, as we have seen, some of the materials used in the construction and decoration of the White Monastery were obviously borrowed from edifices dating from the pharaonic or Roman period. Another architectural element distinguishes the church of the Red Monastery from that of the White Monastery: the two columns before the presbytery. The relative narrowness of the triumphal arch, for reasons of stability, created a discordance between the wide nave and the narrow passage into the presbytery; the addition of two big columns was a clever artistic and architectural invention which brilliantly resolved the aesthetic problem by removing the discrepancy between the dimensions of the nave and those of the entry to the sanctuary. This decorative device was subsequently utilized in practically all churches having a narrow entry into the presbytery.

The triconch sanctuary is splendid: the three apses are embellished by two orders of superposed niches separated by small elegant columns whose completely painted surfaces lend to the spaces' richness and sacredness. The motif of the broken tympanum surmounting each niche is especially interesting. As in the White Monastery, the collapse of the roof and the lack of monastic vocations led sometime in the Middle Ages to the construction of a wall in front of the presbytery, which diminished the space destined for liturgical celebrations.

THE TERRITORY OF AKHMIM

The City of Akhmim

The present name of the city derives from the ancient Egyptian Khent-min and the Coptic Khmin or Shmin. Located on the east bank of the Nile opposite the city of Sohag, Akhmim was the flourishing center of the ninth nome of upper Egypt. Scant traces remain from this glorious past because in the course of centuries the building materials of the temples have been reused for new constructions.

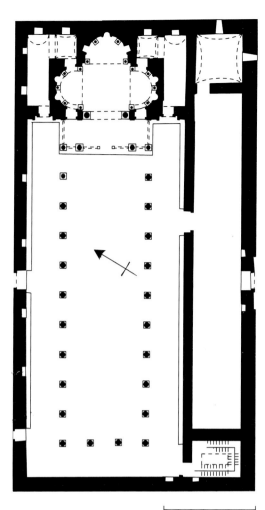

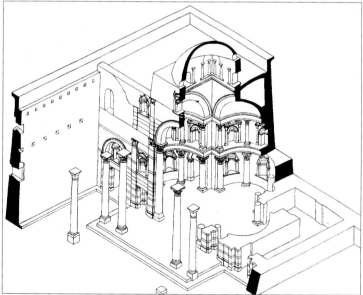

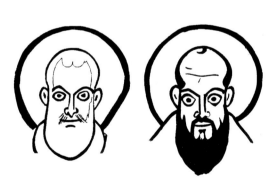

91. Red Monastery.

Above, left: niche of the apse.

Above, right: original plan of the church (second half of 5th century).

Below, left: axonometric section of the choir area.

Below, right: heads of Sts. Mark and Paul (from wall paintings in the apse).

207

The city owes its name to Min, the god of fertility, protector of the Eastern Desert and the cities of Qift and Akhmim. The Greeks identified the god with Pan, which is why the city took the name of Panopolis during classical antiquity.

The Churches of Akhmim

Akhmim has kept some ancient examples of religious Coptic architecture: the churches of St. Dimiana (Sitt Dimiana), the Holy Virgin (al-Adra), and St. Mercurius. The first two, built back to back, are in the north section of the city; St. Dimiana is the older and dates from the sixteenth–seventeenth centuries. Both churches have a triple sanctuary and are roofed with cupolas. The church of St. Mercurius (Abu al-Seifein) stands in the center of the city. It dates from the sixteenth–seventeenth centuries and has a triple sanctuary with semi-circular apses adorned with niches. Originally, the sanctuaries had adjacent rooms on their south and north sides; the south room still exists but the north one was destroyed in the course of the eighteenth and nineteenth centuries to enlarge the church by providing it with three more sanctuaries.

Monasteries and Churches North of Akhmim

Among the many monasteries north of Akhmim, those of St. Pachomius, St. Thomas the Anchorite, and St. Shenute have a certain interest.

The monastery dedicated to St. Pachomius (Deir Anba Bakhum) and his sister Dalusham, who were martyrs at the time of Diocletian, is located about twelve kilometers north of Akhmim in a village on the road to Saqulta. The monastery has been almost entirely destroyed except for the church, from which some elements belonging to the original building dating from the seventh century remain: the main sanctuary with its apse, the south apse, and the additional room in the southeast corner. Initially, the church must have had a triconch sanctuary and a nave with two side aisles, similar but on a more modest scale to that of the White Monastery at Sohag. In subsequent times, the basilican nave was destroyed and the building enlarged on the north. This transformation entailed the destruction of the north apse and the addition of two other sanctuaries.

The monastery of St. Thomas the Anchorite (Deir Anba Tuma) is located at Arab Beni Wasil near Saqulta, some fifteen kilometers north of Akhmim. Thomas lived between the end of the third century and beginning of the fourth. Being a bishop, he took part in the council of Nicaea in 325. The ancient monastery, of which only the small church and some other rooms still exist, is occupied today by a single monk. The plan

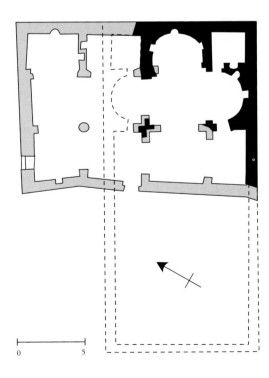

92. Akhmim. Monastery of
St. Pachomius.
Plan of the church.
In black: original construction
still extant (7th century).
In grey: later construction.
Dotted lines: original construction
no longer extant.

0   5

Preceding pages:
71. White Monastery, church of St. Shenute. The great nave (middle of 5th century).

72. White Monastery. Exterior view of the renowned monastic complex which developed in the course of the first half of the 5th century around the charismatic figure of Abbot Shenute.

73, 74. White Monastery, church of St. Shenute. Details of the triconch apse, characterized by niches and superposed columns.

Following pages:
75. Red Monastery. Exterior view of the monastery, founded in the 5th century; its structure is similar to that of the White Monastery, but different in its building material, red brick, whose color gave it its name.

76, 77. Monastery of the Holy Virgin (Deir al-Adra) and Monastery of the Martyrs (Deir al-Shuhada) near the village of al-Hawawish in the region of Akhmim.

of the church comprises a transverse nave with three bays and a triconch sanctuary which possesses an apse decorated with niches. The building dates from the sixteenth-seventeenth centuries.

The Eastern Monastery of St. Shenute (Deir Anba Shenuda al-Sharqi), so named to distinguish it from the well-known monastery near Sohag, is found some twenty kilometers north of Akhmim. Its church dates from the sixteenth-seventeenth centuries and presents the characteristics of the Akhmim churches with three sanctuaries and two side rooms. The nave is divided crosswise by a series of four columns.

The Monasteries of al-Hawawish

Al-Hawawish is a village located five kilometers from Akhmim on the drivable road east of the Nile. About five kilometers east of the village, one sees three fortified monasteries one kilometer or so apart from each other; they are dedicated respectively to the archangel Michael (al-Malak Mikhail), the Martyrs (al-Shuhada), and the Holy Virgin (al-Adra).

The monastery of the archangel Michael is the northernmost. The Arab historian al-Maqrizi makes mention of it, specifying that when he visited the place in the fifteenth century, there was only one monk and the monastic buildings served only for receiving pilgrims and sheltering donkeys and horses. The large church dates from somewhere between the fifteenth and seventeenth centuries. The columns, tympanums, and circular base of the cupola are decorated with motifs in red brick. Like almost all churches in the Akhmim region, its plan has three sanctuaries and two adjacent rooms north and south of the side sanctuaries. Behind the sanctuaries, there is a long connecting passage called a *difir*. From north to south, the sanctuaries are dedicated respectively to St. Mercurius, the archangel Michael, and St. George. On June 19 and November 21, the feast of St.

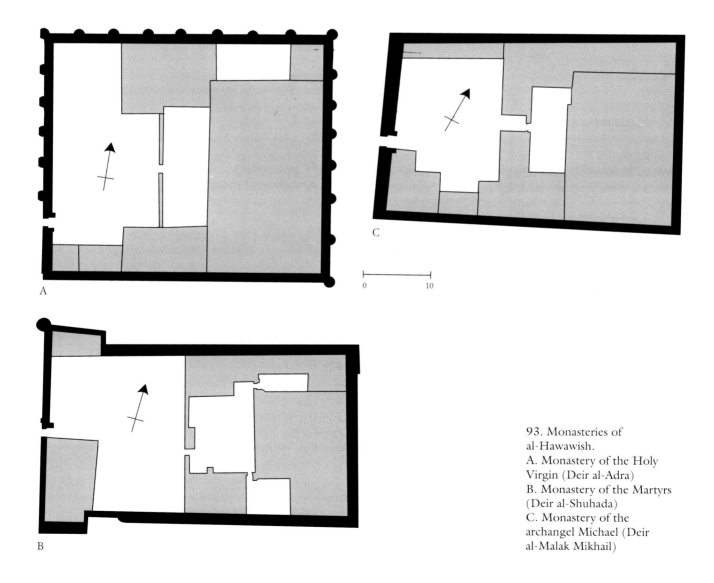

93. Monasteries of
al-Hawawish.
A. Monastery of the Holy
Virgin (Deir al-Adra)
B. Monastery of the Martyrs
(Deir al-Shuhada)
C. Monastery of the
archangel Michael (Deir
al-Malak Mikhail)

217

Michael, the monastery is filled with hundreds of pilgrims who gather to attend the special celebrations in honor of the archangel.

South of the monastery of the archangel Michael, the monastery of the Martyrs (Deir al-Shuhada) is also protected by high walls. With a nearly square plan, the church has a nave, divided into rows of five bays, and three sanctuaries. The middle sanctuary has an apse decorated with niches. Very precious ancient fabrics have been recovered from the many tombs surrounding the monastery. It is probable that this monastery was constructed where the martyrs of Akhmim had been buried in the first centuries of the Christian era.

The monastery of the Holy Virgin (Deir al-Adra) is situated farther south. Its walls delineate a square area with the church in its southeast part. The building dates from the sixteenth-seventeenth centuries and presents the characteristic plan of the Akhmim churches, with three sanctuaries having apses and side rooms. As in the monastery of the archangel Michael, a long vaulted passage called a *difir* runs behind the sanctuaries. Later on, two other chapels were added on the north side. The nave, subdivided into two rows of five bays by a series of four columns, is decorated with red and black bricks laid alternately.

Monasteries South of Akhmim

The districts south of Akhmim have two monasteries possessing a certain interest, those of St. George and St. Psote (Bisada in Arabic). The monastery of St. George (Deir Mari Girgis al-Hadidi) is located some ten kilometers south of Akhmim, on the east road of the Nile; the word *hadidi* means "iron" and refers to the entrance portal of the monastery, which was covered with iron. Originally, the monastery was dedicated to Eulogius and Arsenius, two Syrians who underwent martyrdom at that place. The church conforms to the traditional plan of the Akhmim territory: a transverse nave subdivided by a rank of columns, three deep sanctuaries, and two additional side rooms. The bays formed by the columns as well as the sanctuaries are roofed with cupolas, the largest being before the middle sanctuary. The present edifice probably dates from the sixteenth-seventeenth centuries.

The monastery of St. Psote (Deir Anba Bisada) stands about eighteen kilometers from Akhmim, in the village of Ahaywa Sharq on the east road of the Nile. The central part of the church is very old and probably goes back to the early Christian centuries. The principal apse (on the east) and traces of the south apse are all that is extant today. South of the main sanctuary, the remains of St. Psote, a bishop and martyr of the fourth century, are preserved in a room which belonged to the ancient church. Above its door is a stone in which an ankh is carved, the symbol of life in the time of the pharaohs, a sign reused in the paleo-Christian era to associate the cross with eternal life. Through this room one has access to a further room in which there is a baptismal font.

The Thebaid

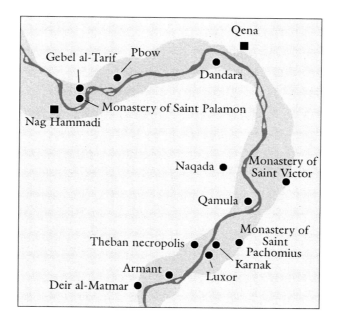

The name Thebaid comes from the name of the ancient pharaonic capital Thebes (today Luxor), in upper Egypt. During the Ptolemaic and Roman periods, this name designated a rather vast geographical and administrative territory; however, we shall use it in the following pages to define the region of Luxor. In the Christian world, the term "thebaid" has taken on the meaning of a place of solitude and asceticism for anchorites and monastics because this region was, above any other, the theater of the extraordinary development of Christian anchoritism.

THE MONASTERIES OF ST. PACHOMIUS

Pachomius and Cenobitism

Pachomius, the father of Christian cenobitic monasticism, was born to pagan parents in upper Egypt about 292–294. Having enlisted in the imperial army at the age of twenty, he was very moved by the charity with which some Christians offered their moral and material help to the recruits. He then decided to consecrate his life to God. He had himself catechized and baptized and three years later withdrew from the world to live an anchoritic life by following the teaching of his spiritual father Palamon. One day after a few years of asceticism, arriving in the village of Tabennisi, he heard a voice which, according to the anonymous author of the *Life of Pachomius,* told him, "Pachomius, struggle, dwell in this place and build a monastery; for many will come to you to become monks with you, and they will profit their souls" (Veilleux, 39). Pachomius stayed in Tabennisi, founded a monastery, and organized his *koinonia* ("congregation") at the time the first anchoritic colonies arose in northern Egypt. For the monks "he established an irreproachable life-style and traditions profitable for their souls in rules [which he took] from the holy Scriptures: absolute equality in their clothing and food, and decent sleeping arrangements" (Veilleux, 46). "He appointed some from among the capable brothers as his assistants to take care of their souls' salvation. [He appointed] one [of them] at the head of the first house, that of the lesser stewards, with a second to help him in preparing the tables and in cooking for [the brothers]. [He appointed] another brother also, with his second . . . to look after the food and the care of the sick brothers. . . . And at the doorway [he appointed] other brothers . . . to receive visitors. Similarly, [he appointed] other faithful brothers to transact sales and make purchases. They performed *in fear and trembling* the task assigned by the housemaster. He appointed still others . . . to work at the shops and at mat-making" (Veilleux, 48–49).

According to the rule he had introduced, the members of the community were to share everything they possessed. The Pachomian monks could not possess anything, dispose of anything since everything belonged to all; they could neither give, lend, nor destroy since they "did not possess anything," and they could not receive anything either since any gift belonged to the community. Cenobitism—a term deriving from the two Greek words *koinos* (common) and *bios* (life)—represented the choice to live in community, implying on the part of the monks the renunciation of their independence and their total devotion to the service of others. The detailed regulations perfected by Pachomius stated with precision what the work, prayer, clothing, and food would be for each monastic and condemned any individual initiative. Pachomius' aim was to arrive at a genuine unanimity, "one heart and one soul," thanks to the services that the monks rendered to one another.

Tabennisi, Pbow, and Chenoboskion, the three principal monasteries of Pachomius, were in the area lying between the present towns of Nag Hammadi and Qena, fifty kilometers apart. The first monastery he founded was Tabennisi in about 320 on the banks of the Nile east of the town of Dishna. Nothing has survived from the ancient monastic establishment—without doubt because the materials used in its construction (mud and unbaked brick) were fragile and because the site of the monastery, set on the banks of the Nile, was subject to the slow erosion caused by the floods of the river.

The monastery of Pbow was located in the present village of Faw Qibli, where Pachomius died in 346. Evocative vestiges of an impressive basilica have survived to our time; in contrast, there remains nothing from the monastery of Chenoboskion, which was located near the present village of Qasr al-Sayyad. However, a large monastery dedicated to St. Palamon, Pachomius' master and spiritual father, although recently constructed, confirms the ancient monastic tradition of the place.

The Monastery of St. Palamon (Deir Anba Balamun)
The monastery of St. Palamon, the great ascetic and master of St. Pachomius, stands one kilometer south of the village of Qasr al-Sayyad, on the right bank of the Nile, some ten kilometers east of Nag Hammadi. Palamon was one of the first anchorites in Egypt and lived not far from the present monastery, in the desertic area on the mountain slopes. His asceticism was characterized by an extreme rigor at the limit of human capacity: he practiced with particular relentlessness prayer, fasting, and all sorts of bodily abstinence. It is perhaps Pachomius' anchoritic training at Palamon's side which caused him to reflect on the necessity of leading a more moderate ascetical life, less physically traumatizing in order not to endanger bodily health, in Pachomius' opinion the indispensable condition to live a fuller mystical life.

The monastery counts three churches, dedicated to St. Mercurius (Abu al-Seifein), St. Palamon (Anba Balamun), and St. Dimiana (Sitt Dimiana). This last one is the oldest building of all; it is about one and a half meters below the level of the courtyard and has a single sanctuary preceded by a nave and a south room intended

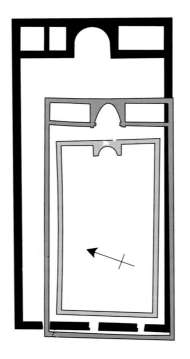
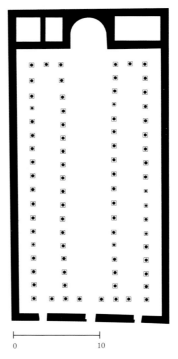

94. Church of the monastery of Pbow.

Left: hypothetical plan of the exterior walls and apse in its three successive phases of construction.
In light grey: first half of the 4th century.
In dark grey: beginning of the 5th century.
In black: middle of the 5th century.

Right: plan of the church dating from the middle of the 5th century (459).

for women. The churches of St. Mercurius and St. Palamon are rather recent in their present structure and do not offer any particular architectural interest.

The Basilica of the Monastery of Pbow
Where the village of Faw Qibli stands today, some fifteen kilometers east of Qasr al-Sayyad, there once stood the great Pachomian monastery of Pbow, from which the present name Faw derives. The monastery was probably established about 330, and the anonymous author of the *Life of Pachomius* depicts it in these terms: "As the number of the brothers increased at the monastery of Tabennisi, he saw that they were cramped for lack of room, and he began to ask the Lord about it. He was told in a vision, 'Go north to that deserted village lying downriver from you which is called Phbow, and build a monastery for yourself. It will become a base and a source of renown for you in all ages to come.' At once, he took some brothers with him, went north to that village and spent some days with the brothers until he had built a wall for the monastery. Later he built the little celebration room with the permission of the bishop of Diospolis (today H'éou [Hiw]), and he likewise built the houses. He appointed housemasters with seconds, according to the rules of the first monastery [Tabennisi]. He himself kept watch over the two communities day and night, as a servant of the Good Shepherd" (Veilleux, 71).

Pbow quickly became the principal monastery of the Pachomian *koinonia,* to such an extent that Pachomius moved there and installed his disciple Theodore as the superior of the monastery of Tabennisi. From then on Pbow became the residence of the superior general of the whole monastic *koinonia.*

From this prestigious Pachomian monastery, only the monumental ruins of the great basilica, built with stone and baked bricks, are still extant, its columns lying in disorder on the ground. In contrast, nothing remains from the other monastic buildings, probably made of unbaked brick, a very fragile material, especially in a region such as Pbow, particularly fertile and rich in water.

Three consecutive phases of construction have been identified in the church area. Of the oldest, one can recognize only a few elements of the east and north walls as well as vestiges of stylobates—which would point to a plan with several aisles. This first phase goes back to Pachomius, and therefore one can place the construction before 346, the year of Pachomius' death. In the beginning of the fifth century, a larger church with a nave and four side aisles was erected. This step was made necessary by the great number of monks who had flocked to the monastery. The nave and aisles were rather narrow, in particular the outer ones connected on the west to form a sort of ambulatory. The sanctuary had a semi-elliptical apse and was flanked by two adjacent rooms. Toward the middle of the fifth century, the church once more proved too small to accommodate the considerable number of monks, and it was necessary to replace it with a new edifice, still larger, which according to written sources was consecrated in 459. This church also had four side aisles, the outer ones especially narrow and serving as an ambulatory by being connected on the west side; the semi-circular apse had several rooms on either side. The great columns, still visible today, belong to this last phase of construction and are made of reused material from Roman edifices of the third century or beginning of the fourth. It is curious to see the nave rather narrow in comparison with the aisles: its width is only one and a half times that of the intermediary aisles of the church built in the beginning of the fifth century and one and two thirds times that of the intermediary aisles dating from 459. These characteristics make the church of the monastery of Pbow a magnificent example of monastic architecture of the purest Egyptian tradition which has not yet acquired and appropriated the traditional models of Byzantine basilicas, which were nevertheless already present and well-known throughout Egypt.

The monastery quickly began to decline and the church slowly fell into ruins. The Fatimid caliph al-Hakim (996–1021) completed its destruction when he ransacked its building materials.

THE GNOSTIC CODICES OF NAG HAMMADI

The Discovery of the Codices at Gebel al-Tarif
The rocky massif of Gebel al-Tarif stands about three kilometers from the village of al-Qasr, on the desert edge. Here on its slopes, the renowned Gnostic codices subsequently called "library of Nag Hammadi" were discovered, one of the major archaeological discoveries of the twentieth century. The story of their discovery reads like fiction and goes back to December 1945 when a peasant from al-Qasr, a certain Muhammad Ali al-Samman, went with his brothers to the slopes of the mountain to gather some fertilizer. While digging near a big rock, he discovered a large jar closed with a lid and sealed with bitumen; having opened it, he

found thirteen codices bound in leather. During the following days, the brothers gave the codices to acquaintances they trusted because, being themselves guilty of a grave crime, they feared that the police might find them out in the course of an eventual search of their home. The truth is that the brothers had avenged their father's assassination by discovering the guilty man, killing him, and ferociously mutilating the corpse—they had drawn and quartered him, ripped his heart out and devoured it.

By chance, one of the codices fell into the hands of a history teacher named Raghib Andarawus, who took it to Cairo in October 1946 and delivered it to the director of the Coptic Museum, Togo Mina. The following year the manuscript was shown to the great French Egyptologist, Jean Doresse, who immediately realized the scientific value of this discovery. Rapidly, thanks to Raghib's precious pieces of information, the other twelve codices were retrieved, one of which was already in the hands of an antique dealer in Cairo.

Today, the thirteen codices are kept in the Coptic Museum of Cairo; only a few sheets and one binding are missing: the mother of Muhammad Ali al-Samman unfortunately used them to light the fire.

Gnosticism and the Thirteen Codices

The codices of Nag Hammadi constitute a fairly complete Gnostic library. Gnosticism is a cultural movement which spread between the first and fourth centuries C.E.; it was born and developed from a disenchanted vision of the world and of the Christian event itself. Pain, suffering, disease, and death, together with the victorious presence of evil prove, the Gnostics thought, the intrinsically negative character of the world and therefore the "non-perfection" of the creator of the world, the demiurge, an evil being cast by its own fault or by ignorance into the emptiness outside divine plenitude. However, beyond and above the demiurge, there is God the Most High, a perfect and merciful being who sent the Savior to reveal God's own existence to the ignorant world. The Most High God is good and superior to the demiurge. But the revelation of Christ is reserved for those who still have within themselves a spark of the divine spirit, the "spirituals," who alone have the ability to understand his real message. For the spirituals, the true Gnostics, this "knowledge" (*gnōsis* in Greek) is a guarantee of salvation. But the knowledge is not the privilege of everyone. Indeed, not all human beings are complete: most of them are only bodies devoid of souls, the "physicals," destined to die without leaving a trace; others have a soul, the "psychicals" or "animals"; but those who possess in themselves the divine spark, the "pneumatics" or "spirituals" for whom is reserved the salvific revelation of Christ, are very few.

The Gnostic texts of Nag Hammadi are 52 in number; the thirteen codices in which they are gathered total 1,240 pages. The homogeneity of their contents and their complementarity prove indisputably that they constitute a fairly complete religious corpus.

The Dating of the Manuscripts and Their Historical Context

Paleographic analyses of the manuscripts enable the experts to date the codices from the latter half of the fourth century. Their leather bindings have shed significant light on the research because they have been

95. The *Apokryphon of John,* codex from the third quarter of the 4th century, part of the "Gnostic library of Nag Hammadi."

96. Gebel al-Tarif, where by chance the thirteen codices in Coptic, which constitute a fairly complete collection of Gnostic texts, were discovered in a large jar in 1945.

222

made rigid by a sort of cardboard made of letters and other private documents whose contents allow them to be dated with a minimal margin of error. These documents comprise contracts concerning the sale of fabrics, private letters to laypersons and monastics probably belonging to the monasteries of Chenoboskion and Pbow, bills for the sale of wine and cereals, receipts for various supplies, official texts mentioning the two provinces of the Thebaid (indeed the Thebaid was divided into two *epitrope* between 298 and 323).

However, if the bindings permit the texts to be dated between the end of the third century and the beginning of the fourth, they do not tell us when the original texts themselves were written. Their content leads one to think that some of them were completed as early as the beginning of the second century C.E. It is possible that the *Apokryphon of John* was used by Iraeneus of Lyons (140–202) in his *Against the Heresies* as the source of his knowledge of the Barbelognostics, Sethians, and Ophites. *The Gospel of Truth* is connected to Valentinian Gnosticism, which Iraeneus also violently attacked; the *Letter of Reginus* shows clearly the divergent interpretations regarding the resurrection of Christ which appeared in the course of the second century; the *Gospel of Thomas* asserts the uselessness of circumcision and on this topic draws upon the vehement debate which occurred in the years 130–135. One may conclude that the codices of Nag Hammadi are translations into the Coptic language, into the dialects of Sahidic and sub-Akmimic upper Egypt, of original texts in Greek written in all likelihood in some Judeo-Christian milieux at the time of Alexandrian Gnosticism.

The question posed by the existence of such a complete library of the Gnostic texts is: In what historical context were these manuscripts concealed? Originally, the hiding place was probably one of the many caves and rocky hollows which abound on Gebel al-Tarif and were used as burial places in former times. Because of a slight landslide, perhaps of recent date, the crevice in which the jar with the manuscripts had been hidden would have been brought to the surface, thus facilitating their discovery. The care with which the codices were hidden, their elegance, and the meticulously made bindings prove without a doubt that the person who concealed them did not have the slightest intention of letting them go but wanted them safely preserved from likely destruction. Who could have destroyed them and for what reason? These questions find a very credible answer in the historical and religious context of the Egypt of the second half of the fourth century.

In 367, Athanasius, patriarch of Alexandria, wrote the *Thirty-ninth Festal (Paschal) Letter,* in which he listed the canonical books of the Old and New Testaments and hurled violent criticism against "heretical" books. It is known that the letter was translated from Greek into Coptic by Theodore, the disciple of Pachomius and abbot of the monastery of Tabennisi, and that the text was circulated in all the monasteries of Egypt. In those years, Christianity was the most widespread religion in the whole empire and was rapidly becoming the state religion. In the cities, the campaigns against the heretics were intensifying, promoted by the bishops and their followers, and it was forbidden to possess books other than those declared "orthodox." It is in this climate of tension and upheaval that the manuscripts were hidden by their unknown owners. One should not rule out—it is even a rather reasonable hypothesis—that these owners were the monks from one of the many Pachomian monasteries of the region, perhaps from the monastery of Chenoboskion, which was only three kilometers away from the place chosen to hide the manuscripts. This would confirm the depth and duration of the influence exercised by the Gnostic heresy on early monasticism.

If Gnosticism caused misunderstandings that tore apart the early Christian communities, it also aroused reactions and contributed to the vitality of the Alexandrian Church, to which the dynamism of doctrinal conflicts gave the strength to grow by vigorously imposing its orthodoxy. The Gnostic heresy had the invaluable merit to be within Christianity a critical element which fostered the evolutionary process of its doctrine and dogmas.

DANDARA

The Sacred Enclosure of Hathor

Dandara is on the left bank of the Nile and opposite the city of Qena. Called Tantere in the ancient Egyptian language and Tentyris in Greek, it was the main city of the sixth nome of upper Egypt and a leading center, especially because of the worship of the goddess Hathor. There are still considerable vestiges of her temple.

The temple and the sacred enclosure of Hathor lie at the edge of the cultivated area and cover a vast area delimited by an enclosure wall. Side by side with Hathor, the goddess of the sky and of love, her divine spouse Horus, the falcon-god, was also worshipped in Dandara, and so was their son Ihy, the young god of music. The most solemn celebrations took place on the occasion of the year-end festivities.

The foundation of the sacred complex of Dandara goes back to the beginnings of the Old Kingdom, probably to the time of the pharaoh Cheops (fourth dynasty) and Pepi I (sixth dynasty). However, in the course of the centuries, the temples were restored or rebuilt several times. Therefore, the edifices still extant today date from more recent periods and comprise, besides the large temple of Hathor (first–second centuries C.E.), two *mammisi*, the sacred space where Ihy was born, the first one built under the pharaoh Nectanebo I (fourth century B.C.E.) and the second under Nero (first century C.E.). South of the temple of Hathor is a small temple dedicated to Isis; west, is the sacred lake, a well, and a *sanatorium* (hospital) dating from Roman times to receive the sick pilgrims who came to the temple in the hope of being miraculously cured. Between the two *mammisi* are the vestiges of a vast Coptic church from the middle of the sixth century.

The Church

Constructed in colored sandstone taken from the neighboring Roman *mammisi*, the church is a perfect rectangle thirty-six meters long and eighteen meters wide. The four exterior walls, which have kept only part of their original height, must have given a stern and severe aspect to the building. It had two entrances, the first one on the south side, a few meters from the southwest corner, and the second, symmetrical to the first, on the north side, a few meters from the northwest corner. Both entrances did not open onto either the nave or the narthex but onto two identical rooms serving as antechambers to the narthex. This complicated access to the church underlines the secret and mysterious character which the Coptic world borrowed from the Egyptian rituals of the pharaonic period; in those days, the architectural structures of the temples immersed the faithful, subjected to a predetermined and rigid route, in an increasingly sacred and mysterious atmosphere as they drew nearer to the *sancta sanctorum* (holy of holies).

As usual, the narthex runs along the west side of the church, and its decoration was especially rich and enhanced by niches with carvings in bas-relief. On its east side, three doors gave access to the *naos* whereas three other doors on the west opened onto two rooms destined for particular liturgical functions and a staircase which must have led to the upper story. The *naos* has a nave, two side aisles separated from the nave by two ranks of columns from which only the bases remain, and an aisle along the west connected to the side aisles. At intervals, niches crowned with decorative shell motifs embellished the north and south walls. The presbytery is especially interesting: the sanctuary is flanked by two rooms in the shape of a capital gamma, each directly connected with the sanctuary and its respective side aisles. The *sancta sanctorum* (holy of holies) is a triconch, the main apse being decorated with five small semi-circular niches while the side apses lack them.

Despite the paucity of its vestiges, the edifice retains even today a great majesty and a remarkable harmony of line and volume: the austerity of the exterior walls, the equilibrium of its proportions, and the gracefulness of its decoration make it one of the most beautiful edifices of Coptic architecture from the sixth century.

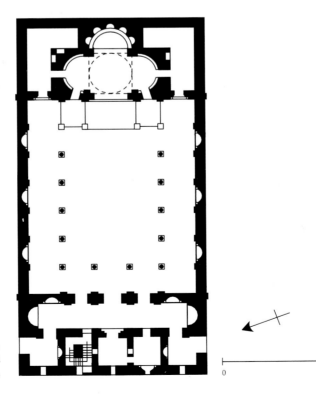

97. Dandara.
Plan of the church
(middle of 6th century).

0   20

78. Remains of the basilica of Pbow (5th century) in today's village of Faw Qibli.

79. Dandara. Ruins of the church from the middle of the 6th century situated between the Roman *mammisi* and that of Nectanebo I, within the sacred enclosure of Hathor.

80. Dandara. Detail of the west part of
the church.

81, 82. Dandara. Decorated niches in the church.

83. Luxor. Vestiges of two churches in the sacred enclosure of the pharaonic temple.

Following pages:
84, 85, 86, 87. Monasteries of the region of Naqada and Qamula: Deir Mari Buqtur—St. Victor (top of page, left), Deir Anba Pisentius—Abbot Bisantawus (bottom of page, left), Deir Mari Girgis—St. George (top of page, right), Deir al-Malak—Archangel Michael (bottom of page, right).

88, 89, 90. Church of the Martyrs (Deir al-Shuhada) near Esna. Details of the sanctuaries.

Bottom of page, right:
91. Monastery of the Potter (Deir al-Fakhuri) in the region of Esna. Interior of the church.

92. Monastery of the Martyrs (Deir al-Shuhada). Exterior view of the monastery founded on the site of the martyrdom of a Christian community of Esna together with its bishop in about 330.

Following pages:
93. Monastery of the Potter (Deir al-Fakhuri). The walls and tower of the monastery, founded probably in the beginning of the 8th century and named after the holy anchorite Matthew, who had plied the trade of potter.

Preceding pages:
94. Monastery of St. Simeon, founded near
Syene (Aswan) in the 7th century
and left vacant in the 13th because either it
was difficult to get sufficient water or the
desert marauders made frequent incursions.

95. Monastery of St. Simeon. Interior of
the church (10th or 11th century).

96. Monastery of St. Simeon. Interior of
the monastery, in the background the
tower *(qasr),* a powerful edifice used by the
monks as a last refuge in case of siege.

Following page:
97. Island of Philae. Church set up inside
the temple of Isis.

The Monasteries of Naqada and Qamula

West of the Nile in the area between Naqada and Qamula are numerous monastic complexes going back to the early Christian centuries, even though the present buildings are more recent. These monasteries are situated on the edge of the desert a few kilometers from the drivable road which runs parallel to the Nile along its west bank. We can mention seven of them within about ten kilometers north to south, only one of which is still active, the others serving only for liturgical celebrations on feast days.

The northernmost is the monastery of the archangel Michael (Deir al-Malak) four kilometers from Naqada; it has three churches built against one another; the structure with its typical cupolas dates from the eighteenth or nineteenth century. Near the village of Danfiq, some four kilometers from Deir al-Malak, stand two monasteries, one dedicated to the Cross (Deir al-Salib), the other, Deir Abu Lif, probably to St. Andrew, since it is also called the monastery of Andrew; however, it is not known whether Abu Lif was a surname of the local St. Andrew or not. The first monastery possesses two churches dedicated respectively to the Holy Cross and to St. Shenute (Shenuda in Arabic); both date from the eighteenth and nineteenth centuries although inside they have kept some architectural elements from the ancient edifices. The churches of these two monasteries are also roofed with cupolas.

About two kilometers south of the monastery of the Cross stands the monastery of St. George (Deir Mari Girgis), also called Deir al-Magma. Originally it had three churches, but now only one still exists, dedicated to St. George and dating from the eighteenth–nineteenth centuries. The iconostasis separating the three sanctuaries from the nave has been built with the columns of the earlier church.

Some two hundred meters from the monastery of St. George, that of Abbot Pisentius (Deir Anba Bisantawus) has a church from the eighteenth–nineteenth centuries roofed with twelve cupolas. About five kilometers south of the monastery of St. George is the monastery of St. Victor (Deir Mari Buqtur) whose buildings are the oldest in the region of Naqada. Constructed on a hill near a village, it has a church whose three sanctuaries were recently rebuilt whereas the *naos* has kept the architecture of the ancient phases of construction: the south, east, and north exterior walls go back to the original edifice from the eighth or ninth century; the square central space is the result of an architectural remodeling in the twelfth century when the church received cupolas in conformity with the customary architectural scheme in upper Egypt during the Middle Ages.

The monastery of the archangel Michael (Deir al-Malak) is the southernmost, a few kilometers from that of St. Victor and is surrounded by a vast cemetery. In the past, it was called the Monastery of the Well because

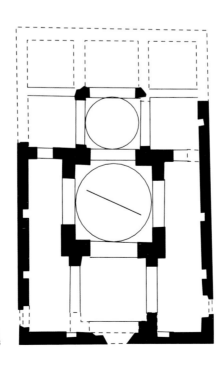

98. Monastery of St. Victor
(Deir Mari Buqtur).
Plan of the church.
In black: original construction
still extant (8th or 9th century).
Dotted lines: later construction.

241

it had a well giving an extraordinarily fresh and wholesome water. It has two churches, the older, dedicated to the archangel, dating from the sixteenth–seventeenth centuries and having a triple sanctuary preceded by a choir and a nave with six equal-sized domed chambers (bays). Today the monastery is occupied by women religious.

The Monasteries of St. Victor and St. Pachomius

North of Luxor on the east bank of the Nile one finds two monasteries whose foundation is ancient but whose buildings are recent. The monastery of St. Victor (Deir Anba Buqtur) is located near the village of Higaza some thirty kilometers from Luxor. It has four churches, the oldest being dedicated to St. Victor and having a triple sanctuary separated from the choir by a stone iconostasis. The monastery of St. Pachomius (Deir Anba Bakhum) stands about ten kilometers east of Luxor near the village of Minshat al-Ammari. The church dates from the seventeenth–eighteenth centuries and has a *naos* comprising a large transverse nave, a *khurus*, and five sanctuaries dedicated to St. Victor, St. George, St. Pachomius, the Holy Virgin, and the archangel Michael. As is the custom in the region, the church is roofed with cupolas. Here and there, decorations and inscriptions belonging to the ancient church are visible on the walls.

Coptic Vestiges in Luxor and Karnak

Luxor and Karnak have preserved interesting architectural and pictorial vestiges from the Coptic period. One can discern the remains of five churches inside the sacred enclosure of the temple of Luxor. The first one stands opposite and to the left of the principal pylon and measures thirty-one meters in length and seventeen in width. It goes back to the sixth–seventh centuries and has a basilican plan with a nave and two side aisles, a sanctuary with an apse, and two adjacent rooms; the side aisles are connected on the west side. The entrance was on the west through two symmetrical doors. The interior presents a very interesting architectural device whose prototype was probably in the Red Monastery: the two large columns placed opposite the back of the apse in order to visually attenuate the difference between the vast middle nave and the narrow semi-circular wall of the apse. At the northwest corner of the church the remains of a square baptistery are still visible; this building, built of bricks, was surmounted by a cupola supported by four columns, the bases of which still surround the baptismal font.

On the west side of the temple, one can detect what remains of two other churches, also basilican in plan with a nave, two side aisles, and an apse with adjacent rooms. Although of smaller dimensions, they are equally representative of the more classical architectural canons of the sixth century. The fourth church occupies the space under the mosque of Abu al-Haggag, inside the courtyard of Ramses II; its windows are

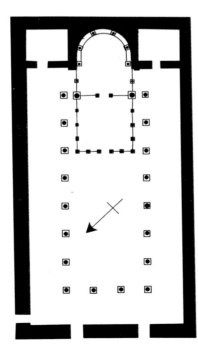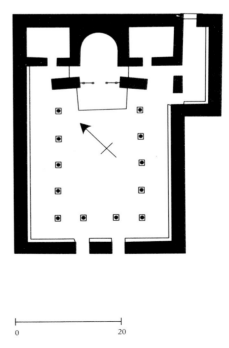

99. Luxor.
Left: plan of the church close to the main pylon of the temple (6th century).
Right: plan of the south church in the sacred enclosure of the temple of Madinat Habu (7th century).

0   20

242

clearly visible under the mosque. But archaeological research is difficult in this area of the temple because the mosque, dedicated to a Muslim saint (Abu al-Haggag) who is the object of a special devotion, is still an active religious center.

In the temple of Amon at Karnak, traces indicate that the Copts made use of certain elements of the temple. In particular, the great "festive hall" of Thutmose III was partially transformed into a church: one can still see the figures of several saints on the shafts of six columns.

The Theban Necropolis
Beyond the Nile, opposite the city of Luxor, the area of the Theban necropolis presents abundant evidence of the past existence of Christian anchoritic communities. In some tombs of the Valley of the Kings (Ramses III, Ramses IV, and Ramses VI), one can see Coptic drawings and inscriptions; in particular, St. Anthony and St. Ammonius, bishop of Esna, are represented in that of Ramses IV. The celebrated temple of Queen Hatshepsut (eighteenth dynasty, fifteenth century B.C.E.) bears the Arabic name Deir al-Bahari, that is, the "north monastery"; this shows that the temple was used by a community of Coptic monks—a fact confirmed, among other proofs, by discoveries made on the upper terrace. South of this temple, traces of other monasteries, called the "south monasteries" in contrast to the "north monastery," are still discernible. Their names were Deir al-Medina (Monastery of the City), which occupied a temple from the Ptolemaic period (third century B.C.E.); Deir Epiphanius (Monastery of St. Epiphanius) and Deir Kyriacus (Monastery of St. Cyriacus), which were located in the area of the Tombs of the Nobles.

More to the south, in the sacred enclosure of Madinat Habu, where the monumental temple of Ramses III (twentieth dynasty, twelfth century B.C.E.) stood, one can see the vestiges of two large churches. From the Roman period on, this area was occupied by Coptic families who built their dwellings among the buildings of the sacred enclosure. Little by little, the village grew into a small town of a certain economic and political importance, as papyri found there attest. The town was abandoned in the ninth or tenth century for unknown reasons. A first church with a nave and two side aisles, perhaps going back to the seventh century, stood next to the south entrance to the enclosure while another with a nave and four side aisles, probably dating from the sixth century, occupied the second courtyard of the temple. One can notice that in the former there was no central column on the east side in order to enlarge the space of the apse and that, in the nave near the west side, the *laqqan,* the basin used for the ritual of the washing of the feet, is still there. About five hundred meters southwest of the temple is the monastery of St. Theodore the Warrior (Deir Shahid Tadrus al-Muharib), whose older parts date from the fifteenth century. The monastery possesses a church roofed with the traditional cupolas; it has five sanctuaries, but only three belong to the original structure.

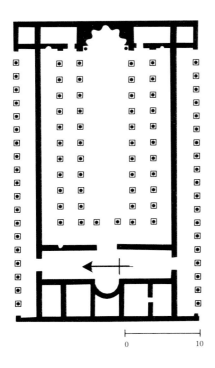

100. Armant (Hermonthis).
Plan of the basilica, probably from the 6th century, no longer extant.
Vestiges of the basilica still visible in Napoleon's time, from *Description de l'Égypte* (1809).

243

Finally, one can see the remains of another monastery, called Deir al-Rumi, on the hill that divides the Valley of the Queens into two parts. Part of the monastery was excavated in the rocky clefts and the rest was built of masonry. Its square church was originally roofed with a cupola.

The Basilica of Armant

The little town of Armant is located about twenty kilometers southwest of Luxor, on the west bank of the Nile. Formerly called Iunu, it was one of the most prestigious shrines of the god of war, Mont; its present name derives from Iunu-Montu, which gave Ermont in Coptic and Hermonthis in Greek. On that spot there was a great basilica with a nave and four side aisles, of which only faint traces remain but which still had a good part of its majestic structure at the time of Napoleon's campaign in Egypt (1798–1799). The basilica was vast (forty-six meters long and twenty-seven wide) and, besides its nave and aisles delineated by four ranks of red granite columns, had a sanctuary with an apse decorated with niches and flanked by two rooms, a narthex placed along the west side as was the custom, and two porticoes with columns along the north and south walls.

The Monastic Complex of Deir al-Matmar

The vestiges of the monastic complex of Deir al-Matmar stretch along some ten kilometers west of Armant, on the edge of the desert, and cover a vast area. The place is also called Deir al-Abiad which means "white monastery." The ruins of the church are interesting: the plan presents a *naos* with a nave and two aisles of modest length (whose columns have disappeared) and a triconch sanctuary. It can probably be dated from the sixth century. In addition, one can see traces of the construction at a later period of a room serving as a *khurus*.

Upper Egypt

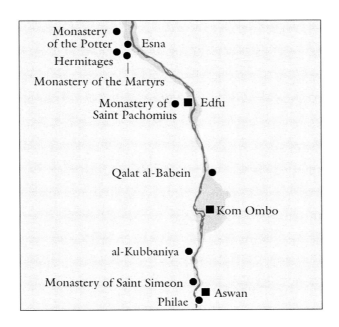

THE REGION OF ESNA

The Church of the Esna Temple

Opposite the Greco-Roman temple of Khnum, the ram-headed Egyptian deity, the ruins of a church of moderate dimensions (about seventeen meters long and eleven meters wide) have been uncovered. The building had a nave, separated from the two side aisles by two series of five columns, while the side aisles were connected by an aisle on the west side. The sanctuary had an apse and two adjacent rooms and was preceded by two columns which served to visually minimize the difference between its narrowness and the nave's width.

The Monastery of the Potter (Deir al-Fakhuri)

This monastery is located northwest of Esna, on the edge of the desert. To reach it, one must leave the road that follows the west bank of the Nile at the village of Asfun al-Matana; the monastery stands some ten kilometers from the village. It is also called the monastery of Matthew the Poor, after an anchorite canonized by the Coptic Church and the founder of the monastery, probably in the beginning of the eighth century. Without doubt, this twofold name derives from the fact that Matthew was a potter. Badly damaged in the tenth century when the Bedouins raided it, it was rebuilt. Subsequently deserted for many years, the site was reoccupied by monks in 1975.

The exterior aspect of the monastery is picturesque. Its massive tower reaches above the enclosure walls, conferring both liveliness to the volumes and austerity to the monastic buildings. It has three stories and, as usual, is accessible through a drawbridge which was lifted when the monks took refuge in it from the incursions of desert plunderers. On the top floor there was a chapel dedicated to the archangel Michael, the traditional defender of Coptic monasteries.

The church possesses a triple sanctuary and in the center of the building a square *naos* roofed with a cupola and surrounded on its four sides by an ambulatory whose east part was used as the *khurus* (choir). The central sanctuary is dedicated to the founder St. Matthew, the side sanctuaries to St. Michael (north) and the Holy Virgin (south). The central square and the *khurus* are the oldest parts, dating from the eighth century and restored toward the end of the twelfth. Wall paintings, unfortunately in very bad condition and fragmentary, decorate the sanctuaries and a part of the central area of the *naos;* inscriptions on the site attribute these to several painters who worked between the thirteenth and fifteenth centuries. The subjects which are still identifiable represent Christ and the apostles, St. Psote (Bisada in Arabic), and St. John

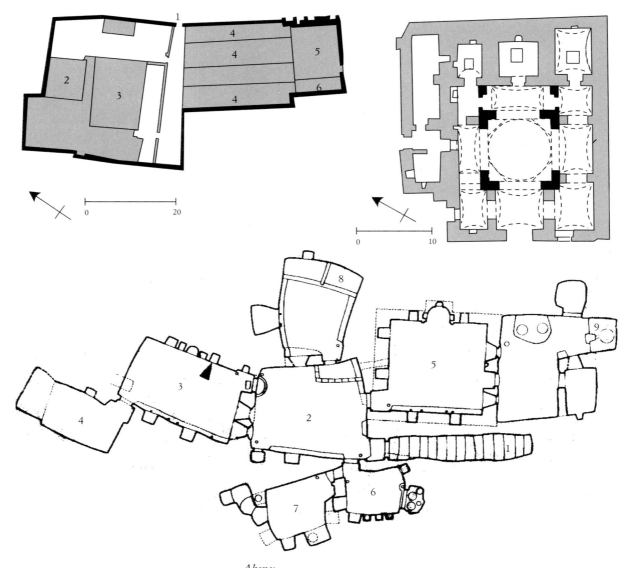

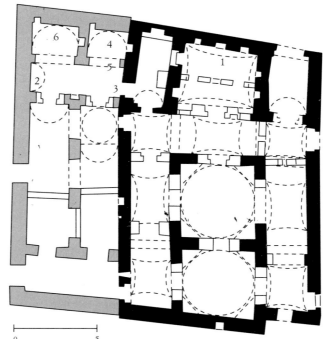

Above:
101. Monastery of the Potter (Deir al-Fakhuri).
Plan of the monastery. 1. Entrance, 2. Tower, 3. Church,
4. Cells, 5. Refectory, 6. Kitchens. Plan of the church.
In black: construction from the 12th century
In grey: later construction.

Center:
102. A hermitage in the desert of Esna.
1. Access staircase, 2. Courtyard, 3. Oratory,
4. Bedroom, 5. Secondary oratory, 6. Kitchen,
7. Storage room, 8. Water supply, 9. Oven.

Below:
103. Monastery of the Martyrs (Deir al-Shuhada).
Plan of the two churches. *In black:* original medieval
construction (11th–12th centuries). *In grey:* later medieval
construction. *In white:* more recent construction.

Wall paintings:
1. Christ between the archangels Michael and Gabriel,
2. St. Theodore, 3. St. Claudius, 4. Christ Pantocrator,
surrounded by the apocalyptic symbols of the four
evangelists and the Holy Virgin enthroned between the
archangels Michael and Gabriel, 5. Sts. Peter and Stephen,
6. Christ Pantocrator and the archangels.

the Baptist, angels, archangels, and prophets. The tomb of St. Matthew is in a little space on the north side of the church.

The south wing of the monastery comprises the monks' cells and the refectory. The cells are arranged on either side of a long vaulted corridor in a two-story building. Originally, each cell accommodated several monks. At the end of the corridor, one has access to the refectory, which is a vast square room with four pillars and is roofed with nine cupolas — one per bay. The kitchens are on the west side of the refectory.

The Hermitages of the Esna Desert

In the desert west of Esna, between Deir al-Fakhuri and Deir al-Shuhada, French archaeologists have unearthed many underground hermitages going back to the fifth and sixth centuries and probably abandoned in the course of the seventh. These hermitages prove that these places were extraordinarily vital centers of anchoritic life in the beginning of the Christian era. Sheltering two monks at the most, each hermitage comprised a sunken courtyard which one entered by a staircase hewn out of the rock; around this courtyard were rooms serving as cells, oratories, and kitchens. The oratories were decorated with paintings and drawings, often representing the cross and birds such as doves and peacocks; but geometrical figures were equally numerous. One of the hermitages still has the painted busts of several saints and the Holy Virgin. The archaeologists have covered a large part of the hermitages with sand in order to protect them.

The Monastery of the Martyrs (Deir al-Shuhada)

The monastery of the Martyrs (Deir al-Shuhada), also called the monastery of St. Ammonius (Deir Manawus), is about seven kilometers south of the large Greco-Roman temple of Esna about one kilometer from the road connecting Esna and Edfu, along the left bank of the Nile. It owes its name to the martyrdom of Ammonius and an entire Christian community massacred on the order of Hadrian, governor of the city of Antinoe. Today's buildings date back at the earliest to the second half of the eleventh century, but many funerary stelae with Greek inscriptions in the adjoining burial grounds attest to the ancient age of the monastic complex. Today, women religious live in this monastery.

Inside the enclosure are two churches attached to each other. The south church, dedicated to St. Ammonius, is the older and probably goes back to the eleventh or twelfth century. Its structure is similar to that of the church of Deir al-Fakhuri: it has a *naos* consisting of a nave divided into two square spaces roofed with cupolas, two small side aisles serving as ambulatories, a *khurus*, and a sanctuary *(haykal)* with two adjacent rooms, the north one used as a baptistery. Certainly built shortly after the south church, the north church has two aisles, a *khurus*, and two sanctuaries. Both churches are especially interesting architecturally and pictorially. Particularly noteworthy is the device which replaces the traditional iconostasis: simple little columns separated by small doors and windows are a screen concealing the sacred spaces.

Sanctuaries and choirs are decorated with fine wall paintings, regrettably in rather bad condition, which are certainly as old as the two churches. In the sanctuary of the south church, Christ is represented between the archangels Michael and Gabriel and two saints (probably Sts. Basil and Gregory). In the choir of the north church, two warrior saints on horseback are depicted, St. Theodore to the north and St. Claudius to the south. The lower part of the south sanctuary is decorated with the image of the Holy Virgin enthroned between the archangels Michael and Gabriel while the concha of the apse has the image of Christ Pantocrator (ruler of the universe) surrounded by the apocalyptic symbols of the evangelists: ox, lion, human being, and eagle. Sts. Peter and Stephen are represented on the arch that separates the choir from the sanctuary. In the north sanctuary, one finds again the iconography of Christ Pantocrator and the archangels.

THE REGION OF EDFU

The Monastery of St. Pachomius (Deir Anba Bakhum)

The monastery of St. Pachomius is located at the edge of the desert, on the west bank of the Nile, about five kilometers from Edfu (the former Apollinopolis Magna). The monastic complex is ancient and was abandoned for a long time; today a community of some thirty monks lives there. The present structure of the church, which dates from the eighteenth–nineteenth centuries and is roofed with cupolas, has a *naos*, three choirs, and four sanctuaries dedicated to St. Pachomius, the Holy Virgin, St. George, and the archangel Michael. The monastery is a place of pilgrimage for the Copts of the vicinity, especially in the month of May on the occasion of the feast of the monastery.

Qalat al-Babein
On the east bank of the Nile, about twenty kilometers south of Edfu, one finds the ruins of two fortresses called Qalat al-Babein, which in the Middle Ages controlled the river and traffic along the road connecting Thebes and Syene (today Aswan). In the center of the south fortress are the vestiges of a church built of unbaked brick. One can still recognize the apse of the church because of its height and because its dimensions suggest those of the Nubian churches of the region of Faras. Although the fortresses have not yet been fully studied by experts, one can consider the fortress and the church to date from the first half of the tenth century at the time of the Nubian occupation of upper Egypt.

THE REGION OF ASWAN

The Monastery of al-Kubbaniya
About twelve kilometers north of Aswan, on the west bank of the Nile not far from the village of al-Kubbaniya, stand the ruins of a monastery whose history and original name are unknown. However, it is probable that it was founded in the sixth–seventh centuries. One can see that the church has an interesting plan although only the lower part of the walls has survived; the church's structure is similar to that of the monastery of St. Simeon and therefore perhaps goes back also to the tenth or eleventh century. The *naos* of the church is a vast square space lined by pillars and roofed with a vast cupola supported by an octagonal drum; formerly an ambulatory ran along the south, west, and north sides. The presbytery was cruciform and comprised a *khurus,* a sanctuary *(haykal),* and two adjacent rooms; two other rectangular rooms in line with the small side aisles flanked the presbytery.

The Monastery of St. George (Deir Mari Girgis)
On the west bank of the Nile, in the area of the Tombs of the Nobles, one kilometer from the island of Elephantine, one can see the vestiges of a monastery probably dedicated to St. George (Mari Girgis). Midway between the Nile and the summit of the hill of Qubbat al-Hawa, the monastic settlement occupies part of the royal tombs from the pharaonic era. Here and there, inscriptions in the Coptic language and decorative motifs are still visible on the walls of unbaked brick covered with plaster. Recently, beautiful wall paintings, dating probably from the eleventh century, have been discovered there; they show Christ, the Holy Virgin flanked by the apostles, and saints.

The Monastery of St. Simeon (Deir Anba Simaan, Deir Anba Hadra)
The monastery of St. Simeon (Deir Anba Hadra) stands on a desertic hill about one kilometer from the west bank of the Nile, opposite the island of Elephantine. Originally dedicated to Anba Hadra, who probably led an ascetic life in that place at the end of the fourth century before becoming the bishop of Syene (now Aswan), the monastery was later incorrectly named after St. Simeon. Little is known about the origins of the monastery except that the area where its imposing ruins stand today was occupied by anchorites from the early centuries of Christianity. The oldest vestiges go back to the seventh century, but the present building shows that extensive reconstruction took place during the tenth century or at the beginning of the eleventh. The monastery was abandoned in the thirteenth century, either because of the difficulty of getting water or because of the frequent raids of desert marauders. Furthermore, in 1173, it suffered a particularly violent attack and heavy damage when the troops of Salah al-Din (Saladin) conducted their expeditions into Nubia.

The aspect of the monastic complex is striking because of the majestic character and severity of its architecture. Set on two terraces on different levels and surrounded by walls more than six meters high, the monastery occupies an area of about one hectare. The enclosure, with its irregular contour, is equipped with towers and lookouts. The lower portion of the walls is made of stone, the upper of unbaked brick; this latter material is also used for the buildings within the walls. The brown-ocher color of the brick contributes to the perfect harmonization of all the buildings with their desert surroundings.

The main entrance to the monastery is placed on the east side where a door in the large defensive tower opens onto the lower terrace. Near the entrance there are the remnants of a vast church dating from the reconstruction that took place in the tenth century or first half of the eleventh. The structure of the edifice is singular and in all respects similar to that of the church of the monastery of al-Kubbaniya, situated some ten kilometers to the north. It is a domed oblong church, a type appearing from the Fatimid period (969–1173) onwards. The *naos* has a nave and two side aisles; the nave, lined with pillars, possesses the particularity of

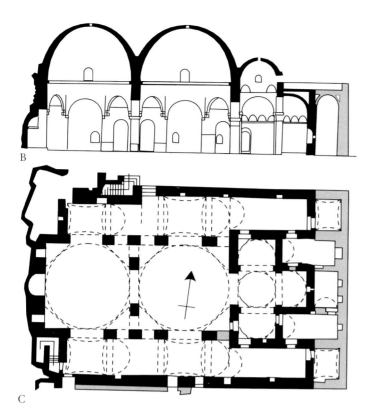

B

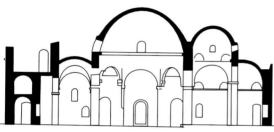

C

A

0   20

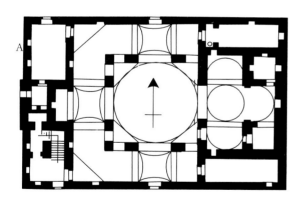

A

B

0   20

Above:
104. Monastery of St. Simeon.
A. Plan of the monastery.
1. Main entrance, 2. Secondary entrance, 3. Church,
4. Dormitory, 5. Refectory, 6. Kitchens, 7. Stables,
8. Oil press, 9. Oven, 10. Wine press, 11. System for
decanting water, 12. System for extracting salt,
13. Latrine.
B. Reconstitution of the elevation of the church
(10th–11th centuries).
C. Plan of the church.

Left:
105. Monastery of al-Kubbaniya.
A. Reconstitution of the elevation
(10th–11th centuries).
B. Plan of the church.

being divided into two square areas which in the past were roofed with cupolas. The cruciform sanctuary was also roofed with a cupola, which has now disappeared, and three semi-circular vaults. There are fragments of wall paintings still visible on the apse: Christ Triumphant between two angels in the middle concha and the twenty-four elders of Revelation on the north wall. The west side of the church rests against the rock which delimits the lower terrace and where there are natural caves which provided refuge for the first Christian anchorites occupying this site. In the northwest corner of the church, one of the caves is decorated with paintings older than the church; going back to the sixth–seventh centuries, they represent saints on the walls and decorative motifs alternating with saints' busts on the ceiling. It may be that this is the original dwelling of Anba Hadra, the holy anchorite who is the patron of the monastery. Behind the church a few monks' cells line the east wall of the monastery; each one has three masonry beds.

North of the church a staircase leads to the upper terrace where a massive edifice *(qasr)* stands; in the past it had three stories and the monks found ultimate refuge there in case of siege. The lowest level has a long central corridor onto which the monks' cells open, each one having at least two masonry beds. On the northwest side, one can see the remains of a large rectangular room which served as a refectory; subdivided into two aisles by a line of columns, of which only the bases are extant, it was roofed with a vault. The kitchen was on the west side in a room adjacent to the refectory. The enclosure of the monastery also includes other buildings and areas necessary to provide for the needs of the monastic community: flour mill, oven, oil press, wine press, stores, baths, latrines, stables, a vat to decant the water and another to extract salt.

The Churches of the Island of Philae
The monumental complex dating from the Ptolemaic period and dedicated to Isis is found in the region of the first cataract of the Nile, in the area between the old Aswan barrage (al-Sadd) and the High Dam (al-Sadd al-Aali). Originally, the temple stood on the island of Philae, but the level of the water rose when first the Old Dam and then the High Dam were constructed. These events aroused an extraordinary mobilization of experts to save this exceptional architectural complex from total disappearance. To achieve this, they proposed to transport the whole to a higher place above the level of the waters. This gigantic operation took eight years, from 1972 to 1980, and entailed the systematic dismantling of the edifices and their reassembling on the island of Agilkia, located about five hundred meters northwest of Philae and reshaped to satisfactorily accommodate the temple and reconstitute as best as possible the physical surroundings of Philae.

When the worship of Isis was forbidden under Justinian, the temples of the island were adapted to Christian worship; in addition, two new churches were built. One of them was made of unbaked brick, the other of stone, but they both disappeared because it was technically impossible to dismantle and reassemble them as had been done for the Ptolemaic temple now in Agilkia. They are now under water in the north part of what was the island of Philae. However, one can discern inside the temple of Isis manifest traces of Coptic modifications. The *pronaos* (vestibule) was transformed into a church in 553 on the order of the bishop Theodore. It was sufficient simply to build walls on the east and south sides (no longer in existence today) in order to redesign the space and to give it the traditional aspect of a church with a nave, two side aisles, and a sanctuary on the east side. One can still see the stone altar, the graceful niche in the east wall, and many crosses carved on the columns and wall.

The Oases

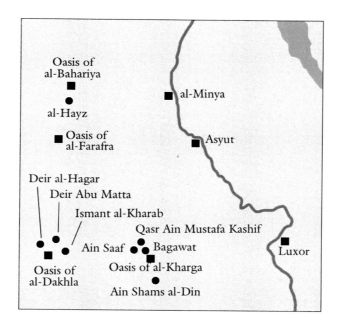

The oases of the Western Desert occupy a series of depressions caused by the winds from the Libyan Desert and are rich in natural springs and wells which have made human settlements possible since the Paleolithic era. There are five main oases: from north to south, Siwa, al-Bahariya, al-Farafra, al-Dakhla, and al-Kharga. For pharaonic as well as Roman Egypt, their importance was due less to their crops of dates and grapes, precious though these were, than to their location on the route of commercial caravans going to faraway lands. Some of these oases contain considerable vestiges from the Coptic era.

THE OASIS OF AL-BAHARIYA

The oasis of al-Bahariya ("the northern one"), formerly called the Little Oasis, is located three hundred kilometers southwest of Cairo.

The Church of al-Hayz

The village of al-Hayz lies about fifty kilometers from the oasis of al-Bahariya on the road which links it to the oasis of al-Farafra. Some three kilometers east of the village, there are the ruins of a large Roman fortress called al-Qasr, a military fortification intended to defend the frontiers of the empire and protect the routes insuring communication between the great Egyptian oases of the Western Desert. Close to the ruins of the fortress, in the middle of burial grounds from the late Roman period, stand the solitary remains of a church in the desertic plain; it is made of unbaked brick covered with a mud plaster, and its exterior walls have practically kept their original height. According to the prevalent opinion, the church dates from the seventh or eighth century. It is nineteen meters long and eight meters wide and has two entrances, one on the north, the other on the south. The north entrance leads to a rectangular narthex located on the west side through which one has access to the *naos* and, by means of a staircase, the upper galleries, no longer in existence. The *naos,* which is also accessible through the south entrance, has a basilican plan with ambulatories on the north, south, and west; those on the north and south have the peculiarity of being interrupted by a concha, a wholly unusual and original architectural element which recalls the pattern of the tetraconch church. The sanctuary is square, has two adjacent rooms, and is separated from the nave by a *khurus* (choir). One can observe the decorative motifs with engaged columns and their capitals, motifs which are repeated inside the nave.

The oasis of al-Dakhla, at the same latitude as Luxor, is about five hundred and fifty kilometers south of al-Bahariya and two hundred kilometers west of al-Kharga. In antiquity, the oasis was, like that of al-Kharga, an important stopping place for caravans and a marketing center where foodstuffs abounded; at the same time, it was a good place of refuge for those who wanted to escape religious persecution or conflict with the law.

The Monastery of the Stones (Deir al-Hagar)

Some ten kilometers west of the little town of al-Qasr, the vestiges of a temple dedicated to Amon and Amonet and dating from the Roman period are still in existence. Locally, it is called *Deir al-Hagar* (Monastery of the Stones) because of the material it is made of. Restored under Nero and Titus, as attested by hieroglyphic inscriptions, the temple has a hypostyle hall, a vestibule, and a few chapels. It was probably occupied by Christian monks in the fifth or sixth century and used as a monastery. The most obvious traces left by the monks are visible in the ruins of the great hypostyle hall which was transformed into a church with a nave and two side aisles.

The Churches of Ismant al-Kharab (Kellis)

At the east end of the oasis of al-Dakhla, near the village of Ismant al-Kharab, about fifteen kilometers from the little town of Mut, one can find the preserved vestiges of a large inhabited center, formerly called Kellis, comprising a temple from the Ptolemaic period and two paleo-Christian churches which one can date from the fifth century. Both churches are in the east section of the complex, southeast of the temple.

The larger one has a basilican plan with a nave and two side aisles, plus a little connecting return aisle on the west, and measures twenty-one meters in length and fourteen in width. The sanctuary apse is singular: in the shape of a horseshoe, it is so diminutive that access to the two adjacent rooms is from the main nave. The use of three columns next to the west corners of the nave is completely original.

Located close to the southeast corner of the first church, the other is smaller and has only one nave. But it too has a sanctuary in the shape of a horseshoe and two rooms which must be entered through the nave. The use of an engaged half-column at the center of the apse wall is most original.

The Church of Deir Abu Matta

The church of Deir Abu Matta is situated about twenty kilometers north of Mut. Built of unbaked brick, it is still in good condition since its external walls have kept most of their original height. Its plan is basilican

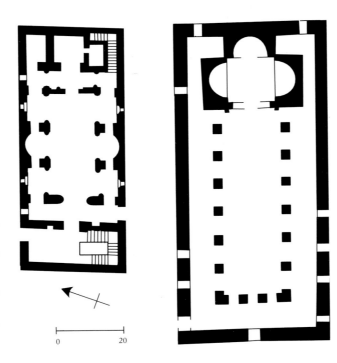

106. Plan of the church of al-Hayz (end of 7th or 8th century), south of the oasis of al-Bahariya.

Right:
107. Oasis of al-Dakhla. Plan of the church of Deir Abu Matta (end of 6th century).

0   20

with a nave, two side aisles, a western return aisle, and a triconch sanctuary with two adjoining rooms in the shape of a capital gamma. The edifice was probably part of a monastic establishment dating from the end of the sixth century.

THE OASIS OF AL-KHARGA

The oasis of al-Kharga, called the Great Oasis in the past, is at the same latitude as Luxor and about two hundred kilometers from it as the crow flies. It is the largest in Egypt and measures almost one hundred kilometers from north to south; from west to east its width varies between twenty and thirty kilometers. From the Nile valley, one can reach the oasis only by the road that connects it to Asyut, about two hundred kilometers away. The oasis has been occupied since the Paleolithic period, as shown by the petroglyphs discovered in the region. From the New Kingdom on, it became an active center of caravan traffic; its prosperity continued and even increased during the Roman period when groups of Greeks, probably from Alexandria and belonging to educated milieux, settled there. This event was also due to the fact that the Great Oasis and its main city, called Hibis in antiquity, had been since the pharaonic period a place of refuge for prominent persons who were exiled there or retired there of their own accord to avoid being harassed by political and religious authorities. Among the exiles and refugees in the oasis, one finds the patriarch of Alexandria, Athanasius, and the patriarch of Constantinople, Nestorius. The former withdrew here on one of his five temporary exiles caused by his fierce struggle against the Arian doctrine, which the emperor sometimes upheld. The latter, who was persecuted as a heretic bishop after the council of Ephesus in 431—convened to settle christological controversies—found a refuge there until his death.

The Necropolis of Bagawat

The Christian necropolis of Bagawat lies on a desertic slope northwest of the oasis. Its some 260 funerary chapels are arranged in a picturesque way along the two opposite sides of a slight depression, which was the route the funerary cortege followed to the church built on top of the hill. The tombs go back to a period extending from the fourth to the seventh century.

The funerary chapels are built of unbaked brick and constitute an extraordinary example of proto-Coptic art. Roofed with cupolas, they are architecturally diversified whether in plan (square, rectangular, circular, composite), elevation, or architectural decoration. The facades and exterior walls are embellished with engaged columns, capitals, niches, arcades, and pilasters, all made of brick.

The wall paintings decorating the two chapels called Chapel of Peace and Chapel of the Exodus are highly interesting. They represent episodes from the Old Testament and figures of early Christianity. Their exceptional character is due first to their date: in all likelihood, the wall paintings of the Chapel of Peace go back to the fifth century and those of the Chapel of the Exodus to the fourth. But their unique value is due most of all to their artistic characteristics. They reveal a taste and style whose origin is certainly Hellenistic and Roman, and it is possible to conclude that both those who commissioned and those who executed this decoration were Greek—as is confirmed, among other indications, by the Greek inscriptions designating persons and places. This particularity is perhaps the result of the Great Oasis' being a refuge for people suspected by political or religious authorities or entangled in serious conflict with them.

The Chapel of Peace is a square building of medium dimensions, roofed with a cupola; its painted decor adopts the traditional themes of the Romano-Byzantine paleo-Christian world: Adam and Eve, St. Paul of Thebes and St. Thecla, the annunciation (with the dove whispering its message in Mary's ear), Noah's ark, the patriarch Jacob, Prayer (*Euchē*), Justice (*Dikaiosynē*) with its scales, Daniel in the lions' den, Peace (*Eirenē*), and the sacrifice of Abraham. The elegance of the draperies and the harmony of the figures are characteristic of the Hellenistic models which manifestly inspired these works.

The paintings of the Chapel of the Exodus are older and less elegant, more sketchy and less detailed. The principal theme is the Exodus of the Jews out of Egypt: the people of Israel are represented walking, guided by Moses, in a long caravan with camels and pursued by the cavalry of the pharaoh. Other traditional themes and figures are also present: Noah's ark, Adam and Eve, Daniel in the lions' den, Daniel's three companions in the furnace, the sacrifice of Abraham, Jeremiah before the Temple, Susanna, Job afflicted, Jonah and the sea monster, Isaiah's torture, Sarah in prayer, St. Thecla in her flaming bush, and Golgotha with the cross of Christ represented as an ankh, the Egyptian symbol of life.

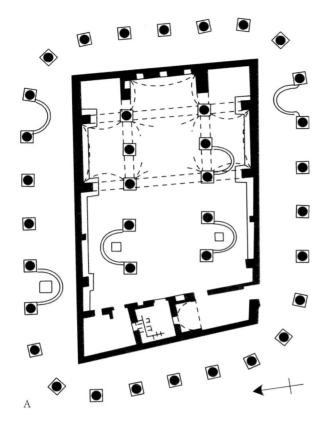

B

C

A

B

C

108–109. Oasis of al-Kharga, necropolis of Bagawat.

Above: the funerary church (5th century).
A. Plan, B. Exterior view, C. Interior view.

Below: Chapel of Peace.
A. Cupola: 1. Adam and Eve, 2. Sts. Paul and Thecla,
3. the annunciation, 4. Noah's ark, 5. the patriarch Jacob,
6. Prayer, 7. Justice, 8. Daniel in the lions' den, 9. Peace,
10. the sacrifice of Abraham.
B. Sts. Paul and Thecla and the annunciation
C. Noah's ark.

A church stands on the hilltop, also built of unbaked brick probably in the fifth century. It may have been used as a funerary chapel and is still in good condition; bases of columns all around its outer perimeter point to the existence of a peristyle. The entrance is on the south side, near the southwest corner and does not lead directly to the *naos* but to a room located on the west side and flanked by two other rooms. From there, one has access to the *naos,* composed of a nave separated from the two side aisles by two ranks of five columns which end on the east in a rectangular presbytery. The edifice served both as a church and as a dining hall for the meals in honor of the dead *(cenae funebres)* as is shown by the seats placed in a semi-circle *(klinai)* and in certain cases the tables whose traces are still visible inside the building along the side aisles and in the peristyle. These tables were probably reserved for the families who, being too poor, lacked the necessary facilities for these meals in their own tombs.

Qasr Ain Mustafa Kashif

The impressive ruins of the monastery called Qasr Ain Mustafa Kashif (meaning "the fortress of Mustafa Kashif's spring") dominate the desertic plain from the arid summit of Gebel al-Tair, about two kilometers from the necropolis of Bagawat. The monastery probably goes back to the end of the fifth or sixth century and was built on the tomb of a holy anchorite who had retired there to lead his ascetical life and whose example had attracted many other anchorites. Some experts think that the edifice was a Romano-Byzantine fortress subsequently occupied by Christian ascetics. The monastery was ransacked and destroyed during the seventh century. It was rebuilt but began to decline from the tenth century on and was completely abandoned later.

The building is fortified, protected by a high enclosure (which still has nearly its original height) and by a strong tower which dominates the entrance. The walls and the structures within the enclosure are made of unbaked brick laid with clay mortar. Although the monastic buildings, which were at least two stories high, have been for a large part destroyed, one can recognize the monks' cells roofed with barrel vaults, the refectory, a hall for assemblies, a church in the south corner of the monastery—there are traces of wall paintings in the church but their subjects are not identifiable—as well as chapels, terraces, corridors, courtyards, and staircases.

From the fifth to the twelfth–thirteenth centuries, the whole surrounding area was certainly rich in monastic settlements. This is proved by the numerous ruins visible on the plain from the height of the monastery, despite the sand which has partially or completely covered them. About one hundred meters to the west one can see the remains of a hermitage with cells for the anchorites, which no doubt depended upon the monastery, and about two kilometers farther away, a watchtower. Furthermore, the desert plain is crisscrossed by a tight and very regular network of rectangular areas outlined by small raised earth edges; these were probably gardens cultivated by the monks, gardens which dried up when they were abandoned. No one

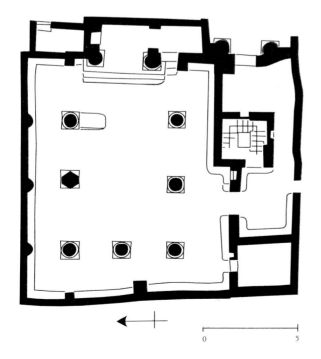

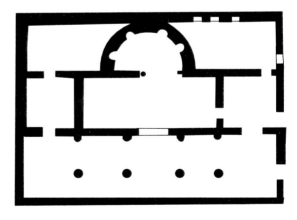

Above:
110. Oasis of al-Kharga, monastery of Ain Saaf.
Plan of the church.

Left:
111. Oasis of Baris, plan of the church of Ain Shams al-Din (4th century).

knows for certain why the monastery and other monastic settlements were deserted at some unknown time. Nevertheless, it is plausible to think that the monks leaving was not due to political, religious, or military events but rather to the progressive desiccation of the region which at some earlier period had enough water to sustain the life of a sizeable monastic community.

The Monastery of Ain Saaf

In the locality of Ain Saaf, about one kilometer from the monastery of Ain Mustafa Kashif, the remains of an anchoritic settlement still exist; it is made of unbaked brick and comprises monastic buildings around a church. This church has a transverse nave, a choir, and a sanctuary with an apse. The nave is divided into two parts by a line of four columns, oriented north-south, whose bases are still visible; engaged columns in the east wall of the nave repeat the pattern and spacing of these four columns. The choir and the sanctuary are each flanked by two rooms, and the sanctuary apse is embellished by four little semi-circular niches.

The Church of Ain Shams al-Din

Some seventy kilometers south of al-Kharga, on the left of the road leading to the frontier of Sudan, about one kilometer from Baris, are the ruins of a small church going back to the first half of the fourth century which was part of a Romano-Byzantine village called Munisis. This church was probably a private dwelling whose U-shaped peristyle was partially modified to transform it into the characteristic structure of a church with nave and aisles. It was built of unbaked bricks covered with plaster; it had an entrance on the south and included the nave, separated from each side aisle by three columns and from the western return aisle by one column, and a sanctuary, with two adjacent rooms, at the end of the nave. There are obvious traces of staircases which led to the upper story. The building probably dates from the time of Constantine, as suggested by the abundance of Greek graffiti and inscriptions on the church walls which are invocations and prayers to God and Jesus Christ. The total absence of any reference to the Holy Virgin and the saints attests to the absolute simplicity of early Christianity. The church of Munisis is without a doubt the oldest Christian monument discovered in Egypt.

98. Church of al-Hayz (7th or 8th century) in the Western Desert, near the road which connects the oasis of al-Bahariya with the oasis of al-Farafra.

Following pages:
99. Church of al-Hayz. Interior with the side ambulatories and embedded columns, a decorative motif.

100. Ruins of the monastery of Ain Saaf near the oasis of al-Kharga.

101. The imposing mass of the monastery called Qasr Ain Mustafa Kashif near the oasis of al-Kharga.

Preceding pages:
102. Oasis of al-Kharga. Necropolis of
Bagawat: 263 funerary chapels (4th–7th
centuries) shelter the remains of inhabitants
of the Great Oasis and of people who were
exiled there for political or religious reasons.

103, 104. Necropolis of Bagawat. Funerary
chapels.

105, 106. Necropolis of Bagawat, chapel of
the Exodus (4th century). Details
of painted decorations.

107. Ruins of the church of Ain Shams
al-Din (4th century) near Baris, south of
the oasis of al-Kharga.

Chronology

THE PTOLEMIES (332–30 B.C.E.)

In 332 B.C.E., when Alexander the Great enters Egypt in the course of his campaign against the Persians, he encounters little resistance. He sojourns only briefly in the country but long enough to found the city which is named after him, Alexandria. At Alexander's premature death in 323 B.C.E., Egypt is part of the territories of the empire divided between his generals. It falls to the lot of Ptolemy, who proclaims himself sovereign and takes the name of Ptolemy I Sōter (Savior). It is governed by Ptolemy's descendants until the death of Cleopatra in 30 B.C.E. and for the three centuries preceding the Christian era is culturally and politically the richest and most influential kingdom in the world of the Middle East. During the last century of the Ptolemaic reign, the relationship between Egypt and Rome becomes progressively closer. It rests on bonds of "friendship" and "alliance" which entails the fact that the Romans influence, sometimes directly, the Ptolemies' politics. The last representative of the dynasty is Cleopatra VII, who seeks to restore luster and prestige to her dynasty by gaining the sympathy first of Caesar then of Mark Anthony. But the queen's dream lasts for only a brief moment and vanishes entirely with her suicide in 30 B.C.E. when Octavian, the future emperor Augustus, enters Alexandria in triumph and definitively subjugates Egypt to the domination of Rome.

THE ROMAN PROVINCE (30 B.C.E.–330 C.E.)

Because of its special importance militarily and, above all, its part in supplying food to Rome, the new Roman province is directly subject to the emperor's authority. However, among the imperial provinces, Egypt enjoys a privileged juridical status: it is not governed by a procurator but by a *praefectus Alexandriae et Egypti* (prefect of Alexandria and Egypt), a sort of governor vested with the powers of a viceroy, directly named by the emperor and answerable to him alone. By this measure Augustus intends to confirm the importance of Egypt as "Rome's granary" and a rich tributary of the Roman public treasury. The strategic role of Egypt and its economic resources justifies the long and frequent visits paid by the emperors and their representatives. First Augustus, then Germanicus, Vespasian, Hadrian, Septimus Severus, Caracalla, Aurelian, Galerius, and Diocletian visit Egypt. It is in

the period of Roman domination that the gospel message, which tradition reports was brought to Egypt by St. Mark, spreads through a milieu intellectually free and particularly open to new philosophical and religious ideas. However, the position of the Roman masters is not as conciliatory, and Diocletian launches the great persecution against Christians. The hatred towards this emperor is such that Christians retrospectively define the first year of his reign as the beginning of the "era of martyrs."

THE BYZANTINES (330–619)

The foundation of Constantinople in 330 affects Egypt in a particular way because Constantine's new imperial capital weakens the prestige of Alexandria, up to then unquestionably the cultural capital of the Mediterranean East. At the same time, however, the diffusion of Christianity, encouraged by the Edict of Milan—which had made the open profession of the Christian faith lawful—contributes to the transformation of the power structure in Egypt by adapting it to its specific needs and by exporting it outside of Egypt itself. Thus, Alexandria recovers its prestige, now as the seat of a supranational church, the beacon of all the Christian East. For the three centuries which separate Constantine's death from the rise of Islam, the church of Egypt, organized around the patriarchate of Alexandria, dominates the religious and civil institutions and so assumes an extraordinarily prominent role on both the religious and political plans, to the point of sometimes opposing the central power of Constantinople. The doctrinal conflicts which arise within Christianity from the fourth century on are a field of battle always ready to be used by the patriarchate of Alexandria to defy and contradict the patriarchate of Constantinople and thus oppose its power, which it owes, not to its own merits, but to its privileged position of immediate proximity to the central imperial authority. The conflict ends in an open and definitive break on the occasion of the controversies concerning Christ's human and divine natures; these disputes culminate in the council of Chalcedon in 451 which, by proclaiming the unity of Christ's person and the duality of Christ's nature—human and divine—openly contradict the Alexandrian doctrine, called Monophysite, teaching the unity of Christ's nature—divine. For Egypt and for the whole Byzantine world, the reign of Justinian (527–565) is a period of tumultuous activity affecting the organization and administration of the state as well as the security and integrity of the empire's territories, increasingly threatened, especially on their eastern frontiers.

THE BRIEF PERSIAN OCCUPATION (619–629)

The golden age of Byzantine history and culture, enhanced by the splendor of the emperor Justinian's architectural achievements, both religious and military, and by his political acumen, lasts but a short time. Indeed, at the end of the sixth century, a severe economic crisis, epidemics, and a crash in population weaken the structure of the Byzantine state, which had already been hard put to protect its eastern frontiers against the violent and determined pressure of the Sassanid Persians. Despite the impressive and ingenious defensive works built under Justinian, the eastern frontier *(limes)* begins to be shaken and in 615 succumbs to the Persian's relentless battering. King Chosroes (Khusrau in Persian, Kisra in Arabic) invades first Syria and Palestine before turning to Egypt, which he occupies in 619. The occupation of the land by the Sassanids lasts for ten years and is no harsher than the Byzantine occupation. In its very first years, the Persian order is characterized by a bloody intolerance, but after that it is careful to preserve the political and religious rights of its new subjects. In 629, the Byzantine emperor Heraclius reconquers Syria, Palestine, and Egypt, and definitively expels the age-old enemy, the Persians. Heraclius makes every attempt to reestablish the unity of the faith disrupted by controversies between Chalcedonians and Monophysites by seeking to impose a theological compromise. To achieve this, he appoints the bishop Cyrus patriarch and also gives him the titles of prefect and viceroy. Heraclius' effort results in a bitter failure because Cyrus' cruelty and violence toward the Monophysites alienate even the Chalcedonian minority and contribute to making his patriarchate the most unpopular period in Egypt for the imperial power. Thus Cyrus' patriarchate contributes to the radical evolution which arises in the East with the advent of Muhammad and the birth of Islam.

Egypt under Islam

THE ARAB CONQUEST (639–661)

A few years after Muhammad's death in 632, his successors, the caliphs, initiate campaigns of military conquest which quickly make them the masters of the Arabian Peninsula, the Middle East, and the provinces of North Africa. The occupation of Egypt begins in December 639 when the emir Amr ibn al-As, the general of the caliph Omar, enters Egyptian territory. The weak Byzantine defense proves unable to resist the smaller Arab army: after a violent battle at Heliopolis in 640, the Byzantine army abandons Egypt, where only two centers of tenacious resistance remain, the fortress of Babylon in Old Cairo and the capital, Alexandria. In April 641, after seven months of siege, the fortress of Babylon falls whereas Alexandria succeeds in resisting for a whole year, capitulating only in September 642. The new Arab order is tolerant toward the Christian faith of the Egyptians, whom they regard as *dhimmi* (protégés) as long as they regularly pay the taxes necessary for the upkeep of the army and the state structure. Nevertheless, a slow but irresistible process of Islamization begins. Islamization is the only way to evade heavy fiscal burdens, to better one's social position, and to have access to public office. It is under Arab occupation that the term "Copt" first appears to designate Egyptian Christians. In reality, the Arabic-speaking Muslims give the name Copt to the native Egyptians (who are all Christians), and when, with the passage of time, a large number of Egyptians convert to Islam, more through opportunism than conviction, people continue to give the name Copt to those who profess the Christian religion. The term, which originally designated Egyptian ethnicity, progressively serves to define the Christian religion professed by Egyptians. The word "Copt" itself is an alteration of the Greek *Aigyptios* (Egyptian) which became *Qibt* in Arabic.

THE UMMAYADS (661–750)

In 661, after a few years of internal strife concerning the attribution of the caliphate, Muawiya wins and founds the Ummayad dynasty, which will last until 750, through fourteen caliphs whose succession is no longer established by election as in the beginning but by direct descent. The Ummayads move the seat of the caliphate of Medina to Damascus, which becomes the capital of the Islamic world. In the conquered lands, the caliph is represented by a governor. This regime applies also to Egypt where the governors' administration is tolerant toward the Coptic world. The few episodes of fanaticism and intolerance remain marginal and are due more to the excesses committed by certain governors than to the Islamic institutions of the caliphate. Under the Ummayad dynasty, Coptic monasticism is at its most flourishing and counts thousands of vocations, perhaps partially prompted by the fiscal exemptions granted to monks. The beginning of the decline of Ummayad power coincides with a profound economic crisis caused by the enormous costs of military campaigns and by a misguided fiscal policy, all of which arouse a covert discontent and then an open disaffection toward the authority of the state.

THE ABBASIDS AND THE TULUNIDS
(750–969)

The accession to the caliphate of the new Abbasid dynasty is favored by internal dissensions and by the severe economic crisis. The founder of the dynasty, Abbas, is descended from an uncle of Muhammad. In 747, he deposes the Ummayad governor of Persia and undertakes his conquests westward. In 749, he is appointed caliph, but it is only in the following year that he succeeds in definitively defeating the Ummayad caliph Marwan II, thus giving birth to the Abbasid dynasty, whose capital is transferred from Damascus to Baghdad. In Egypt, during the years of peace and prosperity corresponding to the first Abbasid period, the process of Islamization continues irreversibly. Greek disappears little by little, and if Coptic survives, its use is limited to the liturgy; Arabic rapidly gains ascendancy, first in public administration and communications, then in ordinary speech. The process of "conversion" to Islam grows to such a point that in a few decades it results in a radical reduction of the number of taxable people which now include only Copts in accordance with the Koranic rule; they see themselves forced to pay heavier and heavier taxes in order to balance the state budget. This situation provokes furious revolts on the part of the Coptic population; these reach their apex in 829 with the uprising of the eastern delta which only the personal intervention of the caliph Mamun could quell. The particularly ferocious repression signals the end of the Coptic irredentism and a fresh rush of conversions to Islam. Conditions take a turn for the better for the Christians when in 868 the Turkish governor Ahmad ibn Tulun rebels against the caliph and decrees Egypt's independence. After his death his successors manage to maintain their independence from the caliph.

THE FATIMIDS (969–1173)

In 969, the Tulunid dynasty is replaced by that of the Fatimids, who belong to the Shiite branch of Islam and are descended from Ali, Muhammad's son-in-law. The caliph al-Muizz (969–975) establishes a city to the north of al-Fustat and calls it al-Qahira ("the Victorious One"), a name which is the origin of the present name of Cairo. The city rapidly becomes the capital of the caliphate and must, according to its founder's intentions, rival Baghdad in prestige. The caliphate of al-Aziz (975–996) is a period of prestigious conquests, artistic efflorescence (especially in the capital of Cairo), and particular tolerance toward religious minorities, whether Christian or Jewish. In contrast, the period corresponding to the caliphate of al-Hakim (996–1021) is a painful parenthesis in the course of the two centuries of the Fatimids' enlightened sovereignty. The cruelty and intolerance of al-Hakim are unleashed with singular ferocity against Christians, Jews, and Sunnite Muslims and thus cause a new spate of conversions to Islam. The Coptic population ends in becoming a weak minority within an Islamized and Arabized world in which the Coptic tongue and writing are now replaced by Arabic. The fall of the Fatimid caliphate nearly coincides with that of the caliphate of Baghdad when in 1173 Salah al-Din Yusuf ibn Ayyub, called Saladin, accedes to power and becomes the founder of the Ayyubid dynasty.

THE AYYUBIDS (1173–1250)

Saladin proclaims himself the sultan of Egypt in 1173. The first years of his caliphate coincide with the Crusades and therefore with the violent combats against the Latin Christian armies. This causes a deep resentment toward the Egyptian Coptic population although it is not directly implicated in the so-called wars of liberation of the holy sepulchre. But after the reconquest of Jerusalem by Saladin in 1187, the Copts are again given influential positions in public administration and receive important commissions such as the planning and building of the new defensive works protecting Cairo and its citadel. The fall of the Ayyubids is due to the sultan's guards who end the dynasty by assassinating Turan Shah, the last descendant of Saladin.

THE MAMLUKS (1250–1517)

The Mamluks rule Egypt for nearly two hundred and fifty years, first under the dynasty of the Bahriyya and then under that of the Burgiyya. This period is characterized by a chronically unstable military regime, but it is also an exceptional time of economic prosperity and development of the arts and sciences. Cairo becomes the brilliant capital of an empire encompassing Syria and Palestine. The Mamluk power is particularly harsh toward the Coptic population, which it oppresses and humiliates because the Muslim majority is envious of the Copts' competence in artisanal and artistic endeavors, their efficiency in the discharge of public duties, and their enterprising commercial ventures. In consequence, there is a return to long-forgotten discriminatory measures and to especially violent and fanatic waves of periodic repression. The Mamluks' domination comes to an end when the Turkish tribe of the Ottomans victoriously enters Cairo in 1517 and kills Tuman Bey, the last sultan. This marks the end of the independence of Egypt, which becomes a province of the Turkish Ottoman Empire.

THE OTTOMANS (1517–1798)

The occupation of Egypt by the sultan Selim I in 1517 opens the most powerful period of the Ottoman Empire: thanks to the conquests of Selim I, Suleyman the Magnificent, and Selim II, this empire reaches its greatest expansion since from Istanbul, the new Constantinople, it rules, with the exception of Morocco, the whole Arab Muslim world. Within this vast empire, Egypt is but one province governed by a Turkish pasha appointed by the sultan. The decline of the country affects of course the spiritual and intellectual life of the Coptic Church, which nonetheless comes closer to the church of Rome than ever before by studiously searching for ways of reunification. The weakness of Ottoman power in Egypt culminates in the eighteenth century when the Mamluks reconquer the central power of Cairo.

MODERN EGYPT

THE FRENCH OCCUPATION (1798–1801)

In 1798, Napoleon Bonaparte, the First Consul, begins a military campaign in Egypt; he is accompanied by scientists, archaeologists, engineers, and economists. Officially, the goal of this expedition is to free Egypt from the medieval Turkish administration in order to transform the country into a modern state conceived on the European model and to reveal to the world the splendors of its past. However, Napoleon's real purpose is to oppose England's commercial supremacy in the region of the eastern Mediterranean and control the sea routes to India. Despite early victories, the military campaign soon fails: a series of political miscalculations and military defeats oblige the French to definitively leave Egypt in 1801. Nevertheless, this brief French presence has the merit of arousing national consciousness, shattering the feudal rigidity of the Mamluk administration, and opening to the Western world the historical and artistic treasures of the pharaohs' world, thereby initiating Egyptology.

THE NATIONALIST AWAKENING (1802–1881)

In order to reestablish his authority against the French invaders, the sultan Selim III sends Albanian troops in whose ranks a Macedonian officer, Mehmet Ali, distinguishes himself and gains recognition. When the French depart from Egypt, Mehmet Ali—whose name is Arabized into Muhammad Ali—with the support of the Albanian troops of which he is the uncontested leader, is named pasha. With lucidity and foresight, he undertakes to transform Egypt into a modern state by giving it necessary infrastructures and introducing Western principles of liberty. At his death in 1849, his sons and grandsons succeed him. But for lack of a personality as strong as his, Egypt rapidly faces a severe economic crisis which the English do not fail to exploit: in 1882, when the country is shaken by upheavals, they occupy the territory after overcoming weak Egyptian resistance.

THE ENGLISH PROTECTORATE (1882–1952)

The English rigorously preserve political institutions and exercise a close control especially in the economic and financial domains. It is only in 1914 that Great Britain officially gives Egypt protectorate status, thus definitively nullifying any Turkish right of sovereignty. But after the first world war, nationalistic movements seeking independence arise, and the English are obliged to abandon their protectorate, formally, and recognize the independence of the country in 1922. However, they retain the right to protect Western interests as well as the security of communications with the British Empire and are in charge of defending Egypt against foreign aggression. The British protectorate comes to a definitive end in 1952 when anglophobic tensions result in a coup d'état: King Farouk is forced to abdicate, while power is assumed by the Committee of Free Officers, led by Gamal Abd al-Nasser. The following year, the monarchy is abolished and the republic proclaimed.

THE REPUBLIC (SINCE 1953)

The new regime inaugurated by Gamal Abd al-Nasser concentrates before all on healing the economy by means of "Arab socialism." This is shown, on the one hand, by the nationalization of the large industrial and financial systems, services, and the infrastructures particularly important to the people, such as the Suez Canal, and on the other, by radical reforms in industry, agriculture, services, and public administration. The building of the Aswan High Dam was begun in 1960 by Gamal Abd al-Nasser in order to increase the yield of arable lands and to produce large quantities of energy for industry. Today, Egypt goes through a difficult period: Islamic fundamentalism nullifies the effects of the enlightened domestic and foreign policies of the government which would enable the country to strengthen its position as a model to which the nations of the Arab world could refer. Mutual tolerance and respect between Egyptian Muslims and Christians—who may, according to the Coptic Church, represent between fifteen and eighteen per cent of the population, that is, about ten or eleven million people—are essential conditions for the development and progress of Egypt.

Selected Bibliography

Some Sources

Athanasius, Saint. *Life of St. Anthony.* Trans. Mary Emily Keenan, S.C.N. In *Early Christian Biographies.* Ed. Roy J. Deferrari. New York: Fathers of the Church, 1952.

_____. *The Resurrection Letters* [Festal or Paschal Letters]. Paraphrased by Jack N. Sparks. Nashville: T. Nelson, 1976.

Besa. *The Life of Shenoute.* Trans. David N. Bell. Kalamazoo, Mich.: Cistercian Publications, 1983.

Cassian, John. *John Cassian: The Institutes.* Trans. Boniface Ramsey. Ancient Christian Writers 58. New York: Newman, 2000.

The Desert Christian: Sayings of the Desert Fathers: The Alphabetical Collection. Trans. Benedicta Ward. New York: Macmillan, 1980.

Eusebius Pamphili. *Ecclesiastical History.* Books 1–5. Trans. Roy J. Deferrari. Fathers of the Church 19. New York: Fathers of the Church, 1953.

Evagrius Ponticus. *Traité pratique, ou, Le moine.* Trans. Antoine Guillaumont and Claire Guillaumont. 2 vols. Sources chrétiennes 170–171. Paris: Cerf, 1971

Jerome, Saint. *The Life of St. Paul, the First Hermit.* Trans. Marie Liguori Ewald, I.H.M. In *Early Christian Biographies.* Ed. Roy J. Deferrari. New York: Fathers of the Church, 1952.

The Life of Saint Pachomius and His Disciples. Trans. Armand Veilleux. Pachomian Koinonia 1. Kalamazoo, Mich.: Cistercian Publications, 1980.

The Lives of the Desert Fathers [History of the Egyptian Monks]. Trans. Norman Russell. Kalamazoo, Mich.: Cistercian Publications, 1981.

Palladius. *The Lausiac History.* Trans. Robert T. Meyer. Westminster, Md.: Newman, 1965.

General Bibliography

Abdel-Sayed, Edris [Idris]. *Les Coptes d'Égypte: Les Premiers Chrétiens du Nil.* Paris: Publisud, 1992.

Abu-Salih, al-Armani. *The Churches and Monasteries of Egypt and Some Neighbouring Countries, Attributed to Abu Salih, the Armenian.* Trans. B.T.A. Evetts. [1885.] Reprint [Frome, England: Butler and Tanner, 1969].

Atiya, Aziz S., ed. *The Coptic Encyclopedia.* 8 vols. New York: Macmillan, 1991.

Camplani, Alberto. *Early Egyptian Christianity. Coptic Studies.* Leiden: Brill, 1989.

Cannuyer, Christian. *Les Coptes,* 2nd ed. Turnhout: Brepols, 1996.

Chevillar, Alain and Évelyne. *Moines du désert d'Égypte.* Lyons: Terre du Ciel, 1990.

Déserts chrétiens d'Égypte. Nice: Culture Sud, 1993.

Du Bourguet, Pierre. *Les Coptes,* 2nd ed. Paris: Presses universitaires de France, 1989.

Griggs, C. Wilfred. *Early Egyptian Christianity: From Its Origins to 451 C.E.* Leiden: Brill, 1990.

Kamil, Jill. *Coptic Egypt: History and Guide.* Cairo: American University in Cairo Press, 1987.

Kamil, Murad. *Coptic Egypt.* Cairo: Printed by Le Scribe égyptien, 1968.

Meinardus, Otto F. A. *Christian Egypt, Ancient and Modern.* Cairo: American University in Cairo Press, 1965.

_____. *Monks and Monasteries of the Egyptian Deserts.* Cairo: American University in Cairo Press, 1961.

_____. *Two Thousand Years of Coptic Christianity.* Cairo: American University in Cairo Press, 1999.

Roncaglia-Martiniano, Pellegrino, *Histoire de l'Église copte,* 2nd ed. Beirut: Librairie St. Paul, 1985.

Viaud, Gérard. *La Liturgie des Coptes d'Égypte.* Paris: Librairie d'Amérique et d'Orient, 1978.

_____. *Les Pèlerinages coptes en Égypte.* Bibliothèque d'études coptes 15. [Cairo]: Institut français d'archéologie orientale du Caire, 1979.

Wansleben, Johann Michael [Vansleb, F.]. *The Present State of Egypt, or, A New Relation of a Late Voyage into That Kingdom . . . 1672 and 1673.* Trans. M.D. and B.D. London: printed by R.E. for John Starkey, 1678.

Watterson, Barbara. *Coptic Egypt.* Edinburgh: Scottish Academic Press, 1988.

Art

Actes du IVᵉ Congrès copte (1988). Institut orientaliste 40. Louvaine-la-Neuve: Université catholique de Louvain, 1992.

Ägypten Schätze aus dem Wüstensand: Kunst und Kultur der Christen am Nil. Catalog. Wiesbaden: Dr. Ludwig Reichert, 1996.

Badawy, Alexander. *Coptic Art and Archaeology: The Art of the Christian Egyptians from the Late Antique to the Middle Ages.* Cambridge: MIT Press, 1978.

Badawy, Alexandre. *L'Art copte: Les influences égyptiennes.* [Cairo]: Institut français d'archéologie orientale du Caire, 1949.

Deneuve, Gustave. *L'Arte Copta.* Florence: Sadea/Sansoni, 1970.

Du Bourguet, Pierre. *Coptic Art.* Trans. Caryll Hay-Shaw. London: Methuen, 1971.

Koptische Kunst: Christentum am Nil. Catalog of exhibition, May 3–August 15, 1963. Essen, 1963.

Rutschowscaya, Marie-Hélène. *La Peinture copte.* Catalog of the Louvre. Paris: Réunion des musées nationaux, 1992.

al-Syriani, Samuel, and Badii Habib. *Guide to Ancient Coptic Churches and Monasteries in Upper Egypt.* [Cairo]: Institute of Coptic Studies, Dept. of Coptic Architecture, 1990.

XXVII Corso di cultura sull'arte ravennate e bizantina: Egitto Copto. Ravenna: Girasole, 1981.

Wessel, Klaus. *Coptic Art.* Trans. Jean Carroll and Sheila Hatton. New York: McGraw-Hill, [1965].

Minor Arts

Bénazeth, Dominique. *Égypte: l'Art du métal au début de l'ère chrétienne.* Catalog of the Louvre. Paris: Réunion des musées nationaux, 1992.

Lorquin, Alexandra. *Les Tissus coptes.* Catalog of the Louvre. Paris: Réunion des musées nationaux, 1992.

____. *Les tissus coptes au Musée national du Moyen Age, Thermes de Cluny.* Catalog of the Museum of Cluny. Paris: Réunion des musées nationaux, 1992.

Martiniani-Reber, Marielle. *Tissus coptes.* Catalog of the Museum of Art and History. Geneva: Musée d'art et d'histoire, 1999.

____. *Soieries sassanides, coptes et byzantines (V^e-XIe siècles).* Catalog of the Lyons Historical Museum of Fabrics. Paris: Réunion des musées nationaux, 1986.

Rutschowscaya, Maire-Hélène. *Catalogues des bois de l'Égypte copte au musée du Louvre.* Paris: Réunion des musées nationaux, 1986.

____. *Les Tissus coptes.* Paris: Adam Biro, 1990.

Stauffer, Annemarie. *Textiles d'Égypte de la collection Bouvier.* Catalog. Musée d'Art et d'Histoire de Bribourg, 1991.

Zanni, Annalisa. *La tunica dell'Egitto cristiano: Restauro e iconographia dei tessuti copti del Museo Poldi Pezzoli.* Turin: Artema, 1997.

Monographs

Antinoe (1965–1968): Missione archeologica in Egitto. Rome: Istituto di Studi del Vicino Oriente, Universita di Roma, 1974.

Breval, Roger, Edmond Pauty, and Étienne Meriel. *Les Églises coptes du Caire.* Cairo: E. and R. Schindler, 1936.

Bridel, Philippe, ed. *Le site monastique copte des Kellia: Sources historiques et explorations archéologiques.* Acts of the Geneva Colloquium, August 13–15, 1984 [Geneva]: MSAC, 1986.

Coquin, Charalambia. *Les Édifices chrétiens du Vieux-Caire.* Bibliothèque d'études coptes 11. [Cairo]: Institut français d'archéologie orientale du Caire, 1974.

Evelyn-White, Hugh G. *The Monasteries of the Wadi 'n Natrun.* 3 vols. 1926–33. Reprint, New York: Metropolitan Museum of Art, 1973.

Grossmann, Peter. *Mittelalterliche Langhauskuppelkirchen und verwandte Typen in Oberägypten.* Koptische Reihe 3. Glückstadt: Abhandlungen des deutschen archäologischen Instituts Kairo, 1982.

Habib, Rauf. *The Ancient Coptic Churches of Cairo: A Short Account.* Cairo: Mahabba Bookshop, 1979.

Les Kellia: Ermitages coptes en Basse-Égypte. Catalog of the Museum of Art and History, Geneva. Tricorne, 1989.

KHS-Burmester, O. H. E. *A Guide to the Ancient Coptic Churches of Cairo.* Cairo: Anglo-Egyptian Bookshop, 1955.

____. *A Guide to the Monasteries of the Wadi 'N-Natrun.* Cairo: Société d'archéologie copte, 1954.

Monneret de Villard, Ugo. *Les couvents près de Sohag (Deyr el-Abiad et Deyr el-Ahmar).* 2 vols. Milan: [Tipografia Pontificia Arcivescovile San Giuseppe], 1925–1926.

____. *Les Églises du monastère des Syriens au Wadi Natrun.* Milan: [Tipografia Pontificia Arcivescovile San Giuseppe], 1928.

Monneret de Villard, Ugo, and Achelle Patricolo. *The Church of Sitt Barbara in Old Cairo.* Florence: Fratelli Alinari, 1922.

Sauneron, Serge, and Jean Jacquet. *Les Ermitages chrétiens du désert d'Esna.* 4 vols. [Cairo]: Institut français d'archéologie orientale du Caire, 1972.

Simaika, Marcus H. *Guide sommaire du Musée copte et des principales églises du Caire.* Cairo: Imprimerie nationale, 1937.

Tusun, Umar, Prince. *Études sur le Wadi Natrun, ses moines et ses couvents.* Alexandria: Société de publications égyptiennes, 1931.

____. *Notes sur le Désert Lybique: "Cellia" et ses couvents.* Alexandria: Société de publications égyptiennes, 1935.

Glossary

abun
(our father)
highest spiritual authority in the Ethiopian Church, given to patriarchs, archbishops, bishops, and monks who were saints.

agape
the community meal following the weekly celebration of the Divine Liturgy (the Eucharist) in a monastery.

bema
(from the Greek *bēma*, tribunal)
the sanctuary, so called because it was raised above the rest of an Egyptian church by several steps.

Epiphany tank
a tank or basin set in the floor of a church, usually in the narthex, and large and deep enough to allow any person who so wished to plunge in on the feast of the Epiphany.

haykal
(from the Hebrew *hekal,* the room in front of the Holy of Holies in the Jerusalem temple) the sanctuary of a Coptic church.

hegumen
(from the Greek *hēgoumenos,* leader, president)
head of a monastery.

hermetarium
the stake to which prisoners were tied to be flogged.

khurus
(from the Greek *choros,* choir)
a room between the apse and the *naos* reserved for the clergy, which developed in the seventh century; not all churches have a *khurus.*

laqqan
a large marble basin set in the floor of a church in the western part of the nave and used for the washing of the feet on Holy Thursday and on the feast of Sts. Peter and Paul.

myron
(from the Greek *muron,* ointment, chrism)
the holy oil prepared by the patriarch on Holy Saturday for all of Egypt.

naos
(Greek, temple)
that part of a Coptic church reserved for the laity, containing the nave, side aisles, and western return aisle, and separate from the sanctuary, *khurus,* and narthex.

presbytery
that part of a Coptic church reserved for clergy where they celebrate the Divine Liturgy (the Eucharist); identical with the sanctuary and sometimes called the bema.

sanctuary
that part of a church which contains the altar and where the Divine Liturgy (Eucharist) is celebrated.

synaxarion
a book containing the short accounts of saints and feasts to be read at the early morning service.

synaxis
(Greek, assembly)
the assembly of a community for the celebration of the Divine Liturgy (the Eucharist) and, in some monasteries, the agape.

synthronon
a raised platform on which the clergy sat, reached by several steps and generally placed against the east wall of the apse of a church.

tetraconch
a rectangular room having apses formed by porticoes or exedras on the four sides.

transitus
passage of a person through death.

triconch
a church or sanctuary having apses on three sides of a rectangular section.

Index of Places